Her Again

BECOMING MERYL STREEP

Michael Schulman

FABER & FABER

First published in the USA in 2016
by HarperCollins Publishers,
195 Broadway, New York, NY 10007

First published in the UK in 2016
by Faber & Faber Ltd
Bloomsbury House, 74–77 Great Russell Street
London WC1B 3DA

Printed and bound in the UK by CPI Group (UK), Croydon CR0 4YY

Photo credits (clockwise):
Pg. 1: Courtesy of the Bernardsville Public Library Local History Collection; Courtesy of C. Otis
Sweezey; Courtesy of Michael Booth. Pg. 2: Photo by William Baker, Courtesy of William Ivey
Long; Photo by Martha Swope/© Billy Rose Theatre Division, The New York Public Library for
the Performing Arts; Photo by George E. Joseph/© Billy Rose Theatre Division, The New York
Public Library for the Performing Arts. Pg. 3: Illustration © Paul Davis; Photofest; Irv Steinberg/
Globe Photos, Inc. Pg. 4: Universal Pictures/Photofest © Universal Pictures; Photo by Mondadori
Portfolio/Getty Images. Pg. 5: United Artists/Photofest © United Artists; Photo by Jack Mitchell/
Getty Images. Pg. 6: Columbia Pictures/Photofest © Columbia Pictures; Columbia Pictures/
Photofest © Columbia Pictures. Pg. 7: Photo by Graham Turner/Getty Images; Photo by Art Zelin/
Getty Images. Pg. 8: Photo by ABC Photo Archives/ABC via Getty Images.

"We're Saving Ourselves for Yale" Copyright © Renewed 1964, David McCord Lippincott
Copyright © 1946, David McCord Lippincott. Lyrics used by permission of the Lippincott family.

The Idiots Karamazov Copyright © 1981 Christopher Durang and Albert Innaurato
Excerpts used by permission of the Authors.

"Surabaya Johnny" from *Happy End.* Text by Bertolt Brecht, Music by Kurt Weill.
English translation by Michael Feingold.
Copyright © 1972 by European American Music Corporation.
Copyright © renewed. All rights reserved. Used by permission.
Originally published in German in 1929 as "Surabaya-Johnny."
Copyright © 1929 by Bertolt-Brecht-Erben / Suhrkamp Verlag.
Used by permission of Liveright Publishing Corporation.

A CIP record for this book
is available from the British Library

ISBN 978-0-571-33098-0

FSC
www.fsc.org
MIX
Paper from
responsible sources
FSC® C101712

2 4 6 8 10 9 7 5 3 1

For Jaime

"Can I just say? There is no such thing as the *best* actress. There is no such thing as the greatest *living* actress. I am in a position where I have secret information, you know, that I know this to be true."

—MERYL STREEP, 2009

CONTENTS

Prologue

NOT ALL MOVIE STARS are created equal. If you were to trap all of Hollywood in amber and study it, like an ancient ecosystem buried beneath layers of sediment and rock, you'd discover a latticework of unspoken hierarchies, thwarted ambitions, and compromises dressed up as career moves. The best time and place to conduct such an archeological survey would undoubtedly be in late winter at 6801 Hollywood Boulevard, where they hand out the Academy Awards.

By now, of course, the Oscars are populated as much by movie stars as by hangers-on: publicists, stylists, red-carpet correspondents, stylists and publicists of red-carpet correspondents. The nominee is like a ship's hull supporting a small community of barnacles. Cutting through hordes of photographers and flacks and assistants trying to stay out of the frame, she has endured months of luncheons and screenings and speculation. Now, a trusted handler will lead her through the thicket, into the hall where her fate lies in an envelope.

The 84th Academy Awards are no different. It's February 26, 2012, and the scene outside the Kodak Theatre is a pandemonium of a zillion micromanaged parts. Screaming spectators in bleachers wait on one side of a triumphal arch through which the contenders arrive in choreographed succession. Gelled television personalities await with questions: Are they nervous? Is it their first time here? And whom, in

1

the unsettling parlance, are they wearing? There are established movie stars (Gwyneth Paltrow, in a white Tom Ford cape), newly minted starlets (Emma Stone, in a red Giambattista Valli neck bow bigger than her head). If you care to notice, there are men: Brad Pitt, Tom Hanks, George Clooney. For some reason, there's a nun.

Most of the attention, though, belongs to the women, and the ones nominated for Best Actress bear special scrutiny. There's Michelle Williams, pixie-like in a sleek red Louis Vuitton dress. Rooney Mara, a punk princess in her white Givenchy gown and forbidding black bangs. Viola Davis, in a lustrous green Vera Wang. And Glenn Close, nominated for *Albert Nobbs*, looking slyly androgynous in a Zac Posen gown and matching tuxedo jacket.

But it's the fifth nominee who will give them all a run for their money, and when she arrives, like a monarch come to greet her subjects, her appearance projects victory.

Meryl Streep is in gold.

Specifically, she is wearing a Lanvin gold lamé gown, draped around her frame like a Greek goddess's toga. The accessories are just as sharp: dangling gold earrings, a mother-of-pearl minaudière, and Salvatore Ferragamo gold lizard sandals. As more than a few observers point out, she looks not unlike an Oscar herself. One fashion blog asks: "Do you agree that this is the best she has ever looked?" The implication: not bad for a sixty-three-year-old.

Most of all, the gold number says one thing: It's my year. But is it?

Consider the odds. Yes, she has won two Oscars already, but the last time was in 1983. And while she has been nominated a record-breaking seventeen times, she has also lost a record-breaking fourteen times, putting her firmly in Susan Lucci territory. Meryl Streep is accustomed to losing Oscars.

And consider the movie. No one thinks that *The Iron Lady*, in which she played a braying Margaret Thatcher, is cinematic genius. While her performance has the trappings of Oscar bait—historical figure, age prosthetics, accent work—they're the same qualities that have pigeonholed her for decades. In his *New York Times* review, A. O. Scott put it this way: "Stiff legged and slow moving, behind a discreetly applied ton of geriatric makeup, Ms. Streep provides, once again, a technically flawless impersonation that also seems to reveal the inner essence of a well-known person." All nice words, but strung together they carry a whiff of fatigue.

As she drags her husband, Don Gummer, down the red carpet, an entertainment reporter sticks a microphone in her face.

"Do you ever get nervous on carpets like this, even though you're such a pro?"

"Yes, you should feel my heart—but you're not allowed to," she answers dryly.

"Do you have any good-luck charms on you?" the reporter persists.

"Yes," she says, a little impatiently. "I have shoes that Ferragamo made—because he made all of Margaret Thatcher's shoes."

Turning to the bleachers, she gives a little shimmy, and the crowd roars with delight. With that, she takes her husband's hand and heads inside.

They wouldn't be the Academy Awards if they weren't endless. Before she can find out if she's this year's Best Actress, a number of formalities will have to be endured. Billy Crystal will do his shtick. ("Nothing can take the sting out of the world's economic problems like watching millionaires present each other with golden statues.") Christopher Plummer, at eighty-two, will become the oldest person to be named Best Supporting Actor. ("When I emerged from my mother's womb I was already rehearsing my Academy speech.") Cirque du Soleil will perform an acrobatic tribute to the magic of cinema.

Finally, Colin Firth comes out to present the award for Best Actress. As he recites the names of the nominees, she takes deep, fortifying breaths, her gold earrings trembling above her shoulders. A short clip plays of Thatcher scolding an American dignitary ("Shall I be mother? Tea, Al?"), then Firth opens the envelope and grins.

"And the Oscar goes to Meryl Streep."

*   *   *

THE MERYL STREEP acceptance speech is an art form unto itself: at once spontaneous and scripted, humble and haughty, grateful and blasé. Of course, the fact that there are so many of them is part of the joke. Who but Meryl Streep has won so many prizes that self-deprecating nonchalance has itself become a running gag? By now, it seems as if the title Greatest Living Actress has affixed itself to her about as long as Elizabeth II has been the queen of England. Superlatives stick to her like thumbtacks: she is a god among actors, able to disappear into any character, master any genre, and, Lord knows, nail any accent. Far from fading into the usual post-fifty obsolescence, she has defied Hollywood calculus and reached a career high. No other actress born before 1960 can even *get* a part unless Meryl passes on it first.

From her breakout roles in the late seventies, she was celebrated for the infinitely shaded brushstrokes of her characterizations. In the eighties, she was the globe-hopping heroine of dramatic epics like *Sophie's Choice* and *Out of Africa*. The nineties, she insists, were a lull. (She was Oscar-nominated four times.) The year she turned forty, she is keen to point out, she was offered the chance to play three different witches. In 2002, she starred in Spike Jonze's uncategorizable *Adaptation*. The movie seemed to liberate her from whatever momentary rut she had been in. Suddenly, she could do what she felt like and make it seem like a lark. When she won the Golden Globe the next year, she seemed almost puzzled. "Oh, I didn't have anything prepared," she said, running her fingers through sweat-covered bangs, "because it's been since, like, the *Pleistocene era* that I won anything."

By 2004, when she won an Emmy for Mike Nichols's television adaptation of *Angels in America*, her humility had melted into arch overconfidence ("There are some days when I myself think I'm overrated . . . but not today"). The hits—and the winking acceptance speeches—kept coming: a Golden Globe for *The Devil Wears Prada* ("I think I've worked with everybody in the room"), a SAG Award

4

for *Doubt* ("I didn't even buy a dress!"). She soon mastered the art of jousting with her own hype, undermining her perceived superiority while putting it on luxurious display.

So when Colin Firth calls her name at the Kodak Theatre, it's a homecoming three decades in the making, a sign that the career rehabilitation that began with *Adaptation* has reached its zenith. When she hears the winner, she puts her hand to her mouth and shakes her head in disbelief. With the audience on its feet, she kisses Don twice, takes hold of her third Oscar, and resumes the time-honored tradition of cutting herself down to size.

"Oh, my God. Oh, *come on*," she begins, quieting the crowd. She laughs to herself. "When they called my name, I had this feeling I could hear half of America going, 'Ohhh, no. Oh, come on—why? *Her. Again.*' You know?"

For a moment, she actually seems hurt by the idea that half of America is disappointed. Then she smirks.

"But . . . *whatever.*"

Having broken the tension with an impeccable fake-out, she proceeds to the business of gratitude.

"First, I'm going to thank Don," she says warmly. "Because when you thank your husband at the end of the speech, they play him out with the music, and I want him to know that everything I value most in our lives, you've given me." The camera cuts to Don, patting his heart.

"And now, secondly, my other partner. Thirty-seven years ago, my first play in New York City, I met the great hair stylist and makeup artist Roy Helland, and we worked together pretty continuously since the day we clapped eyes on each other. His first film with me was *Sophie's Choice*, and all the way up to tonight"—her voice cracks briefly—"when he won for his beautiful work in *The Iron Lady*, thirty years later." With Thatcheresque certitude, she underlines each word with a karate chop: "Every. Single. Movie. In. Between."

She shifts her tone again and continues, "I just want to thank Roy, but also I want to thank—because I really understand I'll never be up here again." (With that, she gives an almost imperceptible side-glance that says, *Well, we'll see* . . .) "I really want to thank all my colleagues, all my friends. I look out here and I see my life before my eyes: my old friends, my new friends."

Her voice softening, she goes for the big finish: "Really, this is such a great honor, but the thing that counts the most with me is the friendships and the love and the sheer joy we have shared making movies together. My friends, thank you, all of you, departed and here, for this, you know, inexplicably wonderful career."

On "departed," she looks skyward and raises a palm to the heavens—or, at least, to the lighting rig of the Kodak Theatre, where showbusiness ghosts lurk. Any number of ghosts could have been on her mind. Her mother, Mary Wolf, who died in 2001. Her father, Harry, who died two years later. Her directors: Karel Reisz, who cast her in *The French Lieutenant's Woman*; Alan J. Pakula, who made her the star of *Sophie's Choice*. Surely, she thought of Joseph Papp, the legendary theater producer, who plucked her from obscurity months after she finished drama school.

But at this moment, seeing her career come to yet another climax, it's hard to imagine that she didn't think back to its beginnings, and its beginnings were all wrapped up in John Cazale.

It's been thirty-four years since she saw him. Thirty-six years since they met, playing Angelo and Isabella in a Shakespeare in the Park production of *Measure for Measure*. Night after night in the sticky summer air, she would beg him to show mercy for her condemned brother: "Spare him, spare him! He's not prepared for death."

John Cazale was one of the great character actors of his generation, and one of the most chronically overlooked. Forever Fredo of the *Godfather* movies, he was her first deep love, and her first devastating loss. Had he lived past forty-two, his name might have become as familiar as De Niro or Pacino. But there was so much he hadn't been around to see. He hadn't seen Meryl win two Academy Awards by the time she was thirty-three. He hadn't seen her age into regal self-possession. He hadn't seen her play Joanna or Sophie or Karen or Lindy or Francesca or Miranda or Julia or Maggie.

John Cazale hadn't lived to see her onstage now, thanking her friends, all of them, for this "inexplicably wonderful career." After one last "thank you," she waves farewell and heads toward the wings, having burnished her reputation once again. Meryl Streep, the Iron Lady of acting: indomitable, unsinkable, inevitable.

BUT IT WASN'T always so.

Forty-two years earlier, Meryl Streep was a pellucid Vassar student just discovering the lure of the stage. Her extraordinary talent was evident to all who knew her, but she didn't see much future in it. Although she possessed an idiosyncratic beauty, she never saw herself as an ingénue. Her insecurity worked in her favor: instead of shoehorning herself into traditionally feminine roles, she could make herself foreign, wacky, or plain, disappearing into lives far beyond her suburban New Jersey upbringing. Neither a classic beauty in the mold of Elizabeth Taylor nor a girl-next-door type like Debbie Reynolds, she was everything and nothing—a chameleon. One thing she knew she was not: a movie star.

What happened next was a series of breaks that every actress on earth dreams of, though few have the raw talent to seize them. By the end of the seventies, she had become the star student at the Yale School of Drama; headlined on Broadway and in Shakespeare in the Park; found and lost the love of her life, John Cazale; found the second love of her life, Don Gummer, and married him; and starred in *Kramer vs. Kramer,* for which she would win her first Academy Award—all within ten dizzying years.

How did she get there? Where did she learn to do what she does? Can it even be learned? The questions don't exist in a bubble: the same decade that made Meryl Streep a star represented a heady, game-changing era in American film acting. But its biggest names were men: Al Pacino, Robert De Niro, Dustin Hoffman. Against her instincts, she joined the cast of *The Deer Hunter* to be with the ailing Cazale and broke into the *Godfather* clique. But it was the nuance and dramatic wit of her performances that earned her a place there. She excelled at the in-between states: ambivalence, denial, regret. Makeup and accents made her unrecognizable, and yet each performance had an inner discontent, a refusal to inhabit any one emotion without coloring it with the opposite emotion. Her interior life was dialectical.

"It's like church for me," she once said, before stumbling on the question of where she goes when she is acting. "It's like approaching the altar. I feel like the more you talk about whatever it is, something will go away. I mean, there's a lot of superstition in it. But I do know that I feel freer, less in control, more susceptible." Her immense craft was not without its detractors. In 1982, Pauline Kael, *The New Yorker*'s maverick film critic, wrote of her performance in *Sophie's Choice*, "She has, as usual, put thought and effort into her work. But something about her puzzles me: after I've seen her in a movie, I can't visualize her from the neck down."

The phrase stuck, as did the idea that Meryl Streep is "technical." But, as she is quick to explain, she works more from intuition than from any codified technique. While she is part of a generation raised on Method acting, rooted in the idea that an actor can project personal emotions and experiences onto a character, she has always been skeptical of its self-punishing demands. She is, among other things, a collage artist, her mind like an algorithm that can call up accents, gestures, inflections, and reassemble them into a character. Sometimes, she doesn't know from what or whom she has borrowed until she sees it up on the screen.

Coming of age during the ascendance of second-wave feminism, her discovery of acting was inextricable from the business of becoming a woman. During her cheerleading days at Bernards High School, she modeled herself on the girls she saw in women's magazines. Her world opened up in 1967 at Vassar College, which was then all-female. By the time she graduated, it had opened its dorms to men, and she had intuited her way through her first major acting role, in August Strindberg's *Miss Julie*. A decade later, she starred in *Kramer vs. Kramer*, as a young mother who has the audacity to abandon her husband and child, only to reappear and demand custody. The film was, on one level, a reactionary slant against women's lib. But Streep insisted on making Joanna Kramer not a dragon lady but a complex woman with legitimate longings and doubts, and she nearly hijacked the movie in the process.

"Women," she has said, "are better at acting than men. Why? Because we have to be. If successfully convincing someone bigger than you are of something he doesn't want to know is a survival skill, this is how women have survived through the millennia. Pretending is not just play. Pretending is imagined possibility. Pretending or acting is a very valuable life skill, and we all do it all the time. We don't want to be caught doing it, but nevertheless it's part of the adaptation of our species. We change who we are to fit the exigencies of our time."

The years that changed Meryl Streep from winsome cheerleader to the unstoppable star of *The French Lieutenant's Woman* and *Sophie's Choice* had their own exigencies, ones that also transformed America, women, and the movies. The story of her rise is also the story of the men who tried to mold her, or love her, or place her on a pedestal. Most of them failed. To become a star—never high on her list of priorities— she would do so on her own terms, letting nothing other than her talent and her otherworldly self-assurance clear her path. As she wrote to an ex-boyfriend her freshman year of college, "I have come to the brink of something very frightening and very wonderful."

Mary

⚘

ON THE FIRST Saturday of November, the student body of Bernards High School gathered for a sacred rite. Homecoming: the ratification of a hard-fought teenage hierarchy. On a crisp green football field tucked behind a Methodist Church, the notoriously hopeless Bernards Mountaineers faced off against their rivals from Dunellen, a New Jersey borough not unlike their own. At halftime, the players cleared the field. Then it was time to crown the homecoming queen of 1966.

Everyone in school knew this year's winner, a blond, blue-eyed senior from 21 Old Fort Road. She was one of those girls who seemed to have it all together: smart, good-looking, with a boyfriend on the football team. They had seen her on the cheerleading squad. And in the choir. And in the school plays—she always got the lead. As the bow-tied student-council president escorted her onto the field, the eyes of Bernardsville fell on her limpid, peculiar face.

She was beautiful. Everyone knew it except her. Alabaster skin. High cheekbones that seemed chiseled like statuary. Hooded eyes, set slightly close. Hair the color of cornsilk. A nose so long and forked it was practically an event.

She wasn't nearly pretty enough to be a movie star, she thought. Movie stars were girlish or voluptuous or demure. They were Audrey Hepburn or Ann-Margret or Jane Fonda. Movie stars were pretty. And no matter how many boys had fallen over one another for her affections, she wasn't pretty, she told herself. Not with that nose.

Pauline Kael would put it this way: "Streep has the clear-eyed blond handsomeness of a Valkyrie—the slight extra length of her nose gives her face a distinction that takes her out of the pretty class into real beauty." No matter that Kael would become her most vocal critic. She was right: Meryl Streep wasn't pretty. She was something else. Something more interesting, or at least harder to categorize. When she arched an eyebrow or twisted a lip, she could be anyone: an aristocrat, a beggar, a lover, a clown. She could be Nordic or English or Slavic. For now, what she wanted to be was all-American.

Last year's homecoming queen, June Reeves, had returned from junior college to fulfill her final duty: placing a twinkling diadem on her successor's head. The newly crowned queen boarded a float bedecked with flowers, flanked by her homecoming court: Joann Bocchino, Ann Buonopane, Ann Miller, and Peggy Finn, all with flipped hair and corsages. As the float traversed the field, she waved to the crowd and smiled, flashing a white glove. She had worked hard to become the queen, primping and peroxiding and transforming herself into the person she was determined to be.

None of her subjects knew how miscast she felt. What they saw was a role she was playing, down to the last golden hair on her head. Even her giggle was a construction: she had practiced it, making it light and lithesome, the way the boys like. She wouldn't have called it acting, but that's what it was. With unwavering diligence, she had spent her high school years immersed in a role. Still, as good as she was at playing it, there would always be cracks in the façade. She didn't look like the women she saw in the magazines, not really. She had fooled these people, or most of them. The girls saw right through her.

Waving to the crowd, she stayed in character. It felt nice to be worshiped, but perhaps a little lonely. Up on that float, she was on her own plane, a few inches closer to the November sky than any of her supposed peers. If only June or Peggy or her best friend, Sue, could join her—but there was only one queen, and her job was to be the best. Perhaps for the first time, and certainly not for the last, Meryl Streep was learning that perfection could be a prison.

She was seventeen years old.

SHE WOULD SOON discover that transformation, not beauty, was her calling card. It had been with her from the beginning. Call it "the zone." Call it "church." It was a place she visited before she knew how to describe it, though she never really figured out how.

"I was six, placing my mother's half-slip over my head in preparation to play the Virgin Mary in our living room. As I swaddled my Betsy Wetsy doll, I felt quieted, holy, actually, and my transfigured face and very changed demeanor captured on Super-8 by my dad pulled my little brothers—Harry, four, playing Joseph, and Dana, two, a barnyard animal—into the trance. They were actually pulled into this little nativity scene by the intensity of my focus, in a way that my usual technique for getting them to do what I want, yelling at them, never ever would have achieved."

That was six. This was nine:

"I remember taking my mother's eyebrow pencil and carefully drawing lines all over my face, replicating the wrinkles that I had memorized on the face of my grandmother, whom I adored. I made my mother take my picture, and I look at it now, of course, I look like myself now and my grandmother then. But I do really remember, in my bones, how it was possible on that day to feel her age. I stooped, I felt weighted down, but cheerful, you know. I felt like her."

The Virgin Mary was a natural first role: Meryl came from a long line of women named Mary. Her mother was Mary Wolf Wilkinson, whose mother was Mary Agnes, shortened to Mamie. When Mary Wolf's first daughter was born, in Summit, New Jersey, on June 22, 1949, she named the baby Mary Louise. But three Marys in one family was a lot, and before Mary Louise had learned to speak her name, her mother had taken to calling her Meryl.

She knew little of her ancestors growing up. Her mother's side was Quaker stock, stretching back to the Revolutionary War. There were stories of someone getting hanged in Philadelphia for horse thievery. One grandmother busted up bars during the Temperance movement. Her grandfather Harry Rockafellow Wilkinson, known as "Harry Pop" to his grandchildren, was a joker and a gesticulator. When Meryl was little, her maternal grandparents still said "thee" and "thou."

Mary Wolf had a wide, warm face and a bright humor inherited from her father; years later, playing Julia Child, Meryl would draw on her mother's immense "joie de vivre." She was born in 1915, in Brooklyn. During World War II, she worked as an art director at Bell Labs, and later studied at the Art Students League in New York. Like most of her peers, Mary gave up her wartime work to be a full-time wife and mother: the kind of woman Betty Friedan wanted to galvanize with the 1963 publication of *The Feminine Mystique*. But Mary didn't suffer from the malaise Friedan observed in so many housewives, perhaps because she never abandoned her artistic pursuits. While she raised the kids, she worked in a studio on the back porch as a commercial artist, drawing illustrations for local publications and businesses. Had she been part of her daughter's generation, she might have gone out and had a career. As it was, she kept her finger in the pie, and the extra income didn't hurt.

Meryl's paternal side had none of the same ebullience. "Streep" was a German name, though for many years she thought it was Dutch. Her father, Harry Streep, Jr., was an only child. (Harrys and Henrys were as plentiful in her family as Marys.) Nicknamed "Buddy," he was born in Newark in 1910 and went to Brown on a scholarship. After a year, the Depression hit and he was forced to leave. For three decades, he worked in the personnel department of Merck & Co. The job was mostly hiring and firing. Meryl noticed some melancholy in her father, possibly inherited from his mother, Helena, who had been institutionalized for clinical depression. Helena's husband, Harry William Streep, was a traveling salesman who left her alone with their son much of the time. As an older man, Meryl's father would watch his grandson, Henry Wolfe Gummer, in a high school production of *Death of a Salesman* and weep, saying, "That was my dad."

When Meryl visited her paternal grandparents' apartment, she could sense a pervading sadness. The shades were drawn so as to let in only a sliver of light—nothing like the warm Wilkinson house. Her grandmother reused absolutely everything. She would save pieces of tinfoil and wrap them into a ball, which she kept under the sink as it grew larger and larger, to Meryl's fascination.

In the postwar glow, a bright, suburban American dream was within reach for families like the Streeps. They moved around central New Jersey as the family got bigger, first to Basking Ridge and then to Bernardsville. After Meryl, there was Harry Streep III, nicknamed "Third." Then there was another boy, Dana, a skinny jokester with freckles. Meryl's parents would bring her to her brothers' Little League games, but she was just as rambunctious and athletic as they were, maybe more so.

In Bernardsville, they lived on a tree-lined street on top of a small hill, just a short walk from the public high school. The town sat on New Jersey's "wealth belt," about forty-five miles west of New York City. In 1872, a new railroad line had transformed it from a tranquil collection of cottages to a bedroom community for affluent New Yorkers, who built summer homes far away from the city din. The tonier among them erected mansions on Bernardsville Mountain. The "mountain people," as some below called them, sent their children to boarding schools and trotted around on horses. In later years, they included Aristotle and Jacqueline Kennedy Onassis, who kept a ten-acre Bernardsville estate.

The railroad bisected the rest of the town: middle-class Protestants on one side; on the other, working-class Italians, many of whom made their living constructing the mountain people's homes. There were few local industries, save for Meadowbrook Inventions, which made glitter. Aside from its equestrian upper crust, the town was like its many cousins along the Erie Lackawanna line: a place where everyone knew everyone, where bankers and insurance men took the train into the city every morning, leaving their wives and children in their leafy domestic idyll.

As members of Bernardsville's earthbound middle class, the Streeps were nothing like the mountain people. They didn't own horses or send their children to private academies. Unlike the Colonial-style houses popular in town, theirs was modern, with a Japanese screen in the family room and a piano where Mr. Streep would play in the evenings. Outside was a grassy yard where the Streep kids could while away summer afternoons.

Harry had high expectations for his children, whom he wanted on the straight and narrow—and in Bernardsville, the straight and narrow was pretty straight and pretty narrow. Mary had a lighter touch, and an irreverent wit. Aside from their birthdays, the siblings would get "special days," when they could do whatever they wanted. For a while, Meryl chose the zoo or the circus, but soon her special days were all about Broadway shows: *Oliver!*, *Kismet*, Ethel Merman in *Annie Get Your Gun*. Meryl adored musicals, which, as far as she knew, were the only kind of theater there was. At a matinee of *Man of La Mancha*, she sat in the front row "shooting out sparks," as her mother would recall.

She was bossy with her little brothers, coercing them into imaginative games, whether they liked it or not. They were, after all, her only scene partners. Third acquiesced, later describing her as "pretty ghastly when she was young." But the other kids in the neighborhood weren't so easy to manipulate. "I didn't have what you'd call a happy childhood," she said in 1979. "For one thing, I thought no one liked me . . . Actually, I'd say I had pretty good evidence. The kids would chase me up into a tree and hit my legs with sticks until they bled. Besides that, I was ugly."

She wasn't hideous, but she certainly wasn't girlish. When she watched Annette Funicello developing curves on *The Mickey Mouse Club*, she saw a gamine cuteness that eluded her completely. With her cat-eye glasses and brown, neck-length perm, Meryl looked like a middle-aged secretary. Some of the kids at school thought she was a teacher.

When she was twelve, she got up at a school Christmas concert and sang a solo rendition of "O Holy Night" in French. The audience leaped to its feet, perhaps stunned to hear the neighborhood terror produce such a pure, high sound. It was the first time she felt the intoxication of applause. Among the surprised were her parents. Where had Meryl been hiding her coloratura?

Someone told them to enroll her in singing lessons, so they did. Every Saturday morning, she would take the train into New York City to see Estelle Liebling. Miss Liebling, as her students addressed her, was a link to a vanished world. Her father had studied with Franz Liszt, and she was the last surviving pupil of the great Parisian voice teacher Mathilde Marchesi. Miss Liebling had sung Musetta at the Metropolitan Opera and toured two continents with John Philip Sousa. Now she was in her eighties, a chic matron in heels and crimson lipstick, imposing despite her petite frame. She knew everyone in the opera world, and she seemed to mint star sopranos as fast as the Met could take them.

With such a lofty teacher, there was nothing stopping the adolescent Meryl from becoming a world-famous soprano. Not that she was crazy about opera—she preferred the Beatles and Bob Dylan. But that voice was too good to waste. Weekend after weekend, she went to Miss Liebling's studio near Carnegie Hall, standing beside the piano as the octogenarian teacher ran her up and down scales and arpeggios. She taught Meryl about breathing. She taught her that breathing is three-dimensional, reminding her, "There's room in the back!"

As she waited outside Miss Liebling's studio for her 11:30 a.m. appointment, a glorious sound would echo from inside. It was the 10:30 student, Beverly Sills. A bubbly redhead in her early thirties, Sills had been coming to Estelle since she was seven years old. Meryl thought Beverly was good, but so was she. And nobody had ever heard of Beverly either.

Of course, that wasn't quite true: Sills had been singing with the New York City Opera since 1955, and was only a few short years from her breakout role, Cleopatra in Handel's *Giulio Cesare*. "Miss Liebling was very strict and formal with me," Sills wrote in her autobiography. "When she was at the piano, she never let me read music over her shoulder, and she got *very* annoyed the few times I showed up unprepared. One of Miss Liebling's favorite admonitions to me was 'Text! Text! Text!' which she said whenever she felt I was merely singing notes and not paying attention to the meaning of the lyrics. Miss Liebling wanted me to sing the way Olivier acts, to deliver what I was singing in such a way that my audience would respond emotionally."

Miss Liebling had another mantra: "Cover! Cover! Cover!" She was speaking of the passaggio, that tricky vocal stretch between the lower and upper register. For some singers, it was a minefield. Cover it, Miss Liebling told her charges, with certain vowels only: an "*ooh*" or an "*aww*," never a wide-open "*ahh*." Make the transition seamless. For a gawky adolescent with braces and knotty brown hair, the idea must have held some extra appeal: cover the transition. Make it seamless.

In the fall of 1962, Meryl's parents brought her to City Center, the home of the New York City Opera. Sills was debuting as Milly Theale in Douglas Moore's *The Wings of the Dove*. It was the first opera Meryl had seen, and she was rapt. Until then, Beverly had been the nice lady whose lessons preceded her own. Now, watching her onstage, Meryl saw what all those drills on Saturday mornings were for—the glory that capped all the grueling hours of work.

She realized something else that night: she didn't have a voice like Beverly's, and she would never be an opera singer.

After four years, she quit her lessons with Miss Liebling. The reason wasn't just that she had given up her dreams of debuting at the Met. Meryl had come through the passaggio of puberty, and what lay on the other side was far more tempting than Verdi: she had discovered boys.

It was time for a metamorphosis.

*   *   *

AT FOURTEEN YEARS old, Meryl Streep took off her braces. She ditched her glasses and started wearing contacts. She doused her hair in lemon juice and peroxide until it gleamed like gold. At night, she wore rollers—it was torturous, but she'd wake up with a perky flip. As Meryl primped for hours in the bathroom mirror, surely to the chagrin of her younger brothers, she discovered that beauty gave her status and strength. But, like most teenagers rushing headlong toward woman-hood, she was barely conscious of what she was leaving behind.

"Empathy," she would say, "is at the heart of the actor's art. And in high school, another form of acting took hold of me. I wanted to learn how to be appealing. So I studied the character I imagined I wanted to be, that of the generically pretty high school girl." She emulated the women in *Mademoiselle* and *Seventeen* and *Vogue*, copying their eye-lashes, their outfits, their lipstick. She ate an apple a day—and little else. She begged her mother to buy her brand-name clothes, and was refused. She fine-tuned her giggle.

She worked day and night, unaware that she had cast herself se-verely against type. She studied what boys liked, and what girls would accept, and memorized where the two overlapped: a "tricky negoti-ation." She found that she could mimic other people's behavior with faultless precision, like a Martian posing as an Earthling. "I worked harder on this characterization, really, than anyone that I think I've ever done since," she recalled. Gone was the ugly duckling, the brassy little bully of Old Fort Road. By fifteen, that Meryl had disappeared. In her place was "the perfect *Seventeen* magazine knockout."

She was an excellent imposter.

NEWS OF THE SIXTIES seemed not to reach Bernardsville, even as the counterculture caught fire elsewhere. Sure, her friends listened to the Beatles and "Light My Fire," but transgression took the form of a beer, not a joint. The place looked like something out of *Bye Bye Birdie*. Girls wore A-line dresses down to the knees, with Peter Pan collars cinched with a small circle pin. Boys wore khakis and Madras jackets and parted their hair. The vice principal would come around with a ruler to measure their sideburns: too long and they'd be sent home.

Fun was a hamburger at the luncheonette in the center of town, or a movie at the local cinema. At the "Baby Dance," the freshmen dressed up in bonnets and diapers. The next year, it was the "Sweater Dance." After that, the Junior Prom, which was themed "In Days of Olde." It was a fitting motif. "We felt like we were in a little shell, that we were protected and everything would be safe there," said Debbie Bozack (née Welsh), who, like Meryl, entered ninth grade in September, 1963, two months before the Kennedy assassination.

Debbie met Meryl in homeroom on one of the first days of class. At Debbie's old school, there were only five kids in her grade, and the crowded hallways at Bernards High terrified her. So did the prospect of changing for gym. Meryl, though, seemed confident and fearless. They had most of the same classes, so Debbie followed her around like a disciple.

As a newfound adherent to American teenage conformity, Meryl longed to join the cheerleading squad. So did Debbie. But Debbie couldn't do a cartwheel to save her life. Meryl, who was not only self-assured but athletic, was a pro. Some days, Debbie would follow Meryl home after school, where Meryl would try to teach her to do a cartwheel on the lawn. As Meryl guided her legs over her head, Debbie's hands would grate against the pebbles that came up after the rain. In the end, it was all for naught. Debbie didn't make the squad. Meryl, naturally, did.

On fall weekends, the student populace would converge at the football games. With the exception of the brainiacs and the greasers, everyone showed up. Everyone had a place. There were the twirlers. There was the color guard, where Debbie landed a spot. There was the marching band, which was quite good, thanks in part to a precocious senior named John Geils, who within a few years would trade in his trumpet for a guitar and start the J. Geils Band.

But the cheerleaders, or "cheeries," stood apart from the rest. Not that they were mean, but they were close-knit, bonded by their good looks and popularity. With the letter "B" emblazoned on their outfits, they would chant, "Thunder, thunder, thunderation!" Meryl became best friends with her fellow cheery Sue Castrilli, who worked at the Dairy Queen. There wasn't much to do in Bernardsville, besides driving on a loop on the 202 between the DQ and the train station and then back again. When Sue was on duty, she would give her friends double dips.

In class, Meryl was attentive when it suited her. She had a knack for languages—the accents, at least. When she didn't care for the teacher, she got C's. She dreaded the geometry teacher, whom the kids called Fang. Even worse was biology. "Just remember Biology and the Biology exam and you'll never sleep again," one boy wrote in her sophomore yearbook. "I don't know what you'd do if I didn't tell you all the answers," wrote another.

As the sister of two brothers, she was comfortable around boys, maybe more so than she was around girls. She loved the guys who sat in the back row, because they were funny; from them she picked up comedic lessons she wouldn't use until much later. For now, Meryl was content to be their audience, careful not to step out of character. At home, the dinner table was a clamorous exchange of ideas. But opinions, Meryl learned, didn't get you a second date—boys didn't like to be contradicted. Opinions, for now, took a backseat.

IN THE SPRING of 1964, when Meryl was a freshman, she met Mike Booth. She had gone on a date or two with his cousin, J. D. Mike was a sophomore with longish dark hair and a toothy grin. He wore Shetland sweaters with the sleeves cut off halfway—the closest Bernards High came to rebellion. His father thought he was a failure, and Mike proved the old man right by drinking and getting into fights. He had barely passed the ninth grade.

"Do you like it here at Bernards High?" Meryl said, when J. D. introduced them.

"I do now."

Mike thought that Meryl was swell. "Her eyes were extremely bright," he would recall. "Her smile was genuine. She didn't smirk or run with a pack, like a lot of girls. Yet there was a slight awkwardness about her, as though she was certain her dress didn't look right, or her shoes didn't fit, or she was just plain ugly."

Mike began walking her home from school—he didn't have a driver's license. During the summer, they'd go to his Aunt Lala's place for picnics and swim in the pond, or play baseball. On nights, they'd go to parties or the Bernardsville movie theater, rushing home to make Meryl's eleven o'clock curfew. Mike wrote her poems, and she gave him a volume of modern American and British poetry, a Christmas present from her father.

In the middle of the summer, Mike began football practice, and Meryl started practicing with the cheeries. They'd meet for lunch; Meryl would share one of her trademark peanut-butter-and-jelly sandwiches, which they washed down with a Tab and a leftover brownie or piece of cake, which Meryl joked was "aged like a fine cheese." Mike liked her self-deprecating humor, which she'd use to brush off anything that irked her. Sometimes she did impressions for him— he thought she was a "terrific mimic." When he asked if she liked to swim, she switched on a Jersey accent and said, "Duh, yeah," flexing her biceps and bragging, "I'm really quite atletik—for a girl."

On their walk to the community pool one day, they spotted a discarded ring glinting up from the side of the road. It was a promotional item from American Airlines, with a metallic eagle encircled with the words JUNIOR PILOT. Mike put it on Meryl's finger. They were going steady.

Harry Streep didn't like the idea at all. At first, he limited Meryl to seeing Mike just once a week. Then it was every two weeks. Then he insisted that she go on dates with other boys, since she was too young to go steady with anyone. One day at the pool, Meryl won a race at a swim meet, and when she got out Mike gave her a kiss on the cheek. Word got back to Mr. Streep, who chastised his daughter for the public display of affection.

Finally, he cut her off from Mike entirely. They met secretly on a path through the woods between their houses, which were a mile apart. Mike handed her a love poem. Meryl's eyes were red from crying. She went home that night and warned her father: If you don't give me some freedom now, I'll be one of those girls who goes berserk once she leaves for college. He relented.

In her notes to Mike, Meryl daydreamed about their future together. After high school, they'd get married and move to a remote island where they'd join the Peace Corps and "civilize the natives." Then Meryl would go to Sarah Lawrence, or maybe Bard, while Mike got his law degree and became a part-time writer. He'd win the Pulitzer Prize. She'd accept the lead in a Broadway play and immediately become rich and famous. They'd buy a villa on an island off of Nice— early-American style, of course—and throw parties twice a weekend.

Mr. Streep watched Mike with a wary eye. Nevertheless, Mike observed, "There was this constant joking and bantering that went back and forth between Meryl, her mother, and her brothers. They made fun of each other, but in a delightful sort of a way. I remember thinking, Jeez, these people really enjoy each other."

Mike and cheerleading may have dominated her time, but they didn't monopolize it. Bolstered by her father's sense of drive, she raced through high school in an extracurricular frenzy. Her freshman year, she was class treasurer. She did gymnastics and became the secretary of the French Club. She was the head of the announcers, who recited the lunch menu into the loudspeaker each morning. She drew art for the yearbook. She swam.

Meanwhile, she kept up her singing. She joined the choir, which performed in stately robes. One year at the Christmas concert, she scored a solo in Vivaldi's *Gloria*, performed at the Short Hills Mall. The 1965 edition of the *Bernardian* yearbook pictured her in a sweater and flipped hair, with the caption: "A voice worth noting."

But Meryl wasn't so sure of her vocal abilities. She confessed to Mike that she thought her voice was "sharp and shrill." He thought it was beautiful. When they approached her house, she would announce herself by wailing, "Ooooo-eee! Ooooo-eee!" Miss Liebling would have killed her.

"I'm going to strangle you, Meryl dear, if I hear that falsetto one more time!" her mother would call back, holding her ears.

It was in part her mania for activities that led Meryl to audition, her sophomore year, for *The Music Man*. She had seen Barbara Cook play Marian the Librarian on Broadway. Now she surprised half the school by winning the role for herself. Third, who was a freshman, played her lisping little brother, Winthrop. When it came time for the big show, she sang "Goodnight, My Someone" with a voice as light and high as a feather. She told Mike that he was the "someone."

Even her chemistry teacher took to calling her "Songbird." The next April, she played Daisy Mae in *Li'l Abner*, singing and dancing in fringed cutoffs. Days after the curtain went down, she was still glowing. "Almost every day for the past two months has been a 'Typical Day' in Dogpatch, so the song goes," the sixteen-year-old Meryl told the school newspaper, adding: "It's pretty hard to put this out of your mind so quickly." The following year, she was Laurey in *Oklahoma!* Her best friend, Sue Castrilli, was in the cast. So was Third. Playing these dainty ingénues, she didn't think about the acting part. "I thought about the singing part," she said later, "the showing-off part, and the dancing part."

It was a way to feel loved, something she hadn't quite convinced herself she was. "I thought that if I looked pretty and did all the 'right things,' everyone would like me," she said of the teenage self she would later abandon. "I had only two friends in high school, and one of them was my cousin, so that didn't count. Then there's that whole awful kind of competition based on pubescent rivalry for boys. It made me terribly unhappy. My biggest decision every day used to be what clothes I should wear to school. It was ridiculous."

Some other part of her was trying to claw its way out. On afternoons after school, she'd come home and put on her parents' Barbra Streisand albums, imitating every breath, every swell. She found that she could express not only the emotions of the song but the other feelings she was having, the ones that didn't fit the character she was playing. Even as she mouthed along to the truism that "people who need people are the luckiest people in the world," its irony was apparent: at school, she was surrounded by people, but she didn't feel lucky. She felt phony.

"Often success in one area precludes succeeding in the other," she would say. "And along with all of my exterior choices, I worked on my, what actors call, my interior adjustment. I adjusted my natural temperament, which tended—tends—to be slightly bossy, a little opinionated, loud (a little loud), full of pronouncements and high spirits. And I willfully cultivated softness, agreeableness, a breezy, natural sort of sweetness, even a shyness, if you will, which was very, very, very, very, *very* effective on the boys. But the girls didn't buy it. They didn't like me; they sniffed it out, the acting. And they were probably right. But I was committed. This was absolutely not a cynical exercise. This was a vestigial survival courtship skill I was developing."

Mike Booth didn't seem to notice. The "slight awkwardness" he had noticed when they met had disappeared, and in its place was "exuberance," he recalled. "Somehow she had become even prettier than the year before."

Meryl had taken up drawing and gave him her cartoons, most of which were at her own expense. She'd render herself with hairy arms and an elongated nose, still in her cheerleading outfit, or as a lifeguard with bulging muscles and a mustache. Her insecurities were practically begging to be noticed, but Mike saw only talent, which he thought he had none of. At seventeen, he was a middling athlete and an even worse student.

In May, Mike took Meryl to the prom at Florham Park. With her white gloves and corsage, she was a "vision of smiling light," he thought. They had been dating for more than a year. That August, Mike brought her to see the Beatles at Shea Stadium. The band was barely audible above the screaming. Luckily, they knew all the songs by heart. Their favorite was "If I Fell," which they called "our song." It told them what they already knew: that love was more than just holding hands.

Pitted against the bigger, badder players across New Jersey, the Bernards High football team was accustomed to humiliating defeats. But the first game of the season in the fall of 1965, against Bound Brook, was different. Thanks to a magnificent fifty-yard run by a junior named Bruce Thomson (sprung loose by a key block from Mike Booth, the left guard), the Mountaineers pulled off a rare win. Mike eyed Meryl on the sidelines, screaming her head off in her red-and-white cheering uniform.

But Meryl's attentions were wandering. She had set her sights on Bruce Thomson, who had brought the Mountaineers their brief moment of glory. Bruce was a sandy-haired, broad-shouldered hunk with an ego to match. His girlfriend was the captain of the color guard. She was a senior, like Mike, and had grown suspicious of Meryl. So had some of the other girls. Meryl was someone who got what she wanted. She wanted Bruce.

Mike was planning a road trip down south with a friend, a last hurrah before the wide world swept them up. The night before they left, he went to a dance and saw Meryl and Bruce in each other's arms. He could only blame himself. A couple weeks earlier, he had broken up with Meryl. He didn't want to be tied down, now that he had a fleeting chance at freedom. He had let Meryl slip away, maybe for good. A few months later, he enlisted in the U.S. Army as a Medical Corpsman.

*   *   *

IN THE FALL of her senior year, Meryl was elected homecoming queen. No one was surprised. By then, she had built a coalition of wary admirers: the cheeries, the chorus girls, the boys who could make her giggle and glance. "Like, okay," Debbie recalled thinking, "we know Meryl will get it."

Her again.

There she was, at the big football game against Dunellen, the senior-class queen of Bernards High. Bruce Thomson had become her new beau, and they looked good together: the homecoming queen and the football star, a high school power couple. From the float, she gazed down on her subjects: the twirlers, the color guard, the jocks, the class clowns from the back row, all arranged in a teenage taxonomy. The plan she had put in motion the day she tore off her old-lady glasses was complete. She had pulled it off, almost too well.

"I reached a point senior year when my adjustment felt like me," she would recall. "I had actually convinced myself that I was this person and she me: pretty, talented, but not stuck-up. You know, a girl who laughed a lot at every stupid thing every boy said and who lowered her eyes at the right moment and deferred, who learned to defer when the boys took over the conversation. I really remember this so clearly, and I could tell it was working. I was much less annoying to the guys than I had been. They liked me better and I liked that. This was conscious, but it was at the same time motivated and fully felt. This was real, real acting."

If only she could see beyond Bernardsville, past the proms and pompoms and tiaras and "Goodnight, My Someone"s. At eighteen, she took her first plane ride. Passing over Bernardsville, she peered down and saw her whole life below: all the roads she knew, her school, her house. All of it fit in the space she could make with two fingers. She realized how small her world had been.

In high school, there had only been one game to play, so she played it. The 1967 edition of the *Bernardian* yearbook revealed just how limited the options were. Beneath each coiffed, combed senior portrait, the descriptions of the graduates read like a generation's collective aspirations, a handbook for what young men and women were supposed to be. Between the genders was a bold, uncrossable line.

Just look at the boys, with their gelled hair and jackets:

"Handsome quarterback of our football team . . . big man in sports . . . likes to play pool . . . partial to blondes . . . usually seen with Barbara . . . Avid motorcycle fan . . . likes cars and working on them . . . fond of drag racing . . . enjoys U.S. History . . . whiz at math . . . future in music . . . future engineer . . . future mathematician . . . future architect . . . looking forward to a military career . . . most likely to succeed . . ."

Compare the girls, miniature Doris Days in pearl necklaces:

"Wants to be a nurse . . . captain of the cheeries . . . keeps the D.Q. swinging . . . a sparkling brunette . . . what beautiful eyes . . . Steve, Steve, Steve . . . loves to sew . . . Twirling is one of her merits . . . a whiz on the sewing machine . . . Cute smile . . . loves shorthand . . . future as a secretary . . . Future nurse . . . giggles galore . . ."

Amid these future architects and future secretaries, the eye is barely drawn to Mary Louise Streep, who spent four years trying to ace conformity and succeeded. Beneath her lustrous portrait is a hard-won summation:

"Pretty blonde . . . vivacious cheerleader . . . our homecoming queen . . . Many talents . . . Where the boys are."

IN THE SOUTHWEST corner of Vermont, Meryl Streep sat in front of a stern-looking administrator at the Bennington College admissions office. Her father was waiting outside.

"What books have you read over the summer?" the woman inquired.

Meryl blinked. Books? *Over the summer?* She was on the swim team, for crying out loud!

She thought back: there had been that rainy day at the library, when she read this one book cover to cover. Something about dreams, by Carl Jung.

But when she said the name of the author, the woman balked.

"Please!" she sniffed. "*Yung.*"

Meryl crumpled in her seat. That was the longest book anyone she knew had read over the summer—anyone on the swim team, at least—and this woman was giving her grief for mispronouncing the author's name?

She found her father outside. "Daddy, take me home." And he did.

So maybe she'd flubbed Bennington. There were other options. She was, in her estimation, "a nice girl, pretty, athletic, and I'd read maybe seven books in four years of high school. I read *The New Yorker* and *Seventeen* magazine, had a great vocabulary, and no understanding whatsoever of mathematics and science. I had a way of imitating people's speech that got me AP in French without really knowing any grammar. I was not what you would call a natural scholar."

Still, she knew she wanted something more than secretarial school, where Debbie and some other girls were headed. She liked languages, enough to fake a little French. Maybe she could be a United Nations interpreter?

The straight and narrow, it turned out, led to Poughkeepsie. In the fall of 1967, she made the ninety-minute trip from Bernardsville for her first term at Vassar College. And this time she knew how to pronounce "Carl Jung."

Julie

❧

"PURITY AND WISDOM" was the motto of Vassar College, though it had long disappeared from the school insignia. Founded in 1861, Vassar was the first of the Seven Sisters schools to be chartered as a college, with the goal of providing a liberal-arts education for young women equivalent to what Harvard or Yale offered young men.

By 1967, though, purity was seriously out of fashion, and the refined living of the all-female campus seemed like something from another century. The expectations were clear: Vassar women were to marry well and raise families, perhaps volunteer or pursue part-time careers if they had the time. Sarah Blanding, the president of Vassar in 1961, assured a luncheon audience that the school was "successful in preparing young women for their part in creating happy homes, forward-looking communities, stalwart states, and neighborly nations."

Step one in creating a happy home: enter a happy partnership, preferably with a boy from the Ivy League. On weekends, the ladies of Vassar would pile onto buses bound for mixers at Princeton or Yale. (If you missed the bus, the bulletin boards were papered with signs for rides.) As the buses pulled onto the men's campus, boys in ties would crowd around, waiting to see the latest haul. If you were lucky, you'd dance with a Whiffenpoof, and if you were that kind of girl, you'd wake up the next morning in the Taft Hotel. Then it was back on the bus to Poughkeepsie.

A decade later, Meryl would star in a television version of *Uncommon Women and Others*, a play by her drama school classmate Wendy Wasserstein. Based on Wasserstein's experiences at Mount Holyoke, another Seven Sisters school, the play captured the vanishing world of midcentury women's liberal-arts education, one in which young ladies in headbands and pleated skirts are trained in "gracious living" by the matronly house mother, Mrs. Plumm. On Father-Daughter Weekend, they sing:

> *Though we have had our chances*
> *For overnight romances*
> *With the Harvard and the Dartmouth male,*
> *And though we've had a bunch in*
> *Tow from Princeton Junction,*
> *We're saving ourselves for Yale.*

Of course, not all the women of 1967 were there to earn an M.R.S. The year before, the newly formed National Organization for Women had released its statement of purpose, in which Betty Friedan called for "a fully equal partnership of the sexes," and the more progressive of the Vassar freshmen were of the same mind.

In *Uncommon Women*, a character describes her conflict between finding Mr. Right and the thornier demands of modern womanhood. "I suppose this isn't a very impressive sentiment," she says to a girl-friend, "but I really would like to meet my prince. Even a few princes. And I wouldn't give up being a person. I'd still remember all the Art History dates. I just don't know why suddenly I'm supposed to know what I want to do."

Meryl arrived on campus oblivious to the changing tides. "On entering Vassar, if you had asked me what feminism was, I would've thought it had something to do with having nice nails and clean hair," she said later.

She was entranced by the school's traditions, its pride—not the rah-rah stuff she'd known as a cheerleader, but the exalted nature of academe. A few days into her first semester, the students assembled for the convocation ceremony, signaling the end of orientation and the beginning of the fall term. It was held in late afternoon on the hills around Sunset Lake, a man-made pond where Vassar girls traditionally brought their dates. Now everyone wore white, and the entire faculty sat in robes on a platform. "A very aesthetically moving scene, right?" Meryl wrote in a letter to her old high school boyfriend Mike Booth. "No. But what really rocked me was just thinking how some of the greatest minds alive were sitting there in front of me. Little Meryl Streep, and they were actually prepared to meet *me* face to face in a seminar. Wow. It's enough to strip your ego to the bone."

She hit it off with her roommate, Liz, and they hung out in the campus coffee shop and played guitar. The repertoire: Eddie Floyd's "Knock on Wood," Simon and Garfunkel's "The Dangling Conversation," "In My Life" by the Beatles, "Hold On, I'm Comin'" by Sam and Dave, "Here, There and Everywhere" (Beatles again), some Otis Redding. Meryl doodled a picture of herself and Liz playing on a couch. Over Liz, she wrote: "sexy dark voice, Jewish, Brooklyn, pot, beat, beads, nice, considerate." Over herself, she wrote: "Mary Louise Streep, 18 years and five months, medium to high wiggly voice, Wasp, Bernardsville, moderate, uncertain, JM"—for Johnny Mathis—"still affectionate, hook nose like Baez, heart of gold."

In reflective moments, she wrote to Mike. He was stationed in Germany, en route to Vietnam. Distance may have made it easier for Meryl to confide her anxieties, as well as her zeal. "I was really apprehensive about coming here," she wrote him, "but there are so many different people [that] I needn't have worried about being thrown amongst debutantes and greasy grimes. There are a lot of both groups here. Some belong to both categories, but there are tons of miscellanies like myself."

She took drama and English and, "just for the hell of it," introductory Italian. There were no boys around to dress up for, or to fight over with other girls. The spawning ground—"where the boys are"—was a bus ride away, and that was far enough that she could finally exhale. People were staying up all night smoking cigarettes and arguing about feminism and race and consciousness. Meryl read *Soul on Ice*, Eldridge Cleaver's account of being black and imprisoned in America—who even knew about the Black Panthers back in Bernardsville? She could wear the same turtleneck for weeks on end, put her hair up in a hasty bun, do Turkish dances in the dorms. No one cared. For once, female friendship was untainted by competition or envy.

"I made some very quick but lifelong and challenging friends," she said later. "And with their help, outside of any competition for boys, my brain woke up. I got up and I got outside myself and I found myself again. I didn't have to pretend. I could be goofy, vehement, aggressive, and slovenly and open and funny and tough, and my friends let me. I didn't wash my hair for three weeks once. They accepted me, like the Velveteen Rabbit. I became real instead of an imaginary stuffed bunny."

Not that boys were out of the picture. She began seeing a Yale junior named Bob Levin, the fullback of the football team—"my new thing at Yale," she'd call him. Her roommate had set them up on a blind date. She would cheer him on at football games, including an infamous Yale-versus-Harvard match that tied 29 to 29. (Tommy Lee Jones was a Crimson guard.) On weekends, she'd go to parties with Bob at DKE, where one of his fraternity brothers was George W. Bush. At the end of his senior year, Bush tried to tap Bob for his secret society, Skull and Bones, but Bob declined, preferring the more informal Elihu Club. Meryl would be his dinner date at Elihu on Sunday evenings. She wouldn't say much, still unsure of a girl's place in the old boys' club.

Her taste in men hadn't changed much since high school, but her sense of their importance was eroding. At Vassar, there was an unspoken rule: if you made plans with a fellow student on the weekend—say, a concert at Skinner Hall—those plans would be immediately usurped if either girl landed a date. The boy took precedence. "I remember when I was, like, a sophomore that someone brought up that probably this was rude and weird and cruel, and that friends were as important as boys," Meryl recalled. "That was a new idea, completely new idea."

She had overpowering reactions to art, to books, to music. One weekend, she went up to Dartmouth to see Simon and Garfunkel. When Garfunkel sang "For Emily, Whenever I May Find Her," she was transfixed. The last line, especially—Garfunkel's wailing, searching declaration of love—moved her for reasons she struggled to articulate. It's an "understatement," she wrote to Mike, in a letter enclosed with a pressed orange maple leaf, "but somehow when he sang the words it was almost like the beautiful feeling you have when someone first tells you the same thing. I can't understand how he can, after singing that song as many times as he has, still make it so earth rocking."

It was a lesson in performance. A lesson in emotional truth.

One night in her dorm, she sat in bed reading James Joyce's *A Portrait of the Artist as a Young Man*. When she got to the last page, she closed the book, the words still ringing in her ears: "Welcome, O life! I go to encounter for the millionth time the reality of experience and to forge in the smithy of my soul the uncreated conscience of my race."

Meryl thought she was having a "severe identity crisis." She went down the hall and asked a girl if she had a fever, just to feel another person's hand on her forehead. The book had confused her, but in a way that felt unbearably exciting. Everything else now seemed trivial: the inane dorm-hall chatter outside her door, her intellectualizing with Bob. She wanted something real, something that hit her in the face and shook her out of her constant preoccupation with herself. But what was "real"? What was Joyce trying to tell her? It was as if he was pushing her somewhere she wasn't ready to go, or wasn't willing.

She started writing a letter to Mike, so many miles away: "I tend now, however, perhaps because of distance (physical/spiritual?) to make you, 'Mike,' what I am searching to find, or something which you represent to me, something I value above all things. I wish so hard you were here always. I miss your presence or at least your word. James Joyce really has me flying around. His 'Portrait,' you know, some sort of autobiography, is so greatly personal. I see you there, me, everybody. There is so much I cannot understand in his work." She signed off in Italian: *Te aspetto e le tue parole come sempre.*

I await you and your words as always.

AT TWO O'CLOCK in the morning, Mike Booth was woken up in his barracks and told to report to the emergency room. The clamor of descending helicopters erased whatever was left of his sleep. The Vietcong had overrun a base down the coast, and now the medics hauled out bleeding soldiers one by one from the choppers.

The 91st Evacuation Hospital, in Tuy Hoa, usually treated Vietnamese civilians, but when something like this happened, they made an exception. Mike darted among the wounded GIs, cutting their fatigues off with scissors. Some of them needed tourniquets, badly—they might lose a limb, but it was their only chance of making it through the night. By daylight, nine Americans were dead.

Such a stupid war, Mike thought to himself. *It shouldn't be going on in the first place.*

Mike hadn't waited for the draft, or evaded it like some of his friends. He enlisted, hoping for a big adventure. Like a lot of people back home, he had his doubts about the war, but he decided that if he became a medic he'd have something to be proud of, no matter what. After three months of basic training and three months of medical training, he shipped out to Germany, where he worked in a dispensary and drove an ambulance.

Most guys were thrilled to be stationed in Germany, but Mike wanted to be where the action was. A friend of his had requested a transfer to Vietnam, and the Army was happy to oblige. After a beer-filled night, Mike decided to do the same. Within two or three weeks, he got his orders and flew to the air base in Guam.

Three times a day, Mike would go to the replacement center, as names and service numbers were called out like in a game of bingo. *Private So-and-So! You're going to Da Nang! Report to Officer So-and-So!* When someone got called to one of the "bad places," the other guys would turn their backs, as if he had a disease. Mike wound up in Tuy Hoa: right in the action. From the plane, he looked down on the Vietnam coastline: all lush jungles and winding beaches, as alien as a Martian landscape. He was finally getting his adventure.

He rode on the back of a truck to the hospital, vaguely aware that he was sniper bait. When he got to the barracks, he dropped his duffel bag on his new bed and went to meet the other men in the unit. Out back, he found twenty or thirty guys, blasting music on a tape deck and smoking dope like there was no tomorrow. Past the barbed wire were an artillery unit and a trucking unit and then sand and cactus as far as the eye could see.

The next day, he reported to the hospital, where there were more patients than beds. He began working twelve-hour shifts, six days a week. He saw traumatic amputations, gunshot wounds, fragmentation wounds, women, children, Vietnamese soldiers. Some had third-degree napalm burns all over their bodies. It was ghastly, but he considered himself lucky. Had he been sent to the front lines as a field medic, he would have been a walking target.

On days off, the guys rode in a truck down to a shantytown, where girls were available and you could get cartons of cigarettes stuffed with marijuana. Mike would wander off to the countryside and amble into Buddhist temples, where the monks would pour him tea. Sometimes, he and a buddy would rent motorcycles and ride them to the edge of town, jumping over ravines like aspiring Steve McQueens. Other days, he would lie in the barracks, reading books from the camp library. "I felt like such a loser being in Vietnam," he recalled, "but I said, 'Well, I'm going to read. I'm going to develop my mind.' And so I read an awful lot of philosophy and existentialism: Dostoyevsky, Camus, Sartre. A lot of poetry—Baudelaire, Rilke, Rimbaud, Yeats. Books about Buddhism and Eastern philosophy."

He knew he was missing out: on college, on rock and roll, even on the antiwar protests that he read about in the paper. When he turned twenty, he got a letter from Meryl. She had just been down to Yale to hear the author William Manchester speak. "I'm not flunking here," she wrote. "It's not hard at all. The reading is fantastic. Read Joyce, 'Portrait of the Artist as a Young Man,' and also very very great is Richard Rubenstein 'After Auschwitz.'"

Back in Bernardsville, Mike had always talked to Meryl about books. But all this breathless rumination over Joyce and roommates and Simon and Garfunkel only made her—and home—seem farther away. "I felt," he recalled, "like I was on the other side of the world."

THOSE FIRST TWO years at Vassar, she walked around campus in a liberated daze. But it wouldn't last. The all-female haven that had emancipated Meryl Streep was under imminent threat. Like her, the school was having a severe identity crisis.

Across the country, single-sex education was falling out of favor. By 1967, nearly two-thirds of the Vassar student body came from coeducational public high schools like Meryl's, and the idea of giving up boys (whatever the benefits) was becoming harder to accept. Alan Simpson, the Oxford-educated historian who had become Vassar's president in 1964, was a firm believer in liberal-arts colleges for women. But applications were drying up. Unlike the other Seven Sisters schools, which were located close to their male counterparts, Vassar was relatively isolated, and it held less and less appeal for young women who wanted to interact with men seven days of the week.

In the fall of 1966, President Simpson formed the Committee on New Dimensions, which would plan for Vassar's future. At its first meeting, he noted that Hamilton was creating a college for women, and Wesleyan and Yale were likely to follow. Ideas were floated: maybe Vassar could create a coordinate men's college, or affiliate with an existing one nearby? The committee began to explore potential "dancing partners."

What the committee didn't know was that Simpson was considering a much more radical plan. In December, he met with Kingman Brewster, the president of Yale, to discuss a possible merger between the two universities. Vassar would sell off its Poughkeepsie campus and relocate to New Haven. He kept the plan quiet, knowing it would be an academic bombshell.

But word got out, and news of an impending "royal marriage" drove Vassar's alumnae to near hysteria. "How unthinkable," one wrote to the alumnae magazine, "to change this quiet and beautiful atmosphere for a huge city complex with its pressures and tensions." Professors were similarly opposed, fearing they would be overshadowed or supplanted by their Yale counterparts. A headline in *Life* magazine echoed the growing sentiment: "How Dare They Do It?"

The undergraduates, though, were intrigued. Sure, they might lose their identity as Vassar students. But "saving ourselves for Yale" would now be a cinch, minus the three-hour round trip. Some took to singing "Boola Boola," the Yale fight song, on the quads. A survey in the spring of 1967 asked students: "Would the presence of men in class improve the quality of discussion?" and "Do you think that the absence of men in Vassar classes involves any important loss in perspective?" Sixty-eight percent said "yes" to both.

Like most everyone at Vassar, Meryl followed the fracas closely. Few students believed the Yale merger would really go through. The relocation would be costly, and those pearl-clutching alumnae might write Vassar out of their wills, to the detriment of students on scholarships. But most of them liked the idea nonetheless, including Meryl.

"I really think they should move to New Haven if we are going to catch up, or maybe loosen up as much as, say, Antioch or even Swarthmore," she wrote to Mike. "It's really so unnatural, especially the social relationships. Hectic, frantic, rushed, etc etc. Now they have affiliations between certain colleges at Yale and houses here at Vassar. That sets up an easier way to have, you know, friends-lovers instead of weekend LOVER babies."

On November 12, 1967, President Simpson informed President Brewster that the Vassar-Yale study was dead. Burying his thwarted enthusiasm, he proclaimed: "Full speed ahead in Poughkeepsie!"

But how? The idea of creating a coordinate men's college still hovered. Then came a dramatic reversal: on May 30, 1968, the faculty voted 102 to 3 in favor of admitting men to Vassar. This option had received minimal scrutiny, but it now seemed like the least apocalyptic scenario. Had Simpson not pursued the Yale merger with such brio, the elders of Vassar might never have considered coeducation. On July 11th, as the students were enjoying the summer of '68, the board of trustees approved the plan. Starting in autumn, 1970, Vassar would admit men for the first time since World War II.

"Vassar to Pursue Complete Coeducation; Method and Cost Under Consideration" ran the front-page headline in the *Miscellany News*, Vassar's student newspaper. As the fall semester began in 1968, the students were abuzz with excitement, angst, even droll curiosity. In a *Miscellany News* column titled "Vassar Men—Facing a Comic Doom," a student named Susan Casteras imagined life for the incoming males. How would a "6 ft. 2 brawny superman" fit into a "female-tailored bed"? Would the bathtubs have to be rescaled to fit more "Amazonian proportions"? "Meals, too would have to be replanned to avoid a starvation diet image. One delicate scoop of cottage cheese on two wilted lettuce leaves, one 3 inch square of meat, one wiggly slab of red jello, and a glass of ice tea (with or without the lemon) are not the stuff of which wonder-strong men are made."

As 1968 turned into 1969, the women of Vassar steeled themselves for the coming boy invasion. But men were far from the first thing on Meryl's mind. Now a sophomore, she was busy acquiring a "genuine sense of identity." And part of that identity was the ability to become someone else. She was discovering acting, and the Drama Department was about to discover her.

Another metamorphosis.

MIKE BOOTH HAD begun to dread coming home. He knew that everyone would look at him differently. It didn't matter that he was against the war, or that he'd been a medic: he'd be branded a "baby killer." Plus, he had gotten used to adventure. Tuy Hoa was starting to feel like where he belonged, if he belonged anywhere.

In late July, 1969, he was on a layover somewhere between Vietnam and home. He had stopped at Fort Lewis for a fresh uniform, an airplane voucher, and one last terrible Army haircut. The televisions in the airports were still playing footage of Neil Armstrong landing on the moon. But Mike didn't share the rest of the country's euphoria.

"It didn't mean anything for me, except I felt like the astronaut," he recalled. "After being in Vietnam for a year and a half, I was in an alien world. Except, instead of being in a spacesuit, I was encased in all my memories." *God,* he thought, *I wonder if I'll ever be what they call normal again.*

He hadn't told his family which day he was arriving, because he didn't want a welcome party. When his mother saw him at the front door, she was overwhelmed. She sat him down and related all the town gossip: who was sick, who was pregnant, who was having money problems. Jet-lagged, Mike was on the verge of falling asleep when she said, "Oh, and one more thing."

"What's that?"

"Meryl's been calling here every day, wondering when you're coming home."

When she walked in the door, he was astonished. Two years had elapsed since they'd seen each other. Her look had become bohemian: hoop earrings, jeans, sandals, and a backless Indian-style blouse, her yellow hair now down to her waist.

Holy cow, he thought, *she's not a girl anymore.*

He told her about the hospital and Buddhist temples and riding motorcycles. She told him about Vassar and drama class and what books she was reading. He couldn't get over how beautiful she was, how confident and self-possessed. To his surprise, she acted like they had never broken up. They started seeing each other every few days, driving around Bernardsville to their old haunts. In the back of his mind, he kept thinking, *What the hell is she bothering with a guy like me for?*

It was as if nothing had changed. Except something had. In their letters, they had communicated their deepest longings. But in person, they felt distant. Mike was restless, not sure what to do with himself. Most people were hesitant to ask him about Vietnam, and when they did, he didn't know quite what to say. The younger kids in town looked at him suspiciously. His elders—the men who had fought in World War II—would slap him on the back. But that didn't feel right either.

Meryl had changed, too. In conversation, she would casually mention the college guys she'd been seeing, like Bob Levin. Mike didn't understand why. He just knew that she was holding back, and so was he. After a while, he asked why she kept coming to see him, then telling him about her other boyfriends. She told him she didn't know what he was really thinking—he'd broken up with her before, and he had barely written to her when he was gone, despite all her letters. "I realized how cowardly I had been with her," he recalled, "because I wasn't going to come out and really let her know how I felt about her. She was kind of playing the same game with me that I was with her."

Mike needed to get out of town. It didn't matter where—his parents' house was too quiet, and Bernardsville was too small. Having missed the Summer of Love, he decided to hitchhike out to San Francisco. Maybe he could still get a taste of it, or at least another adventure. At the end of the summer, Meryl drove him an hour down Route 22, to Easton, Pennsylvania. He gave her some things he'd gotten on a thirty-day leave in India: a silk brocade, an ivory carving of Shiva.

Before he got out of the car, she gave him a kiss and said, "Don't forget to write when you're out there."

"Sure," he said. But he knew that he wouldn't.

ONE DAY IN drama class, Meryl delivered a Blanche DuBois monologue from *A Streetcar Named Desire*. A thickset man with a bushy mustache came rushing up from the back of the room. It was the teacher, Clint Atkinson.

"You're good! You're good!" he told the stunned young Blanche.

He handed her a script. "Read *Miss Julie*," he said.

She looked down at the words from August Strindberg's 1888 masterpiece. Sure, she had gotten the leads in the high school musicals. But this was no Marian the Librarian. Nothing in her experience seemed to match up with that of Strindberg's heroine, a tortured Swedish aristocrat. At least, not at first. But as Meryl read, Atkinson's eyes widened. He saw something in this lissome twenty-year-old, something that she had not yet seen in herself. He had found his Miss Julie.

He went to the head of the department, Evert Sprinchorn, and told him he wanted to do *Miss Julie*. Sprinchorn balked: "You can't do that!" Unlike Atkinson, who was a working director, Sprinchorn was an academic, and a Strindberg scholar at that. Atkinson was up for contract renewal, and Sprinchorn was certain he was trying to butter him up by suggesting a Strindberg play.

But he knew that it wouldn't work. For one thing, he told Atkinson, there are only three characters. To fulfill the student demand, they'd need something with at least five or six parts. Besides, the role was much too demanding. Miss Julie is a psychological minefield, a woman self-immolating from the pressures of her class and the fire in her heart. Playing games with her own authority, she seduces—or is seduced by—her father's servant, Jean. Miss Julie is a rebel, a lady, a lover, and a mess. And she has to carry the entire play. What undergrad could pull that off?

Atkinson pleaded: "Why don't you come to a reading tonight and see what you think?" Sprinchorn agreed. Hours later, he and Atkinson were sitting side by side in the student greenroom, watching Meryl Streep read the part of Miss Julie.

Within ten minutes, Sprinchorn leaned his head in to Atkinson's: "Go ahead with it."

Lights up on the kitchen of a Swedish country manor. It's a midsummer night, and Miss Julie is causing her usual scandal at a dance nearby. Waiting in the wings to make her entrance, Meryl watched the two actors playing the valet and the cook, gossiping about the mistress of the house. ("Tonight she's wild again. Miss Julie's absolutely wild!") Her hands rested on her ruffled blue gown, with an opulent bow atop the bustle. Her lemon-colored hair was pinned up. It was the first serious play she had ever seen, and she was starring in it.

The student theater had once housed a riding academy, and when it rained some of the backstage rooms still smelled of the stables. In the lead-up to the play, Atkinson had asked a couple Vassar girls to go into New York to find lilacs for the set. Since it was not actually midsummer, but midwinter, they had failed. So he sprayed the theater with lilac scent, just enough to cover the whiff of horses. When Meryl heard her cue, she stepped into the light, a lilac dew settling on her brow.

Some of the drama majors, who had put in long hours at the shop, had balked at the casting. Meryl didn't appear to mind. "She just seemed much more mature than I was," said Judy Ringer (née Metskas), who played Christine, the cook. "I'm sure she was in many ways. But in terms of her acting style and her ability to access her emotions, she had much more maturity than anybody else in that department. And who knows where that came from—I can't say."

On the surface, she seemed nonchalant. "I don't remember her having any particular investment in it," recalled Lee Devin, the young instructor who played Jean. Boys had yet to enroll at Vassar, and, as usual, the male roles were played by teachers or hired professionals. Onstage, Devin was her seducer, servant, and tormenter. Offstage, he tried to play professor, but she had no interest in intellectual banter.

"My kind of curioso instructional pompous attitude was not for her," he said. "She just did the stuff."

But the play seemed to work a strange magic on her. "It was a very serious play, and I had no idea what I was doing, really none," she said later. "But oh, my God, it just was a place to tap into all sorts of feelings that I never had I guess admitted to myself, or felt like parading in front of a group of people."

It was as if Miss Julie's emotional landscape had unlocked Meryl's own, transforming it from black-and-white to Technicolor. Strindberg's heroine runs the psychological gamut: imperiousness, lust, entitlement, disgust, self-disgust, self-hatred, pleading, wailing, dreaming, panic—all before wandering back into the night in a suicidal trance, Jean's razor in hand. "She is the first neurotic, with her inner self fighting, and eventually destroying, the outer shell of respectability," the *Poughkeepsie Journal* wrote in its rave on December 13, 1969. "A tall order for any actress . . . one that Miss Streep handles with surprising ease."

She was back in the zone, in the church, in the place she had visited as a child playing the Virgin Mary.

"How did you know how to do that?" her friends asked.

She had no clue.

Evert Sprinchorn had a theory about why the play so transmogrified its leading lady. "Meryl Streep, whether she knew it or not, identified with the character," he said. "Miss Julie sort of hates men. Well, there's an aspect of Meryl Streep—she's rebelling against male society."

"I loved my father," Miss Julie tells Jean, "but I took my mother's side because I didn't know the whole story. She had taught me to hate all men—you've heard how she hated men—and I swore to her that I'd never be a slave to any man." Strindberg wrote *Miss Julie* about a disappearing world, in which the old elite was falling apart in the wake of a new industrial class. Julie and Jean, according to the playwright, are "modern characters, living in a transitional era," one that throws aristocrat and servant into a deadly *danse macabre*.

In other words, it was not unlike the college campus where the play was being staged. It was December, 1969—the eve of a new decade, the eve of a new Vassar. Soon men would be in the classrooms, the dorms, even the bathrooms. Gone would be the demeaning weekend mixers, yes. But what else would be lost? Would the women of Vassar still talk in class when there were boys in the back row? Would they still leave their hair unwashed?

For those first male students to set foot on the Vassar campus, the world had gone topsy-turvy. Women were used to being in places they weren't wanted. Now men were the novelty. Men were the minority. Rarely had they encountered a world so unprepared for their existence. There were no urinals in the bathrooms. Flowery chintz drapes hung in the living room at Raymond House. (They mysteriously disappeared two days into the semester.) One aspiring bodybuilder practiced his five-hundred-pound dead lift in his dorm room, until a space was found for him in the basement. Jeff Silverman, of the class of 1972, transferred from an all-male school, dreaming of a hormonal adventure. "Being the only man—in class, at the dinner table, or just perambulating through the quad—was something we all had to get used to, just as we had to get used to seeing curlers in the morning and nightgowns at night, and making no big deal of either," he recalled. "The rules had yet to be written. Proper etiquette was made up as we went along. At first no one knew what to say at 8 a.m. to the woman sitting next to you at breakfast. But we quickly learned that 'Pass the sugar, please' would do for a start."

The women, meanwhile, were adjusting to the sound of male footfalls in the dining rooms. For Meryl Streep, the change was acute. "The men came my junior and senior years," she recalled. "I lived in Davison and Main, and they moved in with us: demitasse, the dress code, the parietals disappeared. But so did some of the subtler eccentrics. They went underground, I think. I remember the first coed year when suddenly it seemed that the editorships of the literary magazine, the newspaper, the class presidencies, and the leadership of the then very important student political movements were all held by men. I think that was temporary deference to the guests. Egalitarianism did prevail. Vassar evolved. So did we. I think we were ready for them, the men, but I know I was personally grateful for the two-year hiatus from the sexual rat race."

In *Miss Julie*, Jean remembers growing up in a shack with seven siblings and a pig. From his window, he tells Miss Julie, he could see the wall of her father's garden, with apple trees peeking out from the top. "That was the Garden of Eden for me, and there were many angry angels with flaming swords standing guard over it. But in spite of them, I and the other boys found a way to the Tree of Life. . . . I'll bet you despise me."

Miss Julie shrugs and says, "All boys steal apples."

MIKE BOOTH WAS still restless. He had hitchhiked all the way to California. On the way back, he hiked through the Grand Canyon. For a time, he worked in a restaurant in North Carolina. Then he got a job driving a cement truck. Nothing stuck.

His mother had sent his high school transcript to a college-placement center, and every time he came back home she showered him with catalogs.

"Look! Hiram Scott College, out in Nebraska!"

"I don't think so, Mom."

One rainy night, President Nixon came to Morristown, near Bernardsville, to campaign for a gubernatorial candidate. Mike and a friend went to protest. When Nixon's motorcade arrived, he was up front, shouting, "One, two, three, four, we don't want your fucking war!" Nixon flashed a victory sign with his fingers and ducked inside the hotel. When he came out, a half hour later, the protesters were even angrier. Nixon went for his limo, and the crowd surged forward, propelling Mike until he was five feet away from the president. He looked Nixon in the eye and chanted at the top of his lungs.

Once Nixon drove away, Mike heard someone say, "That's the guy!"

Suddenly, three men in suits came over and threw him on the ground. They emptied his pockets, then hauled him inside to an empty office for an interrogation.

"Who are you working for—the Communist Party?" one of them asked.

Mike cackled. "Are you kidding? I'm a vet who just got home from the war, and I don't approve of the shit that's going on there."

They asked what he was doing at the protest.

"I was only trying to get his autograph," he snarled back. "I'm starting a local chapter of the Tricky Dick Fan Club."

The incident made the local papers. When reporters called the house, his mortified father said he had left for college in Colorado. Of course he hadn't. He was right there, even if he seemed worlds away. One week, he'd tell his parents he was going to hike the Appalachian Trail. The next, he wanted to go to Taiwan to study Chinese. All he knew was that he couldn't sit still.

Then he realized what was going on: he missed Vietnam. He missed the excitement. He missed the jungles. He missed riding into town on the back of a truck in the middle of a monsoon rain.

Meryl kept asking when he was going to visit Vassar, and finally he took the train to Poughkeepsie. He hung out with her college friends, who now included men. He drank wine—too much, probably. He was nervous. They talked poetry, and when Mike began extolling Ezra Pound, one of the guys shot back that Pound was an anti-Semite.

"I know that, but he's also a great poet!" Mike said, before pronouncing that "Ballad of the Goodly Fere" was one of the best poems ever written. But what did he know? He'd never been to college.

Before he left, Meryl told him that he should think about enrolling at Vassar, now that it was open to men.

But Mike knew it would never happen. "As a vet, I felt so out of place with all those privileged kids," he recalled. "Maybe I was insecure, but I knew Vassar wasn't the place for me."

*   *   *

THE FALL SEMESTER of her senior year, Meryl did the last thing some-one bemoaning a crumbling matriarchy would do. She spent the term at all-male Dartmouth as part of a twelve-school exchange, one of sixty women on a campus of nearly four thousand. It was the mirror image of Vassar.

When she got to campus in late 1970, she realized what she was in for. Like the men at Vassar, the women who had crash-landed in Hanover, New Hampshire, were a novelty, often an unwelcome one. "They really didn't want us here," she recalled. "There was an us-and-them feel to campus."

One day, Meryl and a girlfriend were studying in the corridor of Baker Library and had to use the bathroom, which was on the other end of the room. They could feel the eyes of male students on them, so they waited and waited, until they couldn't anymore. As they crossed the library, the boys started tapping their toes in rhythm with their footsteps. Then they started pounding their hands on the desks. "It was completely hostile," Meryl said.

Dartmouth's social scene was dominated by the fraternities on Webster Avenue. One night, Meryl's classmate Carol Dudley saw a desk careen out of a window. Moments later, two men in a drunken brawl rolled down three flights of stairs and out into the snow, wearing nothing but shorts. Meryl would balk at the women who would "bust into houses like cattle to the slaughter," disdainful of the rigid gender roles she had only recently learned to transcend at Vassar.

Academic life was similarly jarring. "I got straight A's. My eyes crossed when I got the printout," she would recall. "At Vassar they had a party in the English Department when the first A was given out in twenty years. At Dartmouth, it seemed to me, A's were conferred with ease and detachment. 'Ah,' I said to myself, 'that's the differ-ence between the men's and women's colleges.' We made A's the old-fashioned way. We earned them. At the men's schools, they seemed to be lubricants in the law-school squeeze, and a fond alma mater was anxious to see her boys do well."

Even so, the counterculture was more visible at Dartmouth than it had been at Vassar. The boys wore their hair long—it looked like "Vassar from behind," Meryl recalled. Raggedy clothes were in, and "the social life was incredibly open," Dudley said, "because anybody could afford old T-shirts or whatever from the Army Navy store. Everybody had an old banger. And you could be totally cool without spending anything, other than drinks in the dorms, and the chip was either fifty cents or a dollar for a keg of beer."

In her isolation, Meryl took solace in the beauty of the Upper Valley. When she wasn't waitressing at the Hanover Inn, she would read on the shores of the Connecticut River, or go to Rollins Chapel to sing to herself. It was always empty. That was the way she liked it. She tried out for a play, but lost the only female role to her best friend. She was the only woman in her dance class. In playwriting class, taught by the Trinidadian professor Errol Hill, she wrote feminist dramas: "highly symbolic, metaphorical, serious but funny" treatments of women's lib.

She may have taken some of her zeal from Gloria Steinem, who had delivered the commencement address at Vassar that spring. In a speech titled "Living the Revolution," Steinem told the class of 1970, "Men's hunting activities are forever being pointed to as proof of tribal superiority. But while they were out hunting, women built houses, tilled the fields, developed animal husbandry, and perfected language. Men, isolated from each other out there in the bush, often developed into creatures that were fleet of foot, but not very bright."

Meryl's thesis project at Dartmouth was on costume design. She spent hours on the linoleum floor of her dorm room in the Choates, sketching costumes from different periods of theatrical history: pantaloons and petticoats and corsets and bustles. By winter, she had a portfolio spanning the ages, apparitions of women she might have been, or could become.

Carol Dudley had noticed a difference between Vassar's educational style and Dartmouth's. "The women at Vassar would tend to take notes seriously and regurgitate stuff," she recalled. "Whereas I found the men's thought to be much more freewheeling, that they had more ideas that were theirs and were willing to argue their turf." It wasn't that the men were smarter. They had been pushed to be vocal and argumentative in class, while the Seven Sisters schools still had the vestigial whiff of "gracious living."

Meryl noticed it, too. "I remember thinking, at Vassar, people would sit quietly and answer questions with judicial, thoughtful, ruminative answers," she said. At Dartmouth, no sooner did the professor start asking a question than five guys were trying to answer. "It was very inspiring. It was something I didn't have in me," she said. "The climate and the expectation were playing to the proactive."

As 1970 turned to 1971, Meryl packed her bags and headed back to Poughkeepsie. It hadn't been easy being so outnumbered by men, but those few months in Hanover had fortified her. In class, she mimicked the enterprise she had seen at Dartmouth. Before her professors even finished asking a question, she would thrust her hand up and say, "I don't even think that question is *valid*." It didn't matter that she had no idea what the question was. She had seen both sides of the gender looking glass, and as any Alice in Wonderland knows, things only get curiouser and curiouser.

PROFESSOR ATKINSON COULDN'T stop putting her in plays: Brecht's *The Good Woman of Setzuan*, Molière's *The Miser*. In March of her final term, she was in *The London Merchant*, George Lillo's tragedy from 1731. Atkinson chose the play in part because it offered a good role for Meryl: Sarah Millwood, a prostitute who coerces her lover to steal for her. He winds up murdering his uncle, and the couple is sent to the gallows.

Once again, the action onstage mirrored the gender war in the dorms. Disparaged as a "deceitful, cruel, bloody woman," Millwood unloads on the male sex: "Men of all degrees, and all professions, I have known, yet found no difference, but in their several capacities; all were alike wicked to the utmost of their power."

Meryl tapped into the rage she had displayed in *Miss Julie*. Maybe she was thinking of the Dartmouth boys who had pounded their fists on her way to the library bathroom. Or maybe the times had gotten to her. The previous April, President Nixon had authorized the invasion of Cambodia, and the escalation was hotly debated on campus. Meryl had gotten a taste of the antiwar movement at Yale, where she and Bob Levin hung "We Won't Go!" signs as students heckled them from their dorm windows. But at Vassar she felt disillusioned by the rallies and the bonfires—they all seemed to be dominated by boys, who were still a minority. When Meryl saw them holding forth on the quad, they reminded her of Abbie Hoffman wannabes, performing for a swarm of adoring girls. It was theater, but not the good kind.

Whatever was driving her, it erupted like lava during her final speech in *The London Merchant*. "The audience was just cheering as if it was an operatic aria," said Evert Sprinchorn, who played the merchant Thorowgood. "When I read descriptions of nineteenth-century plays, it sometimes says, when there's a piece of bravura acting, 'The audience rose *at* her.' Well, when I was onstage with Meryl Streep I felt exactly that—the audiences rising at us."

The *Miscellany News* agreed: "Meryl Streep coos, connives, weeps and screams her character alive," it raved. "It is a roll [*sic*] with which Ms. Streep is familiar. Through her performances as 'Miss Julie,' Moliere's Frosine of 'The Miser' and now as Millwood, Ms. Streep is acquiring an image."

Despite the praise, Meryl kept wondering whether acting was a legitimate way to make a living; for a time, she couldn't decide whether to major in drama or economics. But Atkinson believed in her, enough to bring her to New York before she had the chance to graduate. In April of 1971, she made her professional debut, in Atkinson's production of Tirso de Molina's *The Playboy of Seville*, an early Spanish dramatization of the seductions of Don Juan. Meryl played the peasant Tisbea, one of his conquests.

The play went up at the Cubiculo Theater, a subterranean seventy-five-seater nicknamed The Cube, on Fifty-first Street off Ninth Avenue. It wasn't the cleanest part of town, but it was New York. Atkinson had brought a handful of Vassar girls down on their spring break, the talented ones like Meryl who could hold their own against the pros.

Philip LeStrange was a New York actor playing Catalinon. He had acted with Meryl at Vassar, in *The Miser*, and she seemed to him like someone without a care in the world. Backstage, the girls would tally the laughs they were getting night to night—one of them even kept a chart, which she'd check off during the scenes. But Meryl wasn't counting. Meryl was watching. The same was true of *The Playboy of Seville*. "Even in production," LeStrange said, "she would be at a vantage point where she would be, again, watching."

What did she see? Among other things, she saw Michael Moriarty, the thirty-year-old actor playing the title role. Erratic, handsome, with a high forehead and intense eyes, Moriarty had a quavering, disassociated voice, like he was about to snap. He played Don Juan like a cool cat, almost bored to death.

He didn't make it through the three-week run. Midway through, he got cast in a Broadway show and quit. Unlike *The Playboy of Seville*, it was a paying gig. Atkinson scrambled for another Don Juan and found one, albeit with a completely different approach to the part. For Meryl, it was a glimpse at the winds of show business, and far from the last time she'd cross paths with Moriarty.

She returned to Vassar, still unsure what to do with her life. She knew she was good at acting; her friends in the second row at *Miss Julie* had told her so. But when she thought of her holiest moments onstage, her mind kept returning to Sondra Green's speech class.

Meryl had become one of Green's most beloved students at Vassar. She was one of five handpicked for Green's advanced class in "the fundamentals of speech." Green didn't like improvisations, but she was curious about what Meryl would do with the assignment she had in mind.

"I had never given it to anybody before and I never gave it to anybody after," she recalled. "I told all the students I was going to go pick up my mail, and I would be back in five minutes, so they had that much time to prepare the improvisations I would assign to them. It doesn't matter what I told the other students. With Meryl, I told her to simply get up on the stage and that she would be taking her final curtain call after fifty years in the theater." Think of Helen Hayes, Green told her.

When she came back, she had Meryl stand onstage behind a curtain. She instructed the other students to applaud wildly and yell "Brava!" The curtain opened, revealing a girl of no more than twenty-one. But she carried herself like a woman of sixty years or more, someone who had taken countless curtain calls on countless stages.

She stepped forward, clasping her hands and bowing regally to her audience of five. Then she opened her arms and gave a speech.

"This is as much your curtain call as it is mine," she said grandly. "We have done this together, through all of these many wonderful years . . ."

Green was transported. So was Meryl, who was in tears.

"I'd never made myself cry before, even when I wanted to, you know, to get something when I was younger," Meryl recalled, many years, and many curtain calls, later. "I was never able to do that, but this really killed me . . . It was just sort of a glimpse into an imaginative leap that I thought, Ooh, you know, you can thoroughly sort of lose yourself in this thing."

She had gone back into the church of make-believe—and discovered herself, fifty years in the future.

MIKE BOOTH HAD finally found another adventure. His mother, in her unyielding quest to get him to move on with his life, had shown him a catalog for the University of the Americas, in Mexico. On the cover was a picture of two snowcapped volcanoes, Popocatepetl and Iztaccihuatl. It looked beautiful. It looked like a place where he could get away from the past.

Back home on break, he got a job at a shoe store in downtown Bernardsville. A few days after he started, Meryl walked in the door. In her scarf and long coat, she looked worldlier somehow. Her cheerleader skip had become a swagger.

They met up a couple times, just as friends. Mike no longer felt like the sad sack he'd been when he first came home. Now he was a swashbuckler, a globetrotter. And he had met a girl in Mexico. He made sure to mention her to Meryl when they were back at his place.

"She's beautiful, and she's half-Mexican," he said, thinking back to the summer she'd bragged about her Ivy League suitors.

"Really?" Meryl said, perhaps with a flicker of regret. They had watched each other change over these breaks in Bernardsville, each time drifting further and further apart. Back in high school, their world had been so small and safe. Now they no longer made sense together. The boy she had once confided in about James Joyce had found a new chunk of the world to get lost in.

But she had found something, too, something just as entrancing and all her own. On one of their breaks, she had told him excitedly, "I finally did some acting at Vassar."

"No kidding."

Meryl said she'd been in a play called *Miss Julie*. She'd been covered in fake canary blood, and all her friends had come and laughed their heads off.

"Can I do a scene for you?"

Mike snapped to attention as Meryl transformed into Miss Julie at her most withering, after Jean has defiled her: "You lackey! You shoeshine boy! Stand up when I talk to you!"

In hindsight, Mike wondered whether she had chosen the scene for a reason. Was some of Miss Julie's rage directed at him—latent anger or disappointment about the way things had worked out between them?

As he watched, the source of her emotions didn't occur to him. He simply marveled. He hadn't seen her do any acting since Daisy Mae. Nothing like this.

Man, he thought, *has she come a long way.*

SHE GRADUATED FROM Vassar on May 30, 1971. The commencement speaker was Eleanor Holmes Norton, the black feminist leader and future congresswoman. Still wondering whether she should apply to law school, Meryl returned to the Upper Valley. Some friends of hers had started a theater company in New Hampshire. She was all set to join them, until she found a better offer.

One day, she and her friend Peter Maeck, who had been in her playwriting class at Dartmouth, were flipping through the campus newspaper and saw an ad for a new summer-stock company called the Green Mountain Guild. It paid $48 a week—not bad. Peter and Meryl drove to Woodstock, Vermont, to audition. They both got in.

Its founder was Robert O'Neill-Butler, a theater professor who ran the company with his younger wife, Marj. O'Neill-Butler was grand and a bit tyrannical. The actors, who called him "O-B," could never quite tell if he was British. Offstage, Meryl sang jazz standards she'd learned from her mother and played with O-B's six-month-old son, whom she nicknamed Crazy Legs.

They would travel from town to town, putting on plays in Stowe and Killington and Quechee, sleeping in lodges and bunkrooms, everyone crashing together commune-style. One night as they all went to bed, Maeck deadpanned, "So this is the theater." They all cracked up in the pitch-black.

Nothing felt serious, especially acting. In John Van Druten's *The Voice of the Turtle*, Meryl and Peter Maeck had to eat milk and cookies. In the middle of a scene, Meryl raced offstage, then walked calmly back on and said, "Sorry, I had a cookie stuck in my throat. Now, where were we?"

O-B assigned them *Affairs of State*, a hoary 1950 boulevard comedy. Peter Parnell, another Dartmouth friend, was playing a politician who falls in love with his secretary. Meryl played the secretary, a part Celeste Holm had originated on Broadway. Left to their own devices, the young actors found the script so old-fashioned that they secretly rewrote it as a campy genre parody, with Parnell imitating Cary Grant and Meryl doing mousy-secretary-turned-bombshell. When O-B showed up on opening night, he was aghast—but too late to stop them.

As the weather cooled, O-B transformed the summer-stock company into winter-stock. Meryl and three other actors moved into an old farmhouse in Woodstock with a mile-long driveway. When it snowed, which it did almost constantly, the place felt like a colonial homestead, something out of a fairy tale. "It was really quite idyllic," Maeck recalled. "We'd rehearse right in the house and cook for each other and have friends over. It was really quite the life."

They performed in ski lodges and barns and converted restaurants, storing their props on unused tray racks or whatever was at hand. The audiences were tired and sunburnt after a day on the slopes. Sometimes Meryl would hear snoring in the dark. She sold ads for the programs and wrote plays, which she didn't show to anyone. She starred in Shaw's *Candida* in a beautiful old barn, and her parents came from New Jersey to see it. On New Year's Eve, some Dartmouth friends drove up from Boston in two Volkswagen Beetles. The first day of 1972, they woke up bleary-eyed and happy.

But she was feeling restless. Fun as her little "dilettante group" was, she knew that better theater was being done elsewhere. She was ready to be a real actress, whatever that meant. On a day off, she and Maeck went down to New York so Meryl could audition for the National Shakespeare Company, a touring troupe that operated the Cubiculo, where she'd done *The Playboy of Seville*. She thought the audition went well, but they rejected her, "which she just found crazy and unbelievable," Maeck said.

She figured if she was going to act—really act, not frolic around in ski lodges—she would have to study acting. She looked at applications for the two top drama schools in the country, Juilliard and Yale. The application fee for Yale was $15. For Juilliard it was $50, more than she was making in a week. Meryl wrote Juilliard a letter dripping with self-righteousness—something like, "This just shows what kind of cross-section of the population you get at your school."

That left Yale. Like most places, the drama school required two audition monologues, one modern and one classical. For modern, she picked an old standby: Blanche DuBois, *A Streetcar Named Desire*. For classical, something stately: Portia from *The Merchant of Venice*. "The quality of mercy is not strained; / It droppeth as the gentle rain from heaven . . ."

In that snow-covered farmhouse, she drilled her speeches. The thrill of it came in switching back and forth. One minute she was neurotic, sexually frustrated, sweating in the New Orleans heat. The next, she was brainy, cool, pontificating about the quality of mercy. The thrill of it was metamorphosis. That she could do.

From Woodstock, it was a straight shot down to New Haven. In late February, the spires of Yale were just beginning to thaw in the resurgent sun. Wearing a long dress, she was greeted there by Chuck Levin, a first-year acting student. He was the brother of Bob Levin, her Yalie ex-boyfriend. Meryl and Bob had broken up when he graduated and moved to North Carolina. They had talked vaguely about marriage (cohabitation wasn't an option), but once again Meryl's father had kept her on the straight and narrow. His ultimatum to Bob: "You want to provide for her? Pay for her last two years of school." That was the end of that.

At Yale, Chuck ushered her to a former fraternity building that had been taken over by the drama school. Up a musty flight of stairs was a rehearsal room with a small wooden stage. As Chuck waited outside, Meryl stood in front of a panel of professors. She showed them Venice. She showed them New Orleans.

Peter Maeck was staring out the window of the farmhouse when he saw Meryl's Nash Rambler huffing up the snowy driveway. She popped out of the car and climbed up the steps—she was practically strutting. She fixed her glowing eyes on him and smiled.

"I knocked 'em dead."

Constance

✄

SIGOURNEY WEAVER. Christopher Durang. Wendy Wasserstein. Meryl Streep. The talents who converged at the Yale School of Drama between 1972 and 1975 would cement those years as the school's undisputed golden age. They would work together for decades, even as Broadway and blockbusters and Pulitzer Prizes catapulted their careers. For now, they were bright young actors and playwrights and eccentrics, sewing costumes and stumbling through Chekhov amid the ivied walls of Yale.

Sound nice? It was hell.

"I feel instinctively that a school, or a place that professes to be a school, should make an effort not to judge so arbitrarily," Sigourney Weaver would say. "It was all politics. I still don't know what they wanted from me. I still think they probably had this Platonic ideal of a leading lady that I have never been able to live up to. And would never want to."

"The first year sent me into therapy," said Kate McGregor-Stewart, class of 1974. "I was struggling to prove my worth and still be allowed to be there, because a lot of people got cut at the end of the first year. I think we went from eighteen to twelve."

Linda Atkinson, class of 1975: "They didn't take your strong points and build on them from there. The point was to destruct all

61

of that and then find something else to build up in you. Which is sort of stupid, right? You're sort of talented, and So-and-So says, 'Throw that out the window.'"

Wendy Wasserstein called it the Yale School of Trauma.

"When I was in drama school, I was scared," Meryl would recall. "It was the first time I realized this isn't something that is fun, that it had a dark side." Yale "was like boot camp, shaving your head. It made you humble. A lot of it was breaking your spirit, and out of your survival instinct you start gathering what's important."

None of this was apparent when she arrived in New Haven in the fall of 1972, having gotten in on a scholarship. She knew she loved acting and drawing and nature, and she told her new classmates that her favorite place in the world was the Laurentian Mountains, north of Montreal. She had just turned twenty-three.

She moved into a three-story yellow Victorian house on Chapel Street, down the street from the Yale Repertory Theatre. The house had previously been used by Alcoholics Anonymous, and occasionally someone would peer through the windows, looking for a meeting. Now it was the kind of place where students could drift in and out, living there for a few months, or a semester, or a couple. The first night, the housemates gathered in the kitchen to discuss the house rules. Everyone would write their names on the food in the pantry, they decided. Meryl would share the first floor with a directing student named Barry Marshall, along with his wife and their corgi, called Little Dog.

On the second floor was William Ivey Long, a dandyish North Carolinian who had never been this far north. Having studied Renaissance and Baroque architecture at the College of William and Mary, he had recently dropped out of a doctoral program at Chapel Hill (thesis topic: Medici wedding festivals) to study stage design at Yale under the master teacher Ming Cho Lee. He had grabbed the last strip off a "roommate wanted" flyer and was still sleeping on a cot.

Later in the semester, they would get another housemate: a tall, patrician beauty named Susan Weaver, who had decided at thirteen years old that a longer name suited her and started calling herself Sigourney. Everyone knew her father was Sylvester Weaver, the former president of NBC, but you wouldn't guess it from her chaotic fashion sense: hippie rags and motorcycle jackets, selected from color-coded heaps laid around her room like garbage piles. She looked like Athena disguised as a bum. At Stanford, she had spent some time living in a treehouse. When Christopher Durang met her, she was wearing green pajama pants with pom-poms, which she said was part of her "elf" costume.

Now in her second year, Sigourney still baffled the faculty. They saw her as a leading lady. She saw herself as a comedienne. They harped on her appearance, comparing her to an unmade bed. At one evaluation, they told her she looked sullen in the hallways. "I'm sullen in the hallways because I'm not getting cast in anything!" she shot back. When she showed up to her voice lesson the following day in a white blouse and pearls, the instructor sneered, "You know, Sigourney, you don't have to be loved by everybody." For her next evaluation, she found a piece of muslin from the costume department, drew on a giant bull's-eye, and pinned it to her jacket—a symbol of her sartorial persecution. "Hit me," she said.

Disillusioned, she moved off campus to get some distance from the school, and wound up on the same floor as William Ivey Long. "Oh, you've got to come and see the Cabaret," she told him his first night in New Haven. "My friends are performing in it." Soon, he was sitting at a table with Chianti bottles and checkered tablecloth, watching the strangest performance he had ever seen in his life. It was performed by two second-year playwriting students: Albert Innaurato, who was dressed as the Mother Superior from *The Sound of Music*, and Christopher Durang, in a blue taffeta evening gown. After the show, an academic with a droopy mustache sat down and started pontificating on art and the theater. It was Michael Feingold, who would become the chief drama critic at *The Village Voice*.

"I didn't know what was happening," Long recalled. "I didn't understand the theater they were doing." He was ready to pack his bags and go home.

The next day, he was in his kitchen, staring at a "blond goddess" who called herself Meryl Streep. When she heard that Long was studying design, she asked, "Would you like to see my costume sketches?" Then she showed him her drawings, beautifully imagined and rendered. *Oh, my God*, he thought. *She's an actress and she draws like a dream*. Now he was really ready to bolt.

"Every class at the drama school thinks that somebody was a mistake," said Walt Jones, a directing student in Meryl's class. "And I thought it was me." Of course, most of them were worrying the same thing. But who would admit it? Better to keep your eye on your classmates and try to figure out who didn't belong. Because if it wasn't one of them, then it might as well be you.

DRAMA SCHOOLS ARE founded on a dangerous kind of calculus. Attract theatrical personalities, at an age when their ambition vastly outstrips their experience, and place them in a community so small and insular that the most valuable resources—attention, praise, parts— are in perpetually short supply. Still, the Yale School of Drama fed on its own special brand of crazy, and that was thanks to one man: Robert Brustein.

With his booming voice and ironclad ideals, Brustein presided over the drama school like it was his own private fiefdom. Having made his name as the combative drama critic for *The New Republic*, he believed in Artaud's gospel of "no more masterpieces": theater should be challenging, political, and blisteringly new. He loathed the naturalistic dramas of Arthur Miller, extolled the epic theater of Bertolt Brecht. Between semesters, he summered in Martha's Vineyard, socializing with the likes of Lillian Hellman, William Styron, and Joseph Heller. His most famous book was *The Theatre of Revolt*.

Years before he became its dean, Brustein had attended the Yale Drama School as an actor. He found the training archaic. In phonetics lessons, the students were taught to widen their *a*'s and trill their *r*'s. They listened to recordings of John Gielgud and learned to recite their lines in a "mid-Atlantic accent," which Brustein concluded to be unsuitable for the stage, since nobody lives in the mid-Atlantic except fish. "It was all fans and flutterings and bowings and scrapings and Restoration plays," he said. He dropped out after a year.

So when Kingman Brewster, the president of Yale, asked him to take over the program in 1966, he balked. The Yale School of Drama, as far as he was concerned, was one of those "stagnant ponds" where theater went to die. If he did agree, he'd need license to make sweeping changes: new staff, new curriculum, new everything. "My plan was to transform the place from a graduate school, devoted to fulfilling requirements and granting MFA degrees, into a professional conservatory, concerned with developing artists for the American stage," he wrote in *Making Scenes*, his memoir of the "turbulent years at Yale."

When Brustein arrived in New Haven the next term, he was "the liberal on a white horse," according to his first associate dean, Gordon Rogoff. The new Yale School of Drama wouldn't produce "personalities," the kind you see in the movies. It would mint repertory-theater professionals who could tackle anything from Aeschylus to Ionesco. "I wanted to develop an actor capable of playing any role ever written," Brustein wrote, "from the Greeks to the most experimental postmodernists." Imagine his dismay when a promising young actor from the class of 1970, Henry Winkler, went on to become the Fonz on *Happy Days*.

Intrinsic to his vision was establishing the Yale Repertory Theatre, a professional playhouse that would work in tandem with the school. Students would perform alongside hired actors, in bold, genre-busting productions that mocked bourgeois tastes. There was Brustein's production of *Macbeth*, in which the witches were extraterrestrials who beamed in on flying saucers. There was Molière's *Don Juan*, which began with a "blasphemous ritual sacrifice"—blasphemous, because the Yale Rep had made its home in the former Calvary Baptist Church. "The middle-class burghers were in shock," Rogoff said.

When he got to Yale, Brustein vowed to run the school as a participatory democracy. But the turbulent years—radicalism, Black Power, sit-ins—transformed him, like Robespierre, into an autocrat. By 1969, the *Yale Daily News*, which had once applauded Brustein's "open, permissive approach to dissent," was decrying his "authoritarian, repressive policies" and calling for his resignation. Brustein was defiant. "I had tried to be a mellow, reasonable administrator and had presided over uprisings, disruptions, and cancellations," he wrote. "I no longer felt very avuncular."

By the time Meryl arrived, he had alienated almost everyone. Yale undergraduates thought he was shortchanging them by not allowing access to graduate classes. Audiences were confounded by his experimental programming. Graduate students were in constant rebellion. "You know the Sara Lee slogan in the TV commercials—'Everybody doesn't like something, but nobody doesn't like Sara Lee?' " one student told the *New York Times Magazine*. "Well, around here that might be paraphrased to read, 'Everybody doesn't like somebody, but nobody doesn't dislike Robert Brustein.' "

The newly assembled class of 1975 knew, to some extent, that they were entering a cult of personality. But here was the strange thing: when they got to campus for their first semester, Brustein was gone. Exhausted by eight years of turmoil, he had taken a year off to be a guest critic for *The London Observer*. In his place sprang a cadre of petty tyrants, who were about to make Meryl Streep's first year at Yale a torment.

ON WEDNESDAY, SEPTEMBER 13TH, Meryl walked down Chapel Street to attend her first day of classes. Of her thirty-nine classmates, nine were enrolled in the acting program: four men, five women.

The curriculum, according to the official Drama School bulletin, would consist of "a highly disciplined period of training, when all students are serving in an apprentice capacity. It is during this period that the development of their talent, expansion in outlook, and artistic contributions to the theatre are evaluated." If the evaluation went awry, students could, and would, be put on academic probation, the first step toward getting kicked out altogether.

Twice a week, they would gather in the University Theatre for Drama 1, "Introduction to Yale Theatre." It was taught by Howard Stein, whom Brustein had appointed acting dean. Stein was universally beloved; he was Brustein's buffer, the smiling, encouraging good cop you could go to in a bind.

On Monday, Wednesday, and Friday mornings was Drama 128, "Voice Training," with instruction in "correct breathing, tone production, articulation, and corrective tutorial work." On Tuesdays and Thursdays was Drama 138, "Stage Movement," for training in "acrobatics, mime, and studies in the expressiveness of gesture and body composition." This was the domain of Moni Yakim and Carmen de Lavallade, a former prima ballerina who had joined the Rep in hopes of reinventing herself as an actress.

Meryl enjoyed these classes, with their pragmatic focus. "The things that I honestly really think about now and rely on are physical things," she said later. In movement class, they learned about relaxation and strength. In voice, they read sonnets and learned that a thought is a breath and a breath is a thought. "In the singing class, where people were not singers, Betsy Parrish said, 'It doesn't matter, singing is expression, it's undiluted, unobstructed by your brain and all your neuroses. It's pure. It's music. It comes out from the middle of you.' I learned all those things. But acting, however, I don't know how people teach acting."

And yet acting was taught, in Drama 118—the course Meryl would come to dread. Every Tuesday, Wednesday, and Thursday afternoon, the students would file into Vernon Hall, the converted frat house where she'd had her audition. In the basement was the Yale Cabaret, a lovingly disheveled black box where the drama students could let loose and stage their own work, no matter how thrown-together or bizarre. Directly above it was a wide studio with wood floors and weak sunlight, strewn with folding chairs and costume racks. This was where Drama 118 would meet, with the goal of "establishing an Ensemble work approach" and honing specialized skills such as "improvisation, scene study, circus, elementary text breakdown, and masks," under the instruction of Thomas Haas.

"Tom Haas was Meryl's bane," Brustein said. "He was my bane, too, as it turned out. He was an unfortunate human being who had the great capacity to pick out the most talented people in the class and want to throw them out for being talented." Others had a warmer view. Meryl's classmate Steve Rowe called him "one of the luminaries"—so brilliant that Rowe followed him to Yale from Cornell, where the thirty-four-year-old Haas had done part of his Ph.D. But the class of 1975 clashed with him from the start. Privately, they would make fun of his "wall eyes": one went this way, the other went that way. There was talk that his wife had run off to join the women's movement, leaving him with two small sons: the kind of newfangled family dynamic that would inspire *Kramer vs. Kramer.*

His personal troubles might have darkened his mood in the Vernon Hall rehearsal studio, where Haas led the first-year students in improvisational theater games. There was the subway exercise, where you had to walk into a subway car and immediately establish who you are and where you're going. There was the painting exercise, where you had to embody a classic work of art. That first day, Haas gave the class its inaugural assignment: improvising their own deaths. "He said most people didn't die well enough," Linda Atkinson recalled.

To kick off the first round of deaths, Haas called up a cocky acting student named Alan Rosenberg. Rosenberg had double-majored in theater and political science at Case Western Reserve University. His parents, who owned a department store in New Jersey, had given him a couple hundred dollars to apply to graduate schools, but he lost most of it in a poker game. With only enough left for a single application, he had auditioned for the Yale School of Drama and somehow gotten in. Like everyone else, he thought he was the mistake.

When he walked into the studio, Rosenberg saw a gorgeous young woman sitting on a folding chair. "I was knocked out," he recalled. "I looked at her and couldn't stop looking at her." Meryl had a beauty he couldn't quite define, "like a work of art you can contemplate forever."

Unfortunately for him, she had a boyfriend: Philip Casnoff, who had joined the Green Mountain Guild in the summer of 1972. Meryl and Phil had costarred in a play by Peter Maeck, in which they alternated nights in the same gender-neutral role. After the summer, he got a job touring the country in *Godspell*, but would visit New Haven on days off. Phil had flowing hair and a Prince Charming face. As with Bruce Thomson in high school and Bob Levin in college, he and Meryl looked good together.

Rosenberg got up to perform his death scene, hiding his insecurity behind a veneer of goofiness. He performed a pantomime of a guy walking down the street who gets attacked by a swarm of killer bees. The students laughed. Success?

He sat back down and watched the others. One student pretended to set himself on fire. Another shot himself in the mouth and slowly bled to death. Then it was Meryl's turn. Her demise was one that few in the room would forget: she performed an abortion on herself. Not only was this disturbing to watch—and a hell of a way to make a first impression. It was also timely. *Roe v. Wade* was still being argued before the Supreme Court and wouldn't be decided until the following January. In the meantime, women were forced to come up with their own solutions to unwanted pregnancies, often with tragic results.

One thing was clear: Meryl brought a level of commitment to her work that was unmatched in the room. It was "incredibly intense," Rosenberg recalled. He noticed that the colors of her face would change when she was onstage—she was that deep into the character. Rosenberg, however, had been flip. After everyone took a turn at self-destruction, Haas said, "I don't think Alan quite understood what the exercise was about."

Rosenberg went home elated and distraught. On the one hand, he'd met the woman of his dreams. On the other, Haas had asked him to be more "specific," and he was stumped. He called a doctor friend and asked for a specific way to die. The friend said: bone-marrow embolism. Back in class, Haas called Rosenberg up for a second try. He pantomimed a guy driving a car who gets a flat tire. He pulls over and tries to fix it, but the jack splits in two and he breaks his leg. Within twenty seconds, he dies. It was still flip, but it was better than bee stings. And if it didn't impress Haas, maybe it would impress Meryl. In any case, Haas informed them, the class would be practicing its death scenes through Thanksgiving.

SLOWLY BUT SURELY, the students began to realize that Meryl Streep could outdo them in almost everything. "She was more flexible, more limber, had greater command of her body than the rest of us," her classmate Ralph Redpath said. She danced. She could swim three lengths of the pool without taking a breath. She made delicious soufflés with Gruyère cheese. In tumbling lessons with the Olympic gymnast Don Tonry, she surprised everyone by doing a back flip from a standing position. In fencing class, taught by the Hungarian fencer Katalin Piros, she wielded her foil like Errol Flynn. Someone asked if she had fenced before, and she replied, "Not much." Who *was* this person?

In improvisation exercises, she was more inventive, as if dozens of possibilities swarmed her head when one would do. At one point, Haas told them each to walk through a fake door and wordlessly communicate where they were coming from and where they were going. They couldn't use their faces, just their bodies. Meryl was wearing a long caftan with a hood. As she stood facing the door, she pulled her arms inside and turned the caftan around so that the hood was covering her head. Her face was not only expressionless but obscured. "Even in the way she did the exercise, she beat us," Walt Jones said.

In Moni Yakim's movement class, the students were instructed to blow around the room like leaves in the wind. The actors wafted about, arms akimbo, trying not to make eye contact lest they burst into laughter. "All of us were blowing around the room making asses of ourselves, and she was in what looked like a modern-dance position up against the wall," Jones recalled. Another student blew by and asked, "What's up with you?" Meryl answered dryly: "I got caught on a twig."

A new phrase entered circulation: "to Streep it up." William Ivey Long defined it this way: "Take the stage. Own your character. Make us look at you." For better or worse, she was now setting the standard for her own classmates.

She undercut her burgeoning reputation with playful humor. One day after a rehearsal, she and Jones were goofing off at the piano. Jones pretended to be her accompanist in a nightclub act as she sang the Roberta Flack song "The First Time Ever I Saw Your Face." "How long do you think I can hold that note?" she asked him. He played the phrase "the first *tiiime*." As Meryl held the note, Jones ran to the lobby and pretended to make a phone call. When he got back, she was still singing "*tiiime*." He sat down, played the next chord, and the song continued. "It was just for us," he said. "There was nobody else there."

After drilling the students' death scenes for weeks on end, Haas finally moved on. They would perform Chekhov's *Three Sisters*, but with a few twists. Each actor would pull the name of a character from a hat, regardless of gender. Meryl picked Masha, the middle sister. In their scenes, they were allowed to speak only in numbers, or to isolate a single word from each line and repeat it over and over. The idea was to find the potency within the poetry, to dive beneath language and return with pearls of subtext.

Alan Rosenberg was playing Solyony, the boorish army captain. In one scene, he proclaims that when women philosophize, the result is "nothing." Masha snaps back, "What do you mean, you dreadful man?" Meryl reduced the line to the word "what," which she hurled at Rosenberg like a fusillade of darts. "What." "What?" "*WHAT.*" "It had to be thirty times," Jones recalled. "And Alan kind of shrunk back into the floor."

In truth, he was falling into a deep infatuation.

"I was in painfully unrequited love with Meryl," Rosenberg said. Since they both lived in New Jersey, they would travel together on holidays. He visited her over Christmas and met her family. Some weekends, they'd go to New York—maybe to catch the new Ingmar Bergman movie, maybe just to crash at a friend's place, where they'd play guitar and sing and forget to go outside. Rosenberg didn't take Haas's improv games seriously, and his irreverence rubbed off on Meryl. "She'd be a bit of a bad girl with me sometimes," he recalled. In January, 1973, they went to Washington to protest Nixon's second inauguration. Meryl wasn't as politically minded as Rosenberg, but she skipped classes to go. The faculty noted her absence.

The problem, at least for Rosenberg, was Phil Casnoff. When he visited on breaks from *Godspell*, the other students took note of his pretty-boy good looks. Not only was Meryl the perfect fencer, tumbler, singer, and improviser: she had a perfect-looking boyfriend, too. But Phil was barely around, and even when he was, he would float on the margins of the drama students' close-knit, high-stress little world. Meryl drifted closer to Rosenberg, juggling the attentions of two very different suitors: Prince Charming and the Court Jester.

Meanwhile, the *Three Sisters* exercise reached its culmination, a three-hour-long presentation for the faculty. Michael Posnick, a directing teacher, recalled, "Center stage was a sofa. On the sofa was Meryl Streep in the role of Masha with a book. She was lying down on the sofa holding the book, reading the book. And I became aware that she was humping the sofa. And I suddenly saw something about Masha that I had never understood or seen before."

Posnick, like others, had come to realize that Meryl was up to something far more ambitious than her classmates. She was taking more risks, making stranger choices. By the spring term, the first-year students were calling themselves the Meryl Streep Class, though the phrase might have carried a tinge of resentment. And then Haas did something no one anticipated: he put her on probation.

It didn't make sense. "Our class names ourselves the Meryl Streep Class, and this asshole puts the namesake of the class on probation!" William Ivey Long said. "Of course, we all assumed he was jealous of her. Everyone was just in revolt of him because of this behavior." Rosenberg worried that it was because she was spending too much time with him. He never got put on warning, because no one had any expectations of him. With her, it was different.

"What Tom said to us is that there is nothing that she can't do, but I don't think she's pushing herself hard enough," said Walt Jones, who noticed that Haas had been in tears by the end of *Three Sisters*. "And I remember thinking that that was bullshit. I mean, who could do more than she did?"

Even the staff was mystified. In one faculty meeting, Haas said of her talent, "No, I don't trust it. It doesn't seem to have future potential." Posnick couldn't believe what he was hearing: it was like standing in front of the Empire State Building and complaining that it's blocking the sun.

"He said that I was holding back my talent out of fear of competing with my fellow students," Meryl would recall. "There was some truth in that, but there was no reason to put me on warning. I was just trying to be a nice guy, get my M.A. and get out of drama school." Besides, she was beginning to doubt Haas's whole conception of character. "He said, 'The minute you come into a room in a play, the audience should know who you are.' I feel that the minute you leave a room, half the audience should know who you are, and the other half should be in complete disagreement with them."

Branded a problem child for the first time, Meryl burrowed into her work. The acting students were rehearsing Gorky's *The Lower Depths*, set in a Russian boardinghouse for the destitute. This was the first time the older classes at the drama school would see the first-years at work. Albert Innaurato, then a second-year playwright, attended expecting—maybe even hoping for—a train wreck. "Everyone was saying, 'They're awful, they couldn't find anybody good. And the pretty one is just horrible. She's just really bad.'"

The "pretty one" was Meryl Streep, who was playing the keeper's wife. At the climax of Act III, she attacks her own sister in a jealous rage, pushing her down the stairs and scalding her with a bucket of hot water. In the lobby afterward, there was talk of the "charming" actress playing Vassilisa, despite the violence she had just inflicted onstage. "I knew this girl was obviously destined for something very big," Michael Feingold said, "because if you can do that and have everyone talk about how charming you are, you obviously have some hold over an audience."

Even Brustein got a taste of Meryl's abilities. In December, he flew back from London for eight days. On the afternoon of the last day of classes, the school held a Christmas party at the Cabaret. Orange juice and vodka were on the tables, and students performed ribald interpretations of fifties pop songs. After a long semester, it was a welcome opportunity to blow off steam. But, for the first-year students, it was another audition of sorts: their chance to make an impression on the all-powerful dean. In his memoir, Brustein wrote, "I took special note of a very beautiful and talented first-year actress from Vassar named Meryl Streep." He had finally found someone with the "languorous sexual quality combined with a sense of comedy" to play Lulu in Frank Wedekind's *Earth Spirit*, though he never did get to see her in the part. What he didn't realize was how little Tom Haas cared for her supposed talents.

Relief, of sorts, came in the spring, when Haas was pulled away to direct a Brecht play at the Yale Rep. Allan Miller, an associate acting professor, came in to direct the first-years. No one was pained to see Haas go, but they were unnerved. Whereas Haas was academic, Miller was more "street." A Brooklyn guy with no appetite for bullshit, he preferred scene studies to improvisations. It was a completely different approach.

Miller had mentored a young Barbra Streisand when she was just fifteen, and later coached her during rehearsals for *Funny Girl*. When he got to Yale, he thought the student actors were "pretty intelligent" but "hardly ever visceral." He was blunt in his criticisms, and proud of the fact that he didn't filter his thoughts or lard them with tact. He was also coming off an eighteen-year marriage. Meryl was taken aback one day when he asked her out on a date. It was a Friday night, and he was going to see a show at the Yale Rep. Would she come? "She was a little weirded out by it and said no," Rosenberg said. She told him she already had plans with her boyfriend from New York. Rebuffed, Miller asked out Meryl's classmate Laura Zucker, who accepted.

As the term went on, the students became aware that Miller and Zucker were a couple. Meanwhile, his treatment of Meryl hardened. "There was no question about her talent—she was brilliant some of the time, but cold," Miller said. He started calling her the Ice Princess in faculty meetings. In class, he would scold her for not trying hard enough. Maybe, on some level, she wasn't. But the students suspected Miller and Zucker were teaming up on Meryl. "They expressed their vociferous and vindictive feelings passively at first," Walt Jones said, "but it grew."

The semester culminated with a production of Shaw's *Major Barbara*. Miller thought that Meryl's "great galloping zeal" would be right for the title role, the moralistic Salvation Army girl who spars with her father, an arms industrialist. He cast Zucker as Barbara's mother. In rehearsal, she would glower at Meryl with a look that said: "She's not that great, *really*." At night, she'd needle Miller: "How come I'm sleeping with the director and I don't get the part of Major Barbara?"

Miller pushed the students to ground Shaw's pronouncements in rage, disgust, or self-doubt. But no matter how hard Meryl tried, she couldn't please Miller. "She was having a miserable time with him," Walt Jones said. "She didn't know what he was actually trying to say to her. She was doing everything she could, but he was pushing her like she wasn't." The other students were struggling, too. One actor was so irked by Miller that he raised his fist at him, but at the last moment punched the wall instead of the director's face.

During one improvisation, Miller threw out a suggestion and

noticed Meryl shaking it off like a bad scent, turning her back to him. "Come on, Meryl, let it out," he urged her. "She whipped around at me with this terrific look of both desire and pain, and then stopped," Miller recalled. "She stopped the emotional flow. She didn't want to be vulnerable, and that's why her nickname was the Ice Princess."

Meryl found Miller's tactics "manipulative." She was skeptical about the concept of mining her own pain, believing that misery was irrelevant to artistry. What her instructors saw as laziness or evasion was a growing intellectual revolt against the orthodoxy of Method acting, which had shaped the previous generation of actors. She wasn't willing to excavate her personal demons to fuel Major Barbara's. She preferred imagination—and thought that Miller's approach was "a lot of bullshit." "He delved into personal lives in a way I found obnoxious," she said later. Then again, maybe she *was* holding something back.

By most accounts, though, Meryl's Major Barbara was an object lesson in "Streeping it up." "They'd gotten rid of the artificiality," Feingold said. "This was generally true, but not everybody in the class did it with Meryl's fervor."

The Monday after the performance, the cast gathered in the studio for a formal evaluation. (The students had taken to calling them "*de-valuations*.") One by one, the faculty critiqued the actors, starting with the minor parts and working up to the leads. The movement teacher would declare, "Well, you *cahn't* really move." The voice teacher would trill, "Your accent was a *disgrrrrace!*"

"It was a bloodbath," said Walt Jones, who played Barbara's father. "We were all crisped, but Meryl got it between the eyes. A final dose of Allan's vitriol he had been giving her throughout the term."

By the end, she was holding back tears. But then, so was everyone.

The students were stunned. The easiest target, they reasoned, was the most preposterous target. Meryl had delivered something that Miller couldn't recognize, and certainly couldn't take credit for. So better to tear it down, in public.

At the end of the semester, Allan Miller left Yale. So did Laura Zucker. Not long after, they moved to Los Angeles together and got married. The acting class was down one.

Meryl was torn about whether Yale had a place for her. She had friends there, including the smitten Alan Rosenberg. But her teachers had been dismissive at best, authoritarian at worst. Much of this was trickle-down from Brustein. "They were very influenced by Bob's high-handedness and meanness," Innaurato said. In the absence of a coherent power structure, the students had found solidarity in each other. "We were allowed to feel ownership of our time, of our year," William Ivey Long recalled.

In the kitchen of their yellow Victorian house, Meryl poured out her grievances to Long, whom she affectionately called "Wi'm." If she was as flawed an actress as they claimed, why stay? Then again: If she was as talented as her classmates seemed to believe, why give up?

If she had learned anything her first year, it was tenacity. Maybe if she worked hard—even harder than she had on *Major Barbara*—someone with sway would recognize her.

And then Robert Brustein came back.

ON SEPTEMBER 5TH, 1973, the Yale School of Drama assembled in the University Theatre. The man who walked out onstage was known only to the third-year class, which now included Sigourney Weaver and Christopher Durang. To the rest, he had lived only in legend: the indomitable Robert Brustein, here to give his welcome address.

"It's a curious sensation to see so many unfamiliar faces gathered together in this auditorium," he said from the podium. "For the first time since I've been Dean, I find it necessary to introduce myself not only to the incoming class, but to the second year as well." He looked out over those faces, including Meryl Streep's. "Still," he went on, "you can be certain, given the small size of the school and the intimate nature of the work, that we'll all get to know each other fairly fast."

For the uninitiated, Brustein laid out his ideals—and his

disappointment when they weren't met. "I still find it flabbergasting that a performer could turn down a series of challenging roles in exciting plays, earning a decent wage among a community of artists, for a chance at a television series, a film, or a minor part in some commercial play," he proclaimed. "It's rather like a writer working all his life to be a novelist, and when a publisher finally offers him a contract for a book, rejecting the offer for the sake of a more highly paid job in advertising."

Over the summer, Brustein had become obsessed with the unfolding Watergate scandal. He even did a dead-on Nixon impression. As someone who ruled his own small kingdom with a tight fist, he was tickled by the foibles of the powerful. But the scandal troubled him.

"Some years ago," he continued, "in a spirit of optimistic renewal, some Americans were proclaiming that we were a Woodstock nation. From this vantage point, it seems more accurate to call us a Watergate nation. All of us—young and old, culture and counter-culture, men and women, politicians and artists—must bear the taint of that event."

He concluded: "The American theatre is now testing our characters, and our parts in it will determine its future. If the profession fails the test, it has joined the Watergate nation, and helped to deliver the country over to its betrayers. To change the face of theatre, then, we must change our own faces, keep the faith, and try to rekindle the light that once kept our hearts aflame."

Lofty stuff, but not everyone was sold. "He arrived with a red Mercedes that he brought from London," one of the acting students recalled. "Then he gave a big speech about how we never should go into the theater as a way to make money. I'm looking at the red Mercedes, I'm looking at this guy, and I'm thinking: Who *is* this guy?"

Brustein had decided to overhaul the acting program, which he observed was "rife with factionalism, competitiveness, backbiting." He later wrote, "My resolve was strengthened when I discovered, soon after returning from England, that the actress who had impressed me so much the previous year, Meryl Streep, had been put on probation."

Chief among his worries was the absence of a guiding philosophy.

To that end, he had brought in Bobby Lewis as "master teacher." Lewis was a legend in the profession. As an original member of the Group Theatre, along with Harold Clurman, Stella Adler, and Lee Strasberg, he had helped popularize the Method in American acting. In Hollywood, he had acted alongside Charlie Chaplin and Katharine Hepburn.

Some of the students found Lewis (and Method training) old-fashioned. "There was a tradition about him that seemed dated to us," Walt Jones said, "but I don't know who we thought we were." Once again, they were getting instructional whiplash. "Every year, there'd be a coup d'état," Meryl recalled. "The new guy would come in and say, 'Whatever you learned last year, don't worry about it. This is going to be a new approach.'"

Still, it was hard to resist Lewis's Elmer Fudd voice ("I'm *whiting* my *memwaws*") or his eccentric teaching style. With his golden retriever, Caesar, at his side, he would spout anecdotes about himself and the greats: Marlon Brando, Charlie Chaplin. Then he would tell the same stories a second time, or a third. It was a wonder anyone got to act.

And yet they did, occasionally. In one class, Meryl and Franchelle Stewart Dorn performed a scene from Jean Genet's *The Maids*. They were in a dance studio the students called the "mirror room," and the two actors used the mirrored walls to reinterpret the scene, using their reflections as alternate selves. No one in the class quite understood what it meant, but Lewis was rapt.

Consciously or not, Meryl would create her characters as composites of people in her life: a vocal inflection here, a gesture there. Cast as an old woman in a Richard Lees play, she adopted an odd physical tic, twitching her hand like she was strumming a harp. Afterward, she told her classmates that it was borrowed from her aunt. The voice had been her grandmother's.

In November, the second-year class put on Brecht's *Edward II* in the Experimental Theatre (the "Ex"), a cramped space downstairs at the University Theatre. Steve Rowe played the title role, and Meryl was Queen Anne. She kept her focus, even when the *Yale Daily News* ran a caption calling her "Meryl Sheep."

Christopher Durang was cast as her son. "We rehearsed it for a couple of weeks and it wasn't going well," he recalled. "Now, the director had mentioned that he wanted to use a circus conceit in the staging, but when the costume parade came around, Meryl was dressed like a trapeze artist: she had beads on her chest, beads on her crotch—they made noise whenever she walked. Well, Meryl put this on and shot the director a look of daggers. She said there was no way she'd perform in that outfit." The beads went.

Meryl was determined to prove her worth to the people who mattered. One night, William Ivey Long came to drop off a costume in her dressing room and saw blood in the sink. With all the pressure she was putting on herself, Meryl had developed awful stomach problems—she worried she was getting an ulcer. Before the performance, she had thrown up.

She looked at him. "Wi'm," she said. "Don't tell."

THOUGH SHE HAD vanquished her reputation as "the pretty one," Meryl was a radiant presence on campus. Classmates could spot her from down the block flipping her lemon hair—a burst of color amid the ersatz Gothic façades. All the more remarkable, then, that her breakout role at Yale would be one for which she made herself hideously ugly.

The part came courtesy of the school's resident jesters, Christopher Durang and Albert Innaurato. Chris had grown up in Catholic schools, before majoring in English at Harvard. He had got into Yale on the merit of an absurdist play called *The Nature and Purpose of the Universe*. Albert, likewise a lapsed Catholic, had come from Philadelphia. Both were gay, and both were running away from religious backgrounds that had no place for them, finding refuge in menace. (They tended to write plays about evil nuns.) Chris showed up late for the first day of classes with a pronounced limp. Albert saw instantly that he was faking it. They became inseparable.

Unlike some of their classmates, they were too hopelessly flamboyant to hide their sexuality. "We were like Christmas trees walking lit down the street," Innaurato said. But while Albert was openly catty, Chris was sly, with a cherub's face and a viper's wit. Brustein, who took a quick shine to him, called him a "deadly piranha with the manners of an Etonian and the innocence of a choirboy."

When a Yale gallery held an exhibition about William Blake and Thomas Gray, they were asked to write and perform a scene. They dressed as priests and mashed up fifty plays in five minutes. One minute, Chris was Laura from *The Glass Menagerie*. The next, Albert was Eleanor Roosevelt in *Sunrise at Campobello*. Then they sang Mass to the tune of "Willkommen" from *Cabaret*. Midway through, a woman in the audience said to another, "Come, Edith!"—and they left in a huff. But Howard Stein, the associate dean, thought the show was hilarious and urged the duo to perform it at the Cabaret.

Their collaboration continued with a madcap spoof of *The Brothers Karamazov*, performed at Silliman, one of Yale's residential colleges. The play was shot through with allusive glee: Dostoyevsky meets the Three Stooges, with cameos from Djuna Barnes and Anaïs Nin. They billed it as "The Brothers Karamazov, starring Dame Edith Evans" as Constance Garnett, the famed British translator of Russian classics. The audience arrived to discover that "Dame Edith Evans" had broken her hip, and the eighty-year-old "translatrix" would be played by Albert in a mustache and a floral hat. Once again, mischief was their meal ticket: despite complaints, Howard Stein booked it for the Ex in the spring.

But there would be changes. The play was renamed *The Idiots Karamazov*, and the female roles would be played by women. That meant rethinking the Constance Garnett part. The playwrights had conceived her as a witchy, sexually frustrated hag in a wheelchair, serving as absentminded narrator. When she wasn't smashing a monocle or screaming at her butler, Ernest Hemingway, she would vainly try to make sense of the proceedings:

CONSTANCE:

The Brothers Karamazov. This is one of the greatest novels ever writ in any tongue. It deals with the inexorable misery of the condition humain. Hunger, pregnancy, thirst, love, hunger, pregnancy, bondage, sickness, health, and the body, let us not forget the body. *(Shudders luxuriously.)*

Who could pull off this grotesque tour-de-force? The answer was as inspired as it was perverse: the pretty one, Meryl Streep. In *The Lower Depths*, she had shown that viciousness could be charming. Could she make it funny, too?

The catch: the director was the dreaded Tom Haas. When Chris and Albert suggested the idea of casting Meryl as Constance, he balked: "Have you ever *seen* Meryl be good?"

The young playwrights persisted, and got their wish.

Meryl threw herself into the role, shedding whatever vanity she had. Even as Chris and Albert wrote her more and more spastic soliloquies, Haas would leave her off of the rehearsal schedules. Silly as it was, Constance was an enormous part, and she needed time to discover the character. Was the director sabotaging her?

One day, Meryl cornered Albert at the Hall of Graduate Studies. He and Chris and Sigourney Weaver would usually gather there for meals, bouncing jokes off each other or griping about school politics. Now in her third year, Sigourney still wasn't getting any decent parts at the Rep. Instead, she found her own path, starring in whatever absurdist spree Chris and Albert were putting up at the Cabaret.

Sure enough, Meryl found them in the dining hall. "Can I speak to you privately?" she told Albert, pulling him aside. "What can you do to get me to come to rehearsals? Tom won't let me in."

Albert replied that Haas had shut him and Chris out, too. The director had taken to cutting their punch lines and slowing the pace, while instructing the actors to play their scenes with dead seriousness. Startled, the playwrights went to Howard Stein, begging to be let in to rehearsals of their own play. They weren't in a position to lobby for Meryl as well. When they did mention it, Haas insisted that Meryl got worse the more she rehearsed—better to leave her on her own.

A few weeks later, Albert saw Meryl in the alley that connected the University Theatre with the Cabaret. She was visibly upset.

"What's the matter?" he said.

Meryl vented her frustration: "He won't call me to rehearsal. I was going to ask him—he wouldn't even look at me." Her speeches, besides being long, were dense with academic references, and she barely got her own jokes. "I really need work," she said.

"You know," Albert said, "I've played the part."

She had almost forgotten. "How did you do it?"

With that, Albert burst into his grand Edith Evans impersonation: "*Weeell*," he trumpeted like a drunk Lady Bracknell, "I just talked like *thiiis*."

Her mind was turning. "That's actually pretty helpful," she said. She went home and percolated: How to make this camp caricature her own?

When she was finally invited to rehearsal, Meryl came in with a full-fledged comedic persona: the grand, erratic, batty Constance Garnett. She even fashioned her own scratchy wig and prosthetic nose, with a bulging mole on the end. She looked like the Wicked Witch of the West.

Soon Constance—the framing device—dominated the play. In the first act, the Karamazovs sang a vaudeville number called "O We Gotta Get to Moscow." One night, Meryl joined in with an obbligato. It was so funny and unexpected that it got written into the show. "You knew more because she was doing that," said Walt Jones, who composed the score. "You knew more about that character, how central she was to the event, that she was causing this play to happen in her mixed up, crazy mind."

Haas wasn't amused. He still "had it in for Meryl," Durang said. "Haas also thought Meryl took too much focus away from another character's speech at the end; Haas told her to do less. So she did."

Days before tech, fate gave her a boost: Haas came down with the flu and left the second act to his student assistants, who reinstated the original wacky tone.

By the time Haas recovered, he seemed to have caught on to the new screwball pace. During one run-through, he sat in the audience and snapped his fingers—*Faster! Faster!*—as the actors scrambled to keep up. When they came out for notes, Meryl said, in front of everyone, "That was the most unpleasant thing I've ever been through in theater up to now."

Haas looked at her blankly. "Uh-huh," he said. "Here are the notes."

The play opened in the spring of 1974. Nutty and cryptic as it was, the students recognized it as a homegrown hit, with the irreverent sensibility they had forged at the Cabaret. Smack in the center of the action—or, rather, whipping around its perimeter—was Meryl Streep. At the end, for reasons unknown to anyone but the playwrights, Constance morphs into Miss Havisham from *Great Expectations*. In a gossamer wedding dress designed by William Ivey Long ("It was the very first time I worked with silk tulle"), she wheeled into a pink spotlight and sang a lament:

> *You may ask,*
> *Does she cry,*
> *Unassuming translatrix,*
> *Could it be she's the matrix,*
> *The star of the show,*
> *If so, you know*
> *She'll never let it go . . .*

Not only had caricature deepened into pathos; she was also displaying her vocal agility, melting from a Broadway belt into a fragile, floating high note on "let it go," which sputtered away like a deflating balloon. Some people assumed she was a faculty wife, an actress of fifty or sixty, at least.

The first few nights during the curtain call, as the audience howled with approval, she would wheel up and jab the front row with her cane, yelling, "Go home! Go home!" The playwrights loved the ad-lib, but Haas told her to cut it out. So the next night she mimed a heart attack and died dramatically. "We knew that she was upping Tom," Durang said.

Meryl's performance, Michael Feingold said, combined "outrageous extravagance and the completeness of belief." Nothing was fake. Nothing was hammy. Constance's delusions were perfectly reasonable to her, which made them all the funnier. Bobby Lewis thought it was the most imaginative farcical performance he'd ever seen.

Most important, she had impressed the person whose opinion really counted: Robert Brustein. The play fulfilled his vision of antinaturalistic, Brechtian theater, as did its leading lady. "Meryl was totally disguised in this part," he recalled in *Making Scenes*. "Her aquiline nose was turned into a witch's beak with a wart on the end, her lazy eyes were glazed with ooze, her lovely voice crackled with savage authority. This performance immediately suggested she was a major actress." He wrote in his diary: "Meryl Streep, a real find."

Ecstatic, he scheduled *The Idiots Karamazov* for the Rep that fall.

JUST AS MERYL was finding validation onstage, her love life was getting complicated. Her two suitors, Phil Casnoff and Alan Rosenberg, were well aware of each other's existence. Her relationship with Alan was vague: something more than friendship and less than romance. That was enough to irk Phil, who had been cast as the Teen Angel in the Broadway production of *Grease*.

Things came to a head one night in the dead of winter, when both men found themselves at Meryl's place. Phil had come to town on short notice, expecting to spend time with his girlfriend. But she had made plans with Alan. When she broke them, he marched over in a rage. The rivals got into a screaming match.

"Why the fuck are *you* here?"

"*I* was supposed to be with her tonight!"

Before they could come to blows, the two men realized that Meryl was gone. Fed up with their machismo, she had slipped out without a coat. Not only was it freezing, but the streets of New Haven were dangerous after dark, with the students constantly dodging muggers after long hours in the rehearsal room. Alan and Phil went out in search of Meryl, quarreling all the while. But it was no use: she had disappeared into the New Haven night.

She and Phil had been together for more than a year, and Alan knew he was at a disadvantage. Still, he was around when Phil wasn't. They would go for weekends on Cape Cod, and he bought her gifts: glass beads, a Christmas plate from his family's department store. Meryl would confide her anxieties: she was having nightmares about professional failure, what Alan called her "abiding fear of not succeeding." She was obsessed with the book *The Limits to Growth*, about how civilization would someday exhaust the Earth's resources. Her bedroom looked out over a tranquil square, but she missed the woods of Bernardsville. "I later found out that it was the quietest spot in New Haven," she would recall. "The point is I thought it was the noisiest corner on earth, so noisy I couldn't sleep nights."

Alan decided to go for broke. One day, when Meryl was idling in his apartment, he proposed marriage. Knowing it was a long shot, he made it seem off the cuff: no kneeling, no ring. But he meant it. "I think we could do wonderful things together," he told her.

They talked about it a bit and laughed. Somehow, the conversation trailed off to another subject. She hadn't given him a yes or a no, which was, in essence, a no. Alan knew she wasn't serious about him, not like he was about her. Phil was still in the picture, and, regardless, she wasn't ready to settle down with anyone.

In February, Bobby Lewis split the class in two: half would perform Genet's *The Balcony*, the other half Saul Bellow's *The Last Analysis*. Meryl was cast as the Pony Girl in *The Balcony*, a small, kinky part for which she wore a corset, lace-up boots, fishnet stockings, and a horse's tail. Alan was the lead in *The Last Analysis*, a part that Bellow had originally written for Zero Mostel (who had turned it down for *Fiddler on the Roof*). The role intimidated Alan—he was a young man, not a rotund Borscht Belt–style buffoon.

His nerves, like Meryl's, turned physical. He became severely dehydrated, and Meryl had to take him to the campus hospital. After a few days of bed rest, he returned in time to perform. Afterward, his friends gathered backstage and congratulated him on pulling off the impossible. But they also reported that Bobby Lewis had left at intermission. Rosenberg was incensed. At the next class, Lewis gave a detailed critique of the first act. When he started making more general observations about the second act, Alan raised his hand.

"Excuse me," he said, "but I heard you walked out of the play after the first act. So why are you talking about the second act?"

Lewis admitted it. He hadn't liked the direction.

Alan's face went red. "Bobby, we all paid a lot of money to go to this school," he said. "If you didn't like the way we were directed by one of the directing students, then maybe you should have hung in there and watched the play. Maybe we could use your help!"

After leaving the class in a huff, he went to Howard Stein and told him that he was withdrawing from the program. Two days later, he packed up his apartment. There was no time for goodbyes, even with Meryl. And yet he knew that the blow-up with Lewis was just a front. Had Meryl accepted his proposal, he could have endured all the pressure and the egos and the bullshit. Without her, what was the point?

"What I was really running away from," he said, "was her. And my feelings for her."

The acting class was down two.

THE YALE REP ended the spring season with a *ribbit*. In London, Brustein had asked the Broadway director Burt Shevelove to stage a musical version of Aristophanes' *The Frogs* in the swimming pool of the Payne Whitney Gym. The show would serve as a frivolous postseason lark, and a chance to make some quick money for the Rep.

To compose the songs, Shevelove enlisted Stephen Sondheim, with whom he had written *A Funny Thing Happened on the Way to the Forum*. At forty-four, Sondheim was midway through a run of landmark musicals, including *Company* and *Follies*. With Sondheim came his orchestrator, Jonathan Tunick, and with Tunick came a full orchestra. Soon the postseason lark became a splashy extravaganza with a cast of sixty-eight, including twenty-one swimmers in frog costumes and netted jockstraps, drafted from the Yale swim team.

To fill out the chorus, Brustein grabbed whatever drama students he could find, including Christopher Durang, Sigourney Weaver, and Meryl Streep. No one knew quite what was going on. "I remember coming in, getting in that pool, sidling up to Chris Durang, and saying, 'What's happening?'" Kate McGregor-Stewart recalled. "He said, 'I don't know!'" Bored and amused, the chorus members joked about throwing Sondheim in the pool. Ralph Redpath, who had played Ernest Hemingway in *The Idiots Karamazov*, got Meryl to teach him the butterfly stroke.

Sondheim, who found the whole thing mortifyingly unprofessional, saw Brustein as a sneering academic without producing chops. (It didn't help that Brustein had criticized Sondheim's work in print.) Brustein, meanwhile, was aghast at how lavish the show had become, complete with a clown car full of Broadway-size egos. One day at rehearsal, he publicly thanked the company and crew for their hard work. Afterward, Sondheim blew up at him for neglecting to thank the musicians. On top of that, the acoustics of the pool were awful, to the point that Sondheim added a lyric to the opening number: "The echo sometimes lasts for days . . . days . . . days . . . days . . ."

On opening night, a tony Broadway crowd, among them Leonard Bernstein and Harold Prince, descended on New Haven in a circus of air-kissing and quarreling over seats. To Sondheim's unpleasant surprise, Brustein had invited the New York critics, including Mel Gussow of the *Times*, who compared the show favorably to "a splashy M-G-M epic." Had he focused his attention on the bleachers to the left, he would have noticed a slender blonde dressed like a Greek muse, consigned to the chorus for one of the last times in her life.

Despite rapturous reviews, *The Frogs* garnered some backlash. A neurologist from the medical school wrote Brustein an angry letter, complaining that the "scanty" costumes exposed the swimmers' backsides. "In your outrage and embarrassment over the bare buttocks of the swimmers," Brustein replied, "you apparently failed to notice that the show also featured an exposed breast of one of the actresses. Whatever your preference for male behinds as opposed to female mammaries, I hope you will agree that, in this time of equal rights for women, your failure to take note of this fact is an insult to the opposite sex." Meanwhile, the New Haven Women's Liberation Center complained that the show treated women as "sex objects." Brustein retorted, "I think your satire on the humorlessness of the extremist elements of our society is priceless."

The mocking tone was indicative of Brustein's feelings toward second-wave feminism. The go-to response was disdain. When *Ms.* magazine sent him a survey with questions like "How many plays about women have been produced at your theater?" and "How many plays at your theater were written or directed by women?" Brustein sent back a scoffing questionnaire of his own: How many articles by or about men had they published? How many of their editors were men?

Brustein's contempt made life difficult for a first-year playwriting student named Wendy Wasserstein, who had arrived in the fall of 1973. The product of a middle-class Jewish household in Brooklyn, Wasserstein was frizzy-haired, zaftig, and effusive. Having studied history at Mount Holyoke, she was interested in writing plays about women's lives, but her jokey, naturalistic style clashed with Brustein's avant-garde ideals. He would openly question her admission to the school, calling her work "sophomoric"—never mind that Christopher Durang, whose work was overtly sophomoric, was one of his favorites.

In class, she didn't fare much better. At the first reading of what would become *Uncommon Women and Others*, one of the men said, "I just can't get into all this chick stuff."

Wendy hid her insecurity—about her weight, her talent—behind a girlish giggle. Even as her mother called every day at seven a.m. to ask if she had found a husband, she was neglectful of personal hygiene, spending weeks on end in the same velvet dress with a rose embroidered across the bosom. Like Sigourney, she was uninterested in (and incapable of) dressing the way people expected.

She was most comfortable around gay men like Chris, with whom she instantly bonded. They had a writing seminar together, and Chris noticed Wendy zoning out during class. "You look so bored, you must be very bright," he told her after class. (Decades later, she put the line in her Pulitzer Prize–winning play *The Heidi Chronicles*.) They started swapping notes on their messed-up families. "She had her own sadness inside her," Durang said, "but I didn't see it back then."

Women were more nervous around her: everything they feared about themselves she wore on the outside. "There was something about Wendy I found very scary to me," Sigourney told Wendy's biographer. "She was a more naked version of the vulnerability I felt."

Meryl was exactly the kind of woman Wendy spent her life avoiding: the tall, thin, blond shiksa goddess who seemed to breeze through life. She was inclined to distrust such women, who she imagined wanted nothing to do with her. But Meryl was kind, and Wendy would later rank her as No. 8 on her list of "Perfect Women Who Are Bearable." "She'll never pass you a poison apple," she wrote. "Meryl just goes about her business."

On costume duty, required of all the drama students, Meryl and Wendy mended dresses and cracked each other up. But there was a quality to her laughter that unsettled Meryl: it seemed less a genuine release than a contrived offering to the general bonhomie. "To me she always seemed lonely," Meryl would recall, "and the gayer her spirits and the more eager her smile, the lonelier she seemed."

Meryl stayed in New Haven for the inaugural season of the Summer Cabaret, an off-season outgrowth of the student-run theater. Those who remained staged ten (barely rehearsed) plays in ten weeks. One week, Meryl was Lady Cynthia Muldoon in Tom Stoppard's *The Real Inspector Hound*. The next, she was Beatrice in *Much Ado About Nothing*, or the bitter sister in Durang's *The Marriage of Bette & Boo*, for which the Cabaret was transformed into "Our Lady of Perpetual Agony Catholic Church and Bingo Hall." The costumes were whatever junk William Ivey Long found lying around, and the sets were held together with spit and luck. Before a performance of *Dracula Lives*, the smoke machine ran out of juice, and the gang replaced it with drug-store mineral oil, which turned the entire theater into a greasy, acrid swamp.

Without air conditioning, the Cabaret was sweltering. Nevertheless, some company members squatted on the third floor, until the campus police kicked them out. On Saturdays, Meryl would make French toast for everyone at her apartment off campus. Before shows, they would serve Junior's cheesecake and soda, clandestinely sweeping cockroaches off the plates before setting them down. Then they'd stay up late cleaning for the next day. At their favored pub on Chapel Street, they practiced "the Yale Stretch": whenever they were about to badmouth someone, they would crank their heads around to check who might be in earshot.

One week, the company was so exhausted that they decided to put on something completely improvised. The result was *The 1940's Radio Hour*, a wartime spoof. Dressed in fedoras and fur coats (which nearly gave them heat stroke), the actors made up the show as they went, speaking into vintage RCA microphones and hurling crumbled Styrofoam over their heads to signal snow. Meryl's solo was the 1938 standard "You Go To My Head." "You melted when you listened to it," said Walt Jones, who eventually brought the show to Broadway, sans Meryl. By the second night, the line was around the block. Nobody knew how word of mouth had got out that fast.

Amid the frolic, Meryl was looking toward her future. Bobby

Lewis hadn't taught her much about acting, but he had found her an agent at the newly formed ICM: Sheila Robinson, one of the firm's only African-American reps. Meanwhile, through Alvin Epstein, a veteran actor with the Yale Rep, she got her first professional voice-over gig. The married animation team John and Faith Hubley had adapted Erik Erikson's theory of the eight stages of psychosocial development into a series of cartoon vignettes, called *Everybody Rides the Carousel*. Meryl and her classmate Chuck Levin were hired for "Stage Six: Young Adulthood."

The two actors went into a recording studio in New York, where they were shown a storyboard and asked to ad-lib a scene dramatizing the conflict "intimacy versus isolation." They improvised a charming seven-minute scene of a young couple in a rowboat. When the man gets a splinter, the woman tenderly removes it with a safety pin. As they pull away, their faces transform into two-faced masks. They wonder, separately: Will they even be together in two years? The question must have reverberated in Meryl's mind, as she weighed her ambitions against the attentions of guys like Alan and Phil.

On another trip to New York, she saw Liza Minnelli at the Winter Garden. The entertainer's "straight-out, unabashed performing"— miles away from the scene studies she did in class—made her rethink her presumptions about acting.

"If I were not protected by a play, I would die," she said later. "But I learned something from watching Liza Minnelli. Encountering and truth-telling are the initial steps of acting. But there is a further leap to the understanding of the importance of brilliance, sparkle, and excitement. 'Performing' is the final gloss. It's a means to attract the audience to your character."

IN HER THIRD year, Meryl joined the Yale Rep as a company member, for which she got her Actors Equity card. Brustein, by now well aware of her gifts, cast her in the first show of the season, an adaptation of

Dostoyevsky's *The Possessed*, to be directed by the Polish filmmaker Andrzej Wajda. To play Stavrogin, he hired the sinewy young actor Christopher Lloyd.

Wajda spoke through a translator—no one was quite sure how much English he understood. But he was taken with Meryl and Christopher Lloyd, and even added extra dialogue for them. He told Feingold, the Rep's literary manager, "I cut scene in Kraków, but I put back here because your actors are so much better."

With Wajda came the Polish film star Elzbieta Czyzewska, an outcast from her home country since her husband, the American journalist David Halberstam, was expelled for criticizing the Communist regime. Czyzewska had an off-center way of working that fascinated Meryl. She would end the first act by slithering across the stage and screaming at Lloyd—*"Antichrist! Antichrist!"*—with a ferocity that seemed to make the theater quake.

But the significance of Meryl's encounter with Czyzewska wouldn't be apparent for several years. As Brustein's friend William Styron wrote his novel *Sophie's Choice*, he drew on Czyzewska's Polish speech patterns. Several years later, when Meryl played Sophie on film, her Yale classmates noticed something uncanny: there was Czyzewska, or at least elements of her, refracted through both Styron and Streep.

After Dostoyevsky, the Rep turned to a Dostoyevsky spoof: the mainstage production of *The Idiots Karamazov*. Meryl reprised her role as Constance Garnett—without the direction of Tom Haas, whom Brustein had ousted, at the urging of some of the students. Even so, tensions were high as rehearsals got under way. Christopher Durang and Albert Innaurato, Yale's mischievous Tweedledum and Tweedledee, had grown apart. The reason was Wendy Wasserstein.

Wendy's infatuation with Chris disgusted Albert, who felt he was being replaced. He would notice Wendy waiting for Chris after class like a lovesick schoolgirl, clearly barking up the wrong tree. In Albert's mind, Wendy had "poisoned" his friend, exploiting his insecurities.

"When you hate yourself, and then someone comes along and loves you for the very thing you hate in yourself, then it's very hard not to respond to that," he said later.

Brustein lorded over rehearsals, driving the cast up the wall. Even in front of Chris, who was playing Alyosha, Brustein would tamper with the script—Chris was so stressed he developed a rash all over his chest. When Linda Atkinson, who was playing Mrs. Karamazov, objected after Brustein cut one of her lines, he called out, "You can get out of my school!" "*Good*," she yelled back from the stage. (The line in question was: "Yes.")

Even the genteel William Ivey Long, who was doing costumes, reached his breaking point. He had designed a decrepit black-lace-on-magenta number for Grushenka, the prostitute. "She's supposed to be a whore," Brustein told him. "She looks like a duchess!"

"But, Dean Brustein . . ."

"Change it!"

As Brustein walked away, William shouted, despite himself: "Fuck you, Bob!" Brustein turned around and smiled a Cheshire Cat grin.

Meryl, meanwhile, had to re-create the comedic magic of the previous year, this time in a vastly larger space. The stage was steeply raked, and Meryl was constantly on guard to keep her wheelchair from rolling away with her. One night, Durang had to reach out and grab her before she careened into the front row. Still, she loved acting in the wheelchair: "You're limited, and it frees you."

The Rep drew audiences from far beyond the drama school, including critics from every newspaper within driving distance. Meryl's zany Constance Garnett, who had decisively taken over the play, became her coming-out. Raves came from the *Stratford News* and the *Hartford Courant*. Even Mel Gussow, of the *New York Times*, took notice: "The star role is the translator, Constance Garnett. As portrayed by Meryl Streep, she is a daft old witch (the play is daft, too) in a wheelchair, attended by a butler named Ernest, who eventually blows his brains out."

If it wasn't clear to Brustein before, it was now: Meryl was his secret weapon. The rest of the season would be all Streep, all the time, whether she liked it or not.

IT'S DIFFICULT BEING an outcast, but sometimes just as hard to be an asset. Wendy and Sigourney knew what it was like to work in the shadows, at least as far as Brustein was concerned. Meryl was now firmly on the other side, the leading lady in a professional company. In the 1974–75 season, she would act in six out of the seven shows at the Yale Rep. She was miserable.

Under Bobby Lewis, the acting department had become increasingly fractious. The second-year class rebelled after he fired three of the teachers. One student offered to audition *him*. Students were surly, or simply cut class. When Lewis put up a sign reminding them that attendance was mandatory, someone tore it down. Because of her grueling rehearsal schedule at the Rep, Meryl was missing classes as well, but Lewis was hesitant to reprimand her. Brustein was left with the "distressing job" of calling her into his office and telling her that she would have to start attending class regularly if she wanted her degree.

Juggling her multiple roles was hard enough. At the Rep, she appeared in a soap-opera satire called *The Shaft of Love*. One night, Norma Brustein—the dean's wife, who was playing her shrink— missed an entrance. To stall for time, Meryl ambled around the psychiatrist's office, inspecting props. Finally, she looked at one of the Rorschach inkblots on the wall and, pretending that her character had found some deep, horrible truth within it, burst into tears.

In the Brecht-Weill musical *Happy End*, Meryl was cast in the ensemble. Her one line, shrieked amid crowd babble, was *"Where's Lillian?"* "The incisiveness of the moment always knocked people on their asses," said Feingold. Mid-run, the soprano from the music school who was playing Lillian lost her voice. With only an afternoon to rehearse, Meryl stepped in. Far from getting a break in a minor part, she was now the lead. Her first time going on, Brustein sat in the front row in a bright-red tie. At intermission, Meryl sent him an urgent message: the red tie was making her nervous and he needed to clear out if he expected her to make it through the matinee.

Even more stressful was a production of Strindberg's *The Father*, starring Rip Torn. Meryl played his daughter, Bertha. Torn was notoriously erratic, inhabiting his role so fully that the cast worked in perpetual fear. He would stop rehearsals to obsess over a minor costume element or prop. During a tech rehearsal, he announced that he wanted to tear down the door on the set. After yanking it from its hinges, he declared: "More resistant. It's too easy."

Elzbieta Czyzewska was playing his wife, and Torn "tended to treat her offstage with the same cruel contempt with which he regarded her in the play," Brustein recalled. "You just want the *New York Times* to kiss your ass," he would say, to which she countered, "If you care so much about this play, how come you don't know your goddamn lines?" Meryl was stuck between them, like a shuttlecock.

A student dramaturge who was keeping a rehearsal log captured the tumult. From February 1st: "Torn scares everyone by almost throwing Elybieta [*sic*] out the window." February 12th: "Torn starts his scene with Elybieta in Act II by dumping her on the floor." February 19th: "Torn preoccupied with the guns. Doesn't think captain should have an antique gun collection." Meryl, he wrote, "has been having trouble with Bertha because she feels, rightly, that although Bertha is a teenager, the lines are written for a much younger child."

Meanwhile, her status at the Rep was eroding her relationships with her classmates. The women in her class had labored for years, expecting a chance to act on the Rep stage. Now Meryl was getting all the parts. While they couldn't begrudge her her talent, they were demoralized. One actress even went to Kingman Brewster, the president of Yale, and told him, "You know, there are people that are paying to go to this school, and they're never getting a chance to *act*."

At the end of the fall term, the Cabaret once again held a Christmas show. This time, Meryl poked fun at her own ubiquity, singing a winking rendition of Randy Newman's "Lonely at the Top." "A chill went around the room," Walt Jones recalled. "It was icy." She was back on the homecoming float, isolated by her own success.

"The competition in the acting program was very wearing," she would recall. "I was always standing in competition with my friends for every play. And there was no nod to egalitarian casting. Since each student director or playwright was casting his or her senior project, they pretty much got to cast it with whomever they wanted. So some people got cast over and over and others didn't get cast at all. It was unfair. It was the larger world writ small."

That she was on the sunny side of the street didn't make the pressure-cooker atmosphere any better. Instead, she said, "I got into a frenzy about this. It wasn't that I wasn't being cast. I was, over and over. But I felt guilty. I felt I was taking something from people I knew, my friends. I was on a scholarship and some people had paid a lot of money to be there."

She was worn down. Her costar was volatile. Her acting teacher was censuring her. The stress was roiling in her stomach. And her classmates were upset about the stage time she was getting—not that she had any choice in the matter.

Finally, she went to Brustein's office and said, "I'm under too much pressure. I want to be released from some of these commitments."

"Well," Brustein told her, "you could go on academic probation." But that was more threat than compromise; she didn't want to get kicked out of school.

Meryl had been cast as Helena in *A Midsummer Night's Dream*, the final production of the season. Could she get out of that? Brustein blanched: he knew she'd be perfect for it. Instead, he countered, why doesn't she go on as Helena and let her understudy take over in *The Father*?

"Impossible!" Meryl said. "Rip would never stand for it. He really thinks I *am* his daughter. If anybody went on in my place, even if you told him about it beforehand, he would stop the show immediately and say, '*Where's Bertha?*'"

They were at an impasse. She left the office, still booked through the end of the season.

Distraught, she went to see a school psychiatrist, who told her: "You know what? You're going to graduate in eleven weeks, and you'll never be in competition with five women again. You'll be competing with five thousand women and it will be a relief. It will be better or worse, but it won't be this."

Still, those were eleven long weeks, and the tenor of the school was more rancorous than ever. Over Christmas, Bobby Lewis had suffered a heart attack, catalyzed by the pressures of running the acting department. He asked that Norma Brustein, who had been his class assistant, take his place. The second-year students were furious that the dean's wife had been made their teacher without their consultation. They sent a telegram to a bed-ridden Lewis, describing their "surprise" and "disappointment." The *Yale Daily News* ran the headline: "Dissent Stirs Drama School."

Brustein had had just about enough. "Jealousy and meanness of spirit were rife in the School," he wrote. "I think I preferred revolution." He gathered all the second-year actors into the Ex and proceeded to pass out blank withdrawal slips. If anyone was dissatisfied, he informed them, they were free to fill out the forms and leave. No one took him up on it.

Who cared if Brustein was, in his words, a "Genghis Khan presiding over a Stalinist tyranny"? He had a school to run. He fantasized about quitting or disbanding the entire program, but Norma would tear up his resignation letters. For Passover that year, he had Meryl and Chuck Levin over for seder and discussed the turmoil in the acting program, clearly singling them out as students he trusted.

She had one more production left: *A Midsummer Night's Dream*, with Christopher Lloyd as Oberon. Despite her exhaustion, Helena was an irresistible role: beautiful but frenzied, farcical yet melancholy. The director, Alvin Epstein, had a romantic vision, melding Shakespeare's text with Henry Purcell's score for *The Fairy-Queen*. The set featured a gigantic shimmering moon made out of popcorn, and the quarreling lovers—Helena, Hermia, Demetrius, and Lysander—would shed their costumes as the play went along, as if melting into the sylvan scenery.

Epstein was constantly arguing with the conductor, Otto-Werner Mueller, leaving little time to focus on the lovers. This concerned the four actors, who had to pull off one of the most intricate comic scenes in Shakespeare. "Alvin would never direct the scene," said Steve Rowe, who played Demetrius. "He said, 'Go off in a room and work it out.' And we did. We came back and showed it to him. And he would say stuff like, 'Well, it's coming, but I just think you look like pigs in swill. Go off and work on it some more!'"

Robert Marx, the student dramaturge assigned to the production, recorded the mounting anxiety in his rehearsal log. April 21, 1975: "lovers want more rehearsal time—the pressured schedule has led to disjoint[ed] characterizations . . . results in tense discussion with Alvin . . . general feeling of uselessness over pre-rehearsal 'talk' sessions about play . . . actors: too many scenes remain 'unsolved' for them."

April 29th: "evening: scheduled run-through cancelled . . . explosion with Otto: claims he hasn't enough time for preparing and integrating the music . . . Alvin wants to use the time to stage the chorus sequences . . . orchestra dismissed early . . . Otto threatens to resign, but doesn't . . . Staging time used for the chorus."

May 6th: "first complete run-through with live music . . . Chorus moves like death incarnate—they have no freedom of gesture or posture (and they wear the costumes very badly); the enunciation is poor; soloists are generally off-pitch . . . still some question as to how the music will integrate with the text . . . fairy costumes are awkward without being outrageous—a net of Victoriana seems to hang over the big fairy sequences . . . Meryl Streep (Helena) times her melodrama extremely well, but she seems too beautiful for the part; she should be Hermia."

By May 9th—opening night—it somehow came together: "wildly

enthusiastic audience . . . everything coalesces: rustics, lovers, battles, fairies . . . cuts performed seamlessly, although the show is still running just over three hours . . . chorus moves a bit better; orchestra relatively on pitch . . . some rumblings in a few corners of the audience as to whether the play has been sufficiently dealt with from an intellectual point of view; also, some questions about the use of music . . . general consensus—a success."

Most everyone agreed. Brustein called the production "the culmination of everything we had ever done." Linda Atkinson, who played Puck, said that it "just took off like a flying carpet." Mel Gussow, from the *Times*, found it "haunting" and "lustrous," though he added, "The production falters a bit with its star-crossed lovers. Except for Meryl Streep (who clearly is one of the most versatile members of the Yale company) as Helena, they are not quite sportive enough."

Word spread that *Midsummer* was the funniest thing in New Haven, particularly the "Pyramus and Thisbe" scene, led by Meryl's friend Joe "Grifo" Grifasi as Flute. Spectators would crowd in just to see it. "The house manager used to have to pry people away, because he was a retired fire marshal and it was a fire hazard," Feingold recalled. As Helena, Meryl made herself an awkward, teetering mess, someone unaware of her luminous beauty. Amid the reverie, the fall of Saigon, on April 30th, had brought the Vietnam War to an end, closing a nightmarish chapter for the country. The mood on campus, buoyed by the intoxicating *Midsummer*, was one of belated release.

Approaching graduation, Meryl took stock of her Yale experience. What exactly had she learned there? There had been no cohesive training, just a mishmash of techniques. "That kind of grab-bag, eclectic education is invaluable, but only out of adversity," she said later. "Half the time you're thinking, I wouldn't do it this way, this guy is full of crap, but in a way, that's how you build up what you believe in. Still, those years made me tired, crazy, nervous. I was always throwing up."

She had an agent in New York and a fluency with diverse theatrical styles: Brustein's ideal of the repertory player. But there had been darker lessons, too. The pain of not being noticed for one's achievements. The bitterness of competition, even when you win. She had learned what happens when you succumb to powerful men and allow them to rob you of your agency.

And she learned that she was good. Really good.

Brustein begged her to remain with the company after graduation. He knew what he had, and didn't want her to sacrifice her talent to something as banal as stardom. Three days after she turned twenty-six, she wrote to Brustein, apologizing for taking so long with her decision. "The Rep is home," she wrote, "I'm no ingrate, and you've given me opportunities and encouragement that form the basis of my confidence in and commitment to the theatre." However, she continued, "right now everything in me wants to try out what I've learned in New Haven away from New Haven. Just got to see what it's like."

On May 19th, the class of 1975 marched into Old Campus in caps and gowns. Within the sea of black, one woman stood out like a blaze of light. It was Meryl Streep, in a bright white picnic dress. Viewed from the Connecticut sky, she must have looked like a diamond glistening in the muck. Once again, Meryl had done everyone one better.

"All the rest of the women in the class went: '*Bitch*,'" William Ivey Long recalled. "'*Why didn't I think of that?*'"

Isabella

✤

THE SUMMER OF 1975 was a brutal time to start an acting career, and the graduates of the Yale School of Drama had that drummed into their heads. The country had been slogging through a recession, taking the entertainment industry and all of New York City down with it. Times Square had devolved into a wasteland of garbage and strip joints. Broadway theaters were empty, or being turned into hotels. Even day jobs were hard to come by. As Linda Atkinson sighed to the *New Haven Register* shortly after graduation, "Unfortunately, the jobs selling gloves at Macy's are getting as hard to find as acting jobs."

The math was bleak: six thousand more degrees in dramatic arts had been awarded across the country than the previous year. The cast of *A Midsummer Night's Dream* would soon disappear into an ocean of aspiring Pucks and Hermias, each armed with a stack of eight-by-ten glossies. Many would try their luck in New York, while others fanned out to regional theaters. One Yale actor was off to Massachusetts to operate a kite shop.

And where was Meryl Streep, the undisputed star of the class of 1975? Meryl Streep, who had two degrees, four thousand dollars in student loans, and almost no professional credits to her name? Stuck on the interstate from Connecticut, an hour late to meet Joseph Papp, one of the biggest producers in New York City. *I'm twenty-six*, she had told herself. *I'm starting my career. I better make it next year.*

A lot was riding on this one, because she had already screwed up. Before graduation, the acting students had taken a trip to New York to audition for the Theatre Communications Group, which placed young actors at regional theaters across the country. The TCG audition was so important that Yale offered a special class on it. The drama students would be up against their counterparts from Juilliard and NYU, and whoever made it through the New York round would be sent to finals in Chicago. Impress the panel, and you might get hired to join a company in Louisville or Minneapolis. It wasn't New York, it wasn't Hollywood, but it was a job.

Meryl stayed over in New York the night before the audition. When she woke up the next morning, she looked at the clock and went back to sleep. She just didn't go. She couldn't stand the idea of going up against the same seven or eight people again. Perhaps she also knew that she didn't belong in Louisville. As she drifted back to unconsciousness, she could hear her classmates' voices in her head: "Gawd, where's Meryl? Oh, man, she's really fucked herself now!"

Was she finished? Not quite. Because soon after, Milton Goldman, the head of the theater division at ICM, called up Rosemarie Tichler, the casting director at the Public Theater.

"I want you to meet someone," he told her. "Robert Lewis, the acting teacher at Yale, said she's one of the most extraordinary people he's ever taught."

"If Robert Lewis says that, I'd be happy to meet her," Tichler replied from her office in the East Village. Of course, this could be Milton exaggerating, she told herself.

Days later, Meryl was standing onstage on the third floor of the Public, a mazelike red building that had once housed the Astor Library. Now it was the hub of the downtown theater world, the place where *Hair* had originated and where *A Chorus Line* had opened that April to ecstatic reviews.

Like most casting people, Tichler asked for a classic monologue and a modern one. Meryl began with the warlike Queen Margaret from *Henry VI, Part 3*, taunting the captured Duke of York:

Off with the crown, and with the crown his head
And, whilst we breathe, take time to do him dead.

Watching from the house, Tichler smiled. Meryl had captured not just Margaret's viciousness but the glee she takes in torturing her political rival. "She was," Tichler recalled, "a wonderful monster."

Then Meryl shifted her body, becoming girlish, sexy, demure. Her voice melted into a sultry Texas drawl. She was now Southern Comfort, a flirtatious twentysomething wild child from Terrence McNally's *Whiskey*.

"I grew up right here in Houston," she purred. "I was pretty, I was the national champion baton twirler and I only dated football players. Sound familiar?"

It did, to the actress onstage—this was her high school persona, the character she had played to the hilt in Bernardsville, recast as a Southern hussy.

She went on, as Southern Comfort, to describe all the jocks she'd made it with: Bobby Barton, in the backseat of his father's Ford Fairlane; Tiny Walker, who had a blood-red Plymouth Fury with dual carburetors. All the boys were killed on the football field shortly after sleeping with her, but she described their liaisons with delectation—especially the cars.

Tichler was in hysterics. "When she talked about sleeping with them, it was always about the car," she recalled. Meryl had shown some of her chameleonic gift, but Tichler didn't know the full extent of it. "I just knew she had great beauty, she had a lightness of touch," she said. "She had grace."

A few weeks later, Tichler was casting *Trelawny of the "Wells,"* a Victorian comedy by Arthur Wing Pinero, about the ingénue of a theater troupe who gives up the stage for marriage. The show would go up at the Vivian Beaumont at Lincoln Center, which had lately become an outpost of the New York Shakespeare Festival, a sprawling entity that included the Public Theater and Shakespeare in the Park. Tichler was looking for someone to play Miss Imogen Parrott, an actress who doubles as a theater manager. She had to be charming but authoritative, good with money and at telling people what to do. Tichler thought back to the Yale actress who had done that crackling Queen Margaret and called her in for the director, A. J. Antoon.

But Antoon wasn't sold. He liked Meryl, but he liked other people, too. At her second audition at the Public, he hadn't seen what Tichler had seen—that one-in-a-million thing. Tichler kept pushing, but Antoon's wasn't the opinion that really mattered. The person who mattered was Joe Papp, the man who founded the New York Shakespeare Festival and ran the Public and employed just about half of the actors, playwrights, and directors in New York City.

Meryl was still in Connecticut and couldn't make the normal audition times, so Tichler and Antoon had her come in for Papp after hours. Seven o'clock turned to eight o'clock, and there was no Meryl Streep. Papp was getting restless—patience wasn't his strong suit—and the sky was getting dark. As he paced, Tichler nervously kept the conversation going. She wanted him to see this girl. Where in God's name was she?

IN SOME WAYS, Joe Papp was another Robert Brustein. Both were powerful, pugnacious men who started theaters, started fights, and towered over an army of artists from whom they extracted undying loyalty. Both were New York Jews educated in public schools, and both thought that theater could change the world. Between New York and New Haven, they competed over plays and actors, maintaining a (mostly) friendly rivalry.

And there, for the most part, was where the similarities ended. While Brustein operated from the ivory tower, Papp never went to college. Brustein summered in Martha's Vineyard; Papp rented cottages on the Jersey Shore. Born Joseph Papirofsky, to penniless Eastern European immigrants, he had worked as a barker at Coney Island as a teenager and sold tomatoes and pretzels from a pushcart. After serving in World War II, he joined the Actors' Lab in Los Angeles, where he forged his populist ideology: theater was for everyone, not just for the elite. Even as he fought his way to the top of the New York theater world, he felt out of place, a working-class *Yid* in a white-collar universe.

Like Shakespeare's best characters, he was a walking, bellowing contradiction. The critics could never make up their minds about whether he was a cultural paragon or an autodidactic huckster. He spoke of his impoverished Brooklyn boyhood with Dickensian relish, yet two of his four consecutive wives were under the impression that he was Polish Catholic. He joined the Young Communist League when he was fifteen and kept his affiliation through his early thirties, but he rarely spoke of it, wary of putting his theater's funding at risk. As he dashed through the halls of the Public, a trail of assistants would scurry behind, trying to make sense of his conflicting pronouncements. He was punny, allusive. When someone burst into his office to tell him that an actor had been injured rehearsing *Hamlet*, he shot back: "Well, you can't make a *Hamlet* without breaking legs."

With little more than chutzpah (which he had in spades), Papp had built an empire. In 1954, he staged *Romeo and Juliet* in a church on Avenue D, the beginning of what he would call the New York Shakespeare Festival. His dream was to build a home for free Shakespeare in Central Park, leading him into a contentious standoff with the city's all-powerful parks commissioner, Robert Moses, who was in his seventies and had no intention of bending to the will of "an irresponsible Commie." The ensuing battle made Papp a municipal celebrity, a scrappy showbiz Robin Hood who took on the big bad commissioner and brought high art to the masses.

Finally, Moses allowed the plans for a Central Park amphitheater to move forward, and the Delacorte opened in 1962, when Meryl Streep was thirteen. The first Shakespeare in the Park production was *The Merchant of Venice*, starring James Earl Jones and George C. Scott. Four years later, Papp opened the Public Theater, in the East Village, where he would produce bold new plays by writers like David Rabe, whom he treated as a surrogate son.

From the beginning, part of his mission was to forge an American style of Shakespearean acting: muscular and raw, nothing like the plummy British oratory of Laurence Olivier. "We seek blood-and-guts actors . . . actors who have the stamp of truth on everything they say or do," he wrote. "This humanizes the language and replaces verse-reading and singsong recitation—the mark of old-fashioned classical acting—with an understandable, living speech." His actors would look and sound like New York City itself: multiethnic and real and tough.

Although Papp kept up a face of irrepressible bravado, he was plagued by anxiety, usually over the Festival's constant money problems. His attitude was: do something big now, pay for it later. "He always felt under duress and embattled," said Gail Merrifield Papp, who ran the play-development department and in 1976 became the fourth and final Mrs. Papp. The Festival was perpetually in debt, and the fiscal worries of the seventies made the crisis an existential one. Then came a deus ex machina: *A Chorus Line*, the revolutionary musical drawn from the stories and struggles of Broadway dancers. The show opened downtown in April, 1975, and transferred to Broadway that July. Its smash run would bankroll the Festival for years, keeping the Delacorte open and free to the masses and allowing Papp to keep coming up with crazy schemes.

One scheme in particular had him worried. In 1972, the management of Lincoln Center, the massive cultural complex that had revitalized Manhattan's West Sixties, asked him to consult in finding a new director for its theater division. The more he consulted, the more he realized he had the perfect candidate: himself. He loathed the idea of catering to well-to-do matinee ladies uptown, but the Festival was more than a million dollars in debt. Taking over the Vivian Beaumont, Lincoln Center's cavernous eleven-hundred-seat house, he could tap into the kind of cash flow that was unavailable to him at the Public. And, in the process, he could give his brood of audacious young playwrights a national platform.

The addition of Lincoln Center as his new satellite made his reach unprecedented, with outposts downtown, uptown, in Central Park, and on Broadway. Bernard Gersten, his longtime associate producer, called it Papp's "expansionist period." A 1972 *New Yorker* cartoon imagined all of New York City as a Joseph Papp production. But he was uneasy at Lincoln Center, which to him represented the establishment he had spent his life fighting against. The Vivian Beaumont reminded him of a mausoleum. He didn't even keep an office there.

Lincoln Center subscribers returned his disdain. When he announced the lineup for his inaugural season—a rock musical, a "black" play, a working-class drama by David Rabe—they fled in droves. One woman, describing herself as "one of the lily white subscribers who I think you would like to drop anyway," told him: "I'm not interested in a black playwright. I'm interested in a good playwright." "We got bales of mail," Gail Papp recalled. "People protesting the production of black plays on the main stage. Really hateful kind of mail." Within a year, subscriptions plummeted from 27,000 to 22,000. Far from being a goldmine, Lincoln Center was turning into financial quicksand.

Finally, Papp relented. The Vivian Beaumont would now house the classics. He flew to Oslo to persuade the Norwegian film star Liv Ullmann to play Nora in *A Doll's House*, which opened to packed crowds. He booked Ruth Gordon and Lynn Redgrave to star in Shaw's *Mrs. Warren's Profession*. But he gnashed his teeth the whole time. None of this was why he got into theater. Downtown, he was premiering groundbreaking works like Ntozake Shange's *for colored girls who have considered suicide / when the rainbow is enuf*. Uptown, he was a sellout.

He put together the 1975–76 season at the Vivian Beaumont in a hurry. Along with *Mrs. Warren's Profession*, he would transfer the

Delacorte's popular production of *Hamlet* starring Sam Waterston, followed by Ibsen's *Peer Gynt*. The season would open with *Trelawny of the "Wells,"* Pinero's crowd-pleasing comedy of manners. On July 13th, less than two weeks before *A Chorus Line* opened on Broadway, the *Times* ran the headline: "Can Shakespeare, Ibsen, Shaw and Pinero Save Joseph Papp?" He should have been riding high, but he was under fire.

Trelawny wasn't just a chestnut: it was a chestnut *within* a chestnut. Written in the late 1890s, Pinero set the play thirty years earlier. According to the author, the play "should follow, to the closest detail, the mode of the early Sixties—the period, in dress, of crinoline and the peg-top trouser. . . . No attempt should be made to modify such fashions in illustration, to render them less strange, even less grotesque, to the modern eye. On the contrary, there should be an endeavour to reproduce, perhaps to accentuate, any feature which may now seem particularly quaint and bizarre." Nothing could be more antithetical to Papp's vision.

And now here he was, stuck late at work, waiting for some Yale-trained nobody—one of *Brustein's* people—to read for the part of the dainty but determined Imogen Parrott. And she was an hour late.

THE SAME DAY the *Times* had run its dire headline about Joseph Papp, Meryl arrived at the Eugene O'Neill Theater Center, in Waterford, Connecticut. The O'Neill was founded in 1964 on the Hammond farm, a leafy ninety-five-acre expanse not far from where Eugene O'Neill had spent his summers. The following year, the National Playwrights Conference was established there, providing a forum for playwrights to work far away from the critical gaze of New York City. In 1977, Wendy Wasserstein would develop *Uncommon Women and Others* there. The *Times* called it "Tryout town, USA."

For young actors like Meryl Streep, Joe Grifasi, and Christopher Lloyd, it was like theater summer camp. They would sprint from play to play, rehearsing under copper beech trees and spending off hours on the beach. Lloyd was the only actor with a car, a red Triumph convertible. They bunked nearby at Connecticut College, in a dorm affectionately called "The Slammer," which Grifasi later described as "tastefully appointed with glossy enameled cinderblock, sea-green Naugahyde with cigarette-burn appliqué, and each room with a curiously dappled set of linens and a humble Protestant pillow, with the plushness of matzo."

Meryl loved the open air and free-wheeling atmosphere of the O'Neill, with its "motley, idiosyncratic bunch." There was the scholar Arthur Ballet, doused in expensive French suntan oil. There was Edith Oliver, *The New Yorker*'s theater critic and a midwife of plays—a "little old lady with a smile as big as the beach." George C. White, the O'Neill's founder, presided in a white linen suit. From their chatty, exuberant suppers on the sloping lawn, she could see "the lights from the amusement park flickering across the water from the other side of the harbor, the other fun house no one had any time to visit because we were lighting up the sky from our own side as well."

Meryl would perform in five plays in four weeks—the kind of rapid-fire, improvisatory acting she had honed at the Yale Cabaret. There was no time to overthink character choices: just pick something and go with it. In *Marco Polo*, a commedia play for children, she and Grifo played twin Truffaldinos, clowning around like amateur acrobats. "When people saw Meryl in that first play, they realized she wasn't just another pair of fetching cheekbones with a goofy last name," Grifasi recalled. "No one expects a pretty girl to be that funny or insane, but the truth is that others always find Meryl prettier than she considers herself to be."

The most alluring title that year was *Isadora Duncan Sleeps with the Russian Navy*. Meryl played Isadora, the dancer who had famously died when her long, flowing scarf got caught in a wheel of the car she was riding in. Meryl's only prop was the scarf, which she used to ensnare her many lovers before it ultimately strangled her. They had five days to stage the play, and Meryl couldn't manipulate the scarf and hold the script at the same time. So she memorized the whole play, to the amazement of her fellow actors. (A "dull" achievement, if you asked her.)

On a rare night off, she and Grifo went to see the year's inescapable blockbuster movie, *Jaws*. It was the perfect diversion in their carefree summer, the last they'd have before the entertainment industry swallowed them whole—or took a nasty killer-shark bite out of them. The next day, Meryl jumped into Long Island Sound and splashed dramatically, as if daring the great white shark to attack. Under the setting sun, she and Grifo swam out to a float bobbing in the distance. She turned to him and confided:

"I'm going to get married and have a bunch of children by the time I'm thirty-five."

Then they swam back.

Three weeks in, Meryl got a call that turned her peaceful summer on its head. She had a callback for *Trelawny of the "Wells"* at Lincoln Center. When could she be in New York? Her schedule at the O'Neill was jam-packed, but she managed to convince the Public to give her a special audition slot. She would have to get in and out of the city like lightning.

She and Grifo borrowed a car and zoomed down the highway. As Meryl drove and lit cigarettes, Grifo held the script and ran her lines. White-knuckling the wheel at eighty-five miles per hour, she calmly recited her speeches as he fed her cues, the two of them enveloped in a Marlboro cloud. As they passed New Haven, Grifo imagined the *Variety* headline: "Dead Thesps, Dreams Dashed in High-Speed Curtain Call."

By the time they pulled up to Lafayette Street—alive—she was despondent. They were so absurdly late. *They're not going to hire me*, she thought. *I'm going to go, but it's doomed.* She got out of the car while Grifo kept the motor running, like a getaway driver in a bank heist. The air was sticky, and she didn't want to start sweating, so she walked instead of ran. Not that it mattered. She was doomed.

But that's not what Rosemarie Tichler saw. Having desperately tried to keep Papp occupied as the clock ticked, she was about to give up when she stepped outside and took one last look down the street. There was Meryl Streep, an hour and a half late, but *walking*.

She swept Meryl inside and introduced her to Joe. After quickly apologizing for being late, she went right into the scene—no time for fuss.

Tichler watched her in awe. Here she was, fresh out of drama school, meeting the kingpin of downtown theater for the first time, late for a callback for a major part at Lincoln Center. "Ninety-five percent of actresses would get hysterical, but she just . . . handled it," Tichler recalled.

When she left, Tichler let a momentary silence linger. Then she turned to Papp and said: "That's it, right?"

Outside on the curb, Meryl hopped back into the car. She finally breathed. They would have to book it back to Connecticut.

"I saw Joe Papp," she told Grifo.

And?

"He liked me."

She was right. Meryl Streep had just clinched her first role on Broadway. And she hadn't even moved to New York.

FOUR YEARS BEFORE Woody Allen romanticized it in *Manhattan*, New York City was in a rut. Budgetary foibles and urban decay had left a miasma of neon, sleaze, and crime. Murders and robberies had doubled since 1967. Under Mayor Abraham Beame, the city was hurtling toward bankruptcy. In July, 1975, the city's sanitation workers went on a wildcat strike, leaving garbage to pile up and fester in the heat— people were worried about the health risks of flies.

Filmmakers like Sidney Lumet and Martin Scorsese captured the grime and corruption in *Mean Streets*, *Serpico*, and *Dog Day After-noon*, the last of which opened on September 21st, just as the muggy "dog days" of summer were turning into a ruddy fall. Soon after, the city was denied a federal bailout, and the *Daily News* ran the immortal headline "Ford to City: Drop Dead." Like a dirt-smudged orphan, New York was on its own.

For Meryl Streep, who had just moved to Manhattan, it was the place to be. She had a job on Broadway and a room on West End Avenue, in an apartment she shared with Theo Westenberger, a photographer friend she had met at Dartmouth. Westenberger would become the first woman to shoot the cover of *Newsweek* and *Sports Illustrated*. For now, she found an ideal subject in her roommate, whom she shot leaning on a television in a kimono, or straddling a stool in a leopard-print jumpsuit.

Soon after, Meryl got her own place a few blocks away, on West Sixty-ninth Street, just off Central Park West. The neighborhood was rough—there were drug deals on Amsterdam Avenue all the time—but it was the first time she was living alone, free of roommates or brothers. However hazardous, she found the city glamorously lonesome.

"I got three bills a month—the rent, the electric, and the phone," she recalled. "I had my two brothers and four or five close friends to talk to, some acquaintances, and everybody was single. I kept a diary. I read three newspapers and the *New York Review of Books*. I read books, I took afternoon naps before performances and stayed out till two and three, talking about acting with actors in actors' bars."

And, unlike much of New York City, she was employed.

At her first reading of *Trelawny*, she was petrified. The company was large, with veteran stage actors like Walter Abel, who was born in 1898, the same year the play premiered. But there was a younger set, too. A tightly wound twenty-two-year-old Juilliard dropout named Mandy Patinkin was also making his Broadway debut. So was the bug-eyed character actor Jeffrey Jones. At twenty-nine, the broad-faced Harvard graduate John Lithgow was on his third Broadway show. And, in the title role of Miss Rose Trelawny, the bee-voiced, auburn-haired Mary Beth Hurt was on her fourth.

Mary Beth was also twenty-nine, having come out of NYU's drama school in 1972. Her marriage to William Hurt, a drama student at Juilliard, had imploded just as she was finding her professional footing. In 1973, Papp cast her as Celia in *As You Like It* in Central Park, and during rehearsals she became so distraught that she checked into the psych ward at Roosevelt Hospital. "I thought that I had really failed," she said later, "that I was supposed to be the perfect wife." Papp called her every day at the hospital, saying, "We'll hold the role open for you as long as we can. Please come back."

"Once Joe loved you—and it really did feel like love; it didn't feel like trying to use someone—he loved you forever," Mary Beth said. After three days, she checked herself out and went on as Celia.

At the read-through of *Trelawny*, Meryl was trembling. At one point, she realized her upper lip was wiggling, completely independent of the lower one. A. J. Antoon had reset the British play in turn-of-the-century New York, and smack in the middle of one of her lines, she heard a booming voice: "Do a Southern accent."

It was Joe Papp.

"Yessuh," she said, instinctively modeling her drawl on Dinah Shore's. ("See the U.S.A. in your Chevrolet . . .") And suddenly her character started to make sense—an ingénue getting on in years, shifting from Southern belle to savvy theater manager, able to boss people around. Joe was right.

"The curvaceous, desperately subtle flirtation in the cadences moved me toward a way of holding myself and of moving across the room, a way of sitting, and above all an awareness, because a Southern accent affords self-aware self-expression," she said later. "You shape the phrase. Not to get too deep into it, it was a valuable choice and it was not mine, it was his and I still don't know where the hell he got the idea. This is the essence of his direction. *He's* direct. Do it, he says."

John Lithgow had met Meryl a few months earlier, at a reading of a play by a Harvard friend of his—something about hostages in Appalachia. He had noticed "a pale, wispy girl with long, straight, corn-silk hair" and an odd name. "She appeared to be in her late teens," he would recall. "She was so shy, withdrawn, and self-effacing that I couldn't decide whether she was pretty or plain. The only time I heard her voice was when she spoke her lines. She had a high, thin voice and a twangy hillbilly accent. She was so lacking in theatrical airs that I surmised that perhaps she wasn't an actress at all." He wondered whether the play was actually based on her.

When he spotted her at the first rehearsal of *Trelawny of the "Wells,"* she was like a different person, animated and eager and confidently beautiful. As usual, she wasn't letting her nerves show. "I'd been watching actors act my whole life," he recalled. "I wasn't easily taken in. But when I'd mistaken her for a hayseed hillbilly at that play reading a few months before, either I had been a myopic fool or this young woman was a brilliant actress."

OCTOBER 15, 1975: opening night of *Trelawny of the "Wells."* Meryl was backstage at the Vivian Beaumont, waiting to go on. Her upper lip, once again, was trembling. She willed it to stop, but it was no use. She tried not to think about the critics, who were out there scowling in the dark. She told herself: *My student loans are going to be paid off!*

Michael Tucker, the thirty-one-year-old actor playing Tom Wrench, was already onstage. He was nervous, too. Meryl thought of the swanning, confident woman she was about to play, and walked onstage.

"Well, Wrench, and how are you?" was her first line on Broadway.

They played the scene, a little stiffly. Then Tucker caught his sleeve on a prop, and it fell onto the table. Meryl caught it before it broke. She placed it back up.

"And from that moment everything was just fine," she recalled, "because something real had happened, and it pulled us right onto the table, into the world. And then all the work we had done in rehearsal and the life we had lived and who we were, we just located ourselves in the tactile world and there we were."

The critics had other ideas.

"Mr. Antoon has transposed the play to New York at the turn of the century. Why?" Clive Barnes practically screamed in the *Times* the next morning. "What new resonances does he get from it? Is he trying to make it more relevant to American audiences or easier for American actors? Does this make it more meaningful? Or is it merely another example of the Shakespeare Festival determination to do almost anything just as long as that anything is different. This is a folly. And symptomatic folly at that."

Walter Kerr piled on in the Sunday edition, under the headline "'A Chorus Line' Soars, 'Trelawny' Falls Flat." "The lights are no sooner up on a theatrical rooming-house," he wrote, "than the good folk carrying the opening exposition are cackling like wild geese to assure us that something is, or is going to be, hilarious around here." However, he added: "In the overstressed onrush, only two figures emerge at all: Meryl Streep as a glossily successful former colleague who has gone on to 'star' in another theater, tart, level-headed, stunningly decked out in salmon gown and white plumes; and Mary [B]eth Hurt, as Rose Trelawny herself, who is at the very least deeply satisfying to look at."

No doubt, the show was a turkey, at least with critics. The cast was stunned—the audiences seemed to be having a good time.

Meryl wasn't glum. Along with Kerr's peck on the cheek, the show had collateral benefits. Shortly before Thanksgiving, the screen legend Gene Kelly came and greeted the starstruck cast backstage. With him was Tony Randall, famous from *The Odd Couple*. Randall told the actors that he was planning to start a national acting company and he wanted the *Trelawny* cast to join. It sounded heavenly (though it wouldn't materialize until 1991). Still, the young cast didn't take him entirely seriously: Why wait for Tony Randall? They already felt like a repertory company. They had each other.

Meryl's new cohort included Mary Beth Hurt, with whom she shared Dressing Room No. 4. "It was full of smoke," Hurt recalled. "It was fun. We laughed. Mandy would drop in, or Michael Tucker. Everybody was visiting everybody. The doors were open. Nobody ever shut their doors unless they were changing clothes."

And she had a new collaborator: J. Roy Helland, the production's hair designer. The son of a hairdresser, Roy had run a salon in California and moonlighted as a female impersonator before going into theater. The previous spring, he was hired to primp Liv Ullmann for the Lincoln Center production of *A Doll's House. Trelawny* was his second Broadway show. He was painstaking with curlers and wigs, and he knew how to soften facial flaws (say, a crooked nose) with just the right shading. Roy was appalled when the stagehands pinned up naked girlie posters backstage, so he hung up hunky *Playgirl* centerfolds in the wig room, where Meryl and Mary Beth became habitués. Roy told them that Ullmann was trying to lure him to Norway to style her for Ingmar Bergman films. The two young actresses straightened their backs and said, "Well, when *we* get to do movies, we'll take you, too!"

"He wasn't just a guy down there in the darkness doing wigs," Jeffrey Jones recalled. "He had strong opinions and good taste, and he decided immediately that she was the person to whom he would hitch his wagon." When Roy watched Meryl in rehearsal, he noticed a professionalism similar to Ullmann's—she didn't act like it was her first Broadway show. He saw Meryl as a living canvas, someone who seemed to work from the outside in and the inside out at the same time. When she needed a touch-up, she would slink down to the wig room and yodel, "Oh, *Rooooooy!*" Soon, everyone in the cast was doing it.

MERYL STREEP CAME to New York with a primary goal: not to get typecast. At Yale, she had played everyone from Major Barbara to an eighty-year-old "translatrix." In the real world, it wasn't so easy. "Forget about being a character actress. This is *New York*," people kept telling her. "They need an old lady, they'll get an old lady—you're going to get typed, get used to it." More than once, she was told she would make a wonderful Ophelia.

But she didn't want to play Ophelia. And she didn't want to be an ingénue. She wanted to be everything and everybody. If she could just hold on to that ability to carousel through identities—that repertory

"The girls didn't buy it," she said of her high school persona. "They didn't like me; they sniffed it out, the acting."

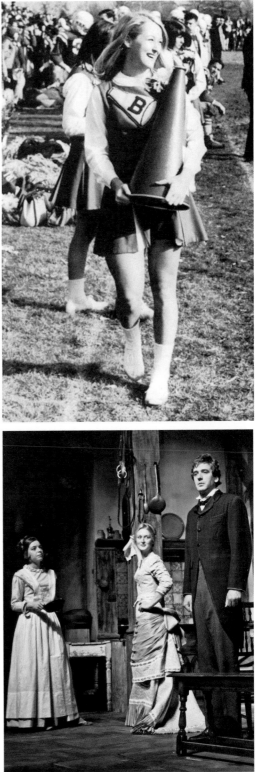

Above, at the prom with Mike Booth. Right, as Miss Julie at Vassar in December, 1969. It was the first serious play she ever saw, and she was starring in it.

Her breakout role at the Yale School of Drama, the eighty-year-old "translatrix" Constance Garnett in *The Idiots Karamazov*. Christopher Durang, kneeling on right, played Alyosha.

Left, her Broadway debut, in *Trelawny of the "Wells."* Right, as Hallelujah Lil in *Happy End*.

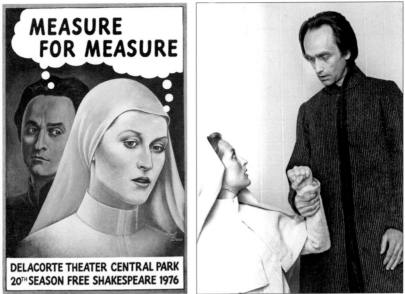

"We sense the sexual give-and-take between her and Angelo," the *Times* critic wrote of her performance as Isabella in *Measure for Measure*, opposite John Cazale.

With Cazale at Lee Strasberg's seventy-fifth birthday party. "The jerk made everything mean something," she said later. "Such good judgment, such uncluttered thought."

Above, shooting *The Deer Hunter* with Michael Cimino and Robert De Niro. Below, with Chuck Aspegren, De Niro, and Cazale, in the wedding scene that seemed to go on forever. Cazale didn't survive to see the film. Of the five movies he acted in, all were Oscar-nominated for Best Picture. He never got a nomination.

"I think he just hated my character," she said of Woody Allen, who cast her as his ex-wife in *Manhattan*. Below, reading Germaine Greer backstage at *The Taming of the Shrew*.

Above, Joanna leaves Ted in the opening scene of *Kramer vs. Kramer*. Below, Ted's lawyer asks, "Were you a failure at the one most important relationship in your life?"

Above, meeting the queen at a royal screening of *Kramer vs. Kramer*. Below, trying and failing to share a private moment with Don Gummer.

thing she had mastered at Yale and the O'Neill—she could be the kind of actress she wanted to be. Had she landed in a movie or a Broadway musical right out of school, she might have been pegged as a pretty blonde. Instead, she did something few svelte young actresses would do: she played a 230-pound Mississippi hussy.

The Phoenix Theatre company had been around since 1953, when it opened a play starring Jessica Tandy in a former Yiddish theater on Second Avenue. Since then, despite its shoestring existence, it had produced dozens of shows, from the Carol Burnett vehicle *Once Upon a Mattress* to *The Seagull*, starring Montgomery Clift. Its gentlemanly cofounder, T. Edward Hambleton (his friends called him "T"), wasn't ideological like Papp. His guiding principle was: produce good plays.

By 1976, the Phoenix was operating out of the Playhouse, a small Broadway theater on West Forty-eighth Street. Like other theater companies in town, it was planning an all-American season to celebrate the coming Bicentennial. First up: a double bill showcasing the twin titans of mid-century American playwriting, Tennessee Williams and Arthur Miller. Both men were in their sixties, their reputations secure enough to render them slightly out of date. And yet the contrast would give the evening some frisson: Williams, the lyrical, sensuous Southerner; and Miller, the lucid, pragmatic Northerner.

When Meryl saw the part she was reading for, she couldn't quite believe it. Set on a front porch in the Mississippi Delta, Williams's *27 Wagons Full of Cotton* is a tour de force for whoever plays Flora, a raunchy Southern sexpot with a big cup size and a low IQ. Flora is married to the unsavory owner of a cotton gin who calls her "Baby Doll." When a rival cotton gin mysteriously burns down, the superintendent comes by asking questions. Flora suspects her husband (who of course is guilty as sin), and the superintendent traps her in a randy cat-and-mouse game, wangling information out of her with coercion, threats, and sex. In *Baby Doll*, Elia Kazan's 1956 film adaptation, Carroll Baker had immortalized the role as a Lolita-like seductress, her sexuality practically bursting from her dress—nothing like the 125-pound slip of a thing that called itself Meryl Streep.

Exhausted after an eight-hour *Trelawny* rehearsal, Meryl arrived at the audition in a plain skirt, a blouse, and slip-on shoes. Carrying a supply closet's worth of tissues she had swiped from the ladies' room, she introduced herself to Arvin Brown, the director. Sitting next to him was John Lithgow, who was directing another Phoenix show. Lithgow recalled what happened next:

"As she made small talk with Arvin about the play and the character, she unpinned her hair, she changed her shoes, she pulled out the shirttails of her blouse, and she began casually stuffing Kleenex into her brassiere, doubling the size of her bust. Reading with an assistant stage manager, she began a scene from *27 Wagons Full of Cotton*. You could barely detect the moment when she slipped out of her own character and into the character of Baby Doll, but the transformation was complete and breathtaking. She was funny, sexy, teasing, brainless, vulnerable, and sad, with all the colors shifting like mercury before our eyes."

Arvin Brown hired her immediately. But he must not have noticed the transformation that had occurred right in front of him, because when rehearsals began, he took a good look at his leading lady and panicked. Her magic trick had worked so well he hadn't realized it was all an illusion. "She was so slim and blond and beautiful, and somehow or another in the audition she had convinced me that she was this really slatternly, sluggish redneck," Brown recalled. He thought, *Is this going to work?*

Meryl was getting worried, too. Her fake D cup had been a way to trick not just the audition room but herself. Without the reams of paper stuffed in her brassiere, she was losing her grip on the character. "Let me try something," she told Brown.

She went out and returned with a slovenly old housedress and prosthetic breasts. She had found Baby Doll—and Brown once again saw a "zaftig cracker." Far from playing a femme fatale, Meryl tapped into

Flora's innocence and vulgarity, which should have contradicted each other but didn't. Like Evert Sprinchorn at Vassar, Brown sensed a hint of rebellion: "I had the feeling she was kind of kicking the traces of a fairly conventional background."

Onstage at the Playhouse in January, 1976, Meryl's Baby Doll announced herself with a squeal in the dark:

"Jaaaaaake! I've lost m' white kid purse!"

Then she clomped into view in high heels and a loose-fitting dress, a buxom, babbling dingbat with a voice like a bubble bath. Between her lines, she cooed, cackled, swatted at imaginary flies. At one point, sitting on the porch with her legs splayed, she looked down at her armpit and wiped it with her hand. Moments later, she picked her nose and flicked away her findings. It was the funniest and most grotesque thing Meryl had done since *The Idiots Karamazov*. But, like Constance Garnett, her Flora was rooted in a goofy kind of humanity.

The *Village Voice* called her

> a tall, well-upholstered, Rubenesque child-woman; a sexy Baby Snooks, tottering around on dingy cream-colored high-heeled shoes, giggling, chattering in her little-girl voice, alternately husky and shrill, mouthing her words as if too lazy to pronounce them properly (and yet you can understand every word), tonguing her lips, smiling wet smiles, playing with her long blonde hair, cuddling her boobs in her arms, lolling and luxuriating in her body as if it were a warm bath. And all this extravagant detail is as spontaneous and organic as it is abundant; nothing is excessive; nothing is distracting; everything is part of Baby Doll. What a performance!

Few people in New York—Rosemarie Tichler, John Lithgow—had known the extent of Meryl's talent for metamorphosis. While her Baby Doll was a bravura feat of physical comedy, the true shock of *27 Wagons Full of Cotton* was what came after. The play was on a double bill with Arthur Miller's *A Memory of Two Mondays*, set in an auto-parts warehouse in Depression-era New York City. The look and feel couldn't have been more different: where the Williams play oozed sex and lemonade, the Miller was pert, industrial, like a dry martini. The cast included Lithgow and Joe Grifasi, with Meryl in the throw-away part of Patricia, a secretary.

But that's where she played her trump card. At the end of the Williams play, the lights went down on Flora, singing "Rock-a-bye Baby" to her purse in the Mississippi moonlight. After intermission, she marched back on as Patricia: black marcelled hair, smart dress, hand on her hip, showing off her pin from a date the night before. As if on cue, there was a rustling of paper in the dark as playgoers thumbed through their programs: Could this possibly be the same actress?

"It's not just that she was playing these two wildly different characters," Arvin Brown recalled, "but she also had created two entirely different energy outlays. *27 Wagons* was all languorous and at times almost bovine. And all of a sudden, there would be this slash of energy as she walked onstage in the second play, and she had this dark wig and everything was urban, steely, fast. It was just a jolt."

Tennessee Williams and Arthur Miller avoided being seen together. They knew that the pairing of their plays would inevitably play like a competition, and they didn't want to encourage the question of who was the great American playwright. So Miller came to the final dress rehearsal and Williams came to opening night. When the curtain came down on *27 Wagons*, Meryl ran backstage to transform from blowsy hillbilly to steely secretary. Aiding her was J. Roy Helland, who had followed her from Lincoln Center and helped mastermind the two competing looks. In the lobby, Williams cornered Arvin Brown to tell him how much Meryl's performance had astounded him.

"It's never been played like that!" he kept saying, which Brown took to mean her naïveté—nothing like the purposeful, pouty bombshell Carroll Baker had played in the film.

Brown slipped into the dressing room to tell Meryl about the playwright's euphoria. After the show, he would bring Williams backstage so he could praise her in person. But Williams never showed up at their appointed meeting place. By curtain call for *A Memory of Two Mondays,* he had vanished.

No one knew why until the next day, when the director got an apologetic call from Williams's agent. What happened was this: Meryl had an understudy named Fiddle Viracola, whose round face and kooky personality made her a natural Baby Doll. Viracola had a bizarre pastime: she would go up to celebrities and ask them to draw her a picture of a frog. At the dress rehearsal, she'd approached Arthur Miller and requested a frog for her collection.

On opening night, Williams had been walking into the lobby to meet Brown when a woman bore down on him yelling something about a frog. The playwright panicked and ran for a taxi. He never made it backstage to tell Meryl how much he loved her Baby Doll.

DESPITE HER ADVANCEMENTS, she still didn't see herself as a movie star, and neither did the rest of the world. Or so it appeared one afternoon, as she sat across from Dino De Laurentiis, the Italian film producer whose credits included everything from Fellini's *La Strada* to *Serpico.* De Laurentiis was casting a remake of *King Kong,* and Meryl had come in to audition for the part made famous by Fay Wray—the girl who wins the heart of the big gorilla.

De Laurentiis eyed her up and down through thick square spectacles. From his office at the top of the Gulf and Western Building, on Columbus Circle, you could see all of Manhattan. He was in his fifties, with slicked-back salt-and-pepper hair. His son, Federico, had seen Meryl in a play and brought her in. But whatever the younger De Laurentiis saw in her, the older certainly did not.

"*Che brutta!*" the father said to the son, and continued in Italian: *This is so ugly! Why do you bring me this?*

Meryl was stunned. Little did he know she had studied Italian at Vassar.

"*Mi dispiace molto,*" she said back, to the producer's amazement.

I'm very sorry that I'm not as beautiful as I should be. But this is what you get.

She was even more upset than she let on. Not only was he calling her ugly—he was assuming she was stupid, too. What actress, much less an American, and a blonde at that, could possibly understand a foreign language?

She got up to leave. This was everything she feared about the movie business: the obsession with looks, with *sex*. Sure, she was looking for a break, but she had promised herself she wouldn't do any junk. And this was junk.

When she learned that Jessica Lange had gotten the part, she didn't pout. She hadn't wanted it that badly, to tell the truth. She knew she wouldn't have been any good in it. Let someone else scream at a monkey on top of the Empire State Building. They wanted a "movie star," and she wasn't one.

She was too *brutta*.

Theater was where her heart was. After the victory in *27 Wagons Full of Cotton*, she stayed on with the Phoenix for another play that spring: *Secret Service*, a Civil War melodrama by William Gillette. Her old friend Grifo was in the cast. So were her *Trelawny* castmates John Lithgow and Mary Beth Hurt.

The play was a thriller from 1895—nothing revelatory, but it was fun to play Edith Varney, a Richmond belle who falls for a Union spy, cannons booming in the background. In her plaid dress and bonnet, she and a mustache-twirling Lithgow played love scenes that would have seemed overblown in *Gone With the Wind*:

"What is it—love and Good-bye?"

"Oh no—only the first!—And that one every day—every hour— every minute—until we meet again!"

It was borderline camp, and the actors never quite figured out how tongue-in-cheek to play their scenes. But the Phoenix kids just wanted to work together, on anything. A close-knit ensemble formed, onstage and off: spunky, squeaky Mary Beth; impish Joe Grifasi; chin-stroking leading man John Lithgow; and Meryl, the Waspy blonde who could do just about anything. They would drink at Joe Allen after shows, then bike home together to the Upper West Side, like New York transplants from *Jules and Jim*. They felt, Mary Beth recalled, like "princes of the city."

Meryl was still riding the success of *27 Wagons* and *A Memory of Two Mondays*. "Those two plays at the Phoenix Theatre did more to bring me attention, along with *Trelawny*, than any three plays I could have done on Broadway in three years playing three blondes," she said later. She won her first professional theater prize, the Theatre World Award, and was nominated for a Drama Desk. Then, in late March— less than a year out of drama school—she was nominated for a Tony Award for the Phoenix double bill. She was up against her own cast-mate Mary Beth, who was nominated for *Trelawny*.

On April 18th, a few days after *Secret Service* opened at the Play-house, both actresses filed into the Shubert Theater for the ceremony. Backstage were the heavies of the entertainment world: Jane Fonda, Jerry Lewis, Richard Burton. Onstage was the bare set of *A Chorus Line*, which was up for nearly every musical category. Its cast members kicked off the ceremony with the already iconic opening number, "I Hope I Get It." For the nominees in the audience, the sentiment was apt.

It was Easter Sunday. Mary Beth showed up in oversize glasses and her trademark red bob. Meryl still had Civil War ringlets falling across her brow. Sitting in the audience, she felt "profoundly uncomfortable." During commercial breaks, she could sense the nominees licking their lips. It all felt so silly.

Sure enough, *A Chorus Line* made a clean sweep, winning half of the eighteen award categories. By the time it beat out *Chicago* and *Pa-cific Overtures* for Best Musical, the orchestra seemed to have "What I Did for Love" playing on a loop. No one could deny it now: Joe Papp had a juggernaut.

Alan Arkin came out to present Best Featured Actress in a Play. When he read Meryl's name, her lips tensed. But the winner was Shirley Knight, for *Kennedy's Children*. Both Meryl and Mary Beth went home empty-handed. When they showed up for work the next Tuesday, it was back to Richmond, Virginia, 1864.

AT THE DRESS rehearsal for *Trelawny of the "Wells,"* Joe Papp had told her, cryptically, "I may have something for you." Then, on Christmas Eve, 1975, the phone rang.

"How would you like to play Isabella in *Measure for Measure* in the park?" the producer said. "And maybe Katherine in *Henry V*?"

Meryl was . . . confused. Had he lost his critical faculties? She knew he had his favorites, and anyone let into Joe's inner circle was employed for life, like at a Japanese corporation. But Isabella? Wasn't that the lead?

"What I thought was great about him was that he treated me as a peer," she said. "Right from the beginning, when I was this unknown, completely ignorant drama student, way before I was ready for it, he admitted me to the discussion as an equal." The two of them had the same birthday, June 22nd, and they felt like they were cosmically linked.

"His conviction about me was total," she recalled, "but somewhere in the back of my brain I was screaming: 'Wow! Wow! Look at this! Wow!'"

Winter turned to spring, and she rode her bicycle everywhere. Downtown to the Public, where she was rehearsing *Measure for Measure*. Uptown to Lincoln Center, where Papp was rehearsing *Henry V*. One day in May, she deposited her bike in the checkroom at Café des Artistes, on West Sixty-seventh, two blocks from her new apartment. A bit early, she wandered the wood-paneled dining room, staring at the bucolic murals of wood nymphs dancing merrily in the nude. The surrounding trees had something of Bernardsville about them—the old Bernardsville, when she was a bossy little girl. Now there were expressways going up, and the whole place was different. Besides, her father had just retired, and he and Mary Wolf were relocating to Mason's Island, in Mystic, Connecticut.

By any actor's standards, her first season in New York had been charmed: back-to-back Broadway plays, a Tony nomination, and, coming up, two roles in Shakespeare in the Park. Plus, a few days earlier, there was a phone call.

Them: "Would you like to fly to London?"

Meryl: "Sure." (Pause.) "What for?"

The answer was an audition for *Julia*, a film based on a chapter from Lillian Hellman's memoir *Pentimento*. The story (of questionable veracity) concerned the playwright's childhood friend, who was always more daring than she. Julia becomes an anti-Nazi activist, and enlists Lillian to smuggle money to Resistance operatives in Russia. Unlike *King Kong*, this was the kind of movie Meryl saw herself in: a tale of female friendship and daring—i.e., not junk. Jane Fonda was playing Lillian. The director, Fred Zinnemann, was thinking about casting an unknown for Julia.

For now, Meryl couldn't stop staring at the plane ticket to London: $620.

"When I was at Yale, people on partial assistance like me got $2.50 an hour when we were on stage," she told her lunch date at Café des Artistes, a *Village Voice* reporter named Terry Curtis Fox. It was her first professional interview. "Before this year the most money I ever made was waitressing. $620. And that's only for an *audition*. It's crazy."

Another thing: she didn't have a passport. She had never needed one.

Meryl was deep into rehearsals for *Henry V*. Papp's vision was simple: the bigger, the better. Down at the harbor, historical ships were converging for the coming Bicentennial, like a flotilla of ghosts. Papp would re-create the pomp and pageantry in Central Park, staging the Battle of Agincourt like a bloody reprise of Lexington and Concord. The success of *A Chorus Line* had given some respite from his cash-flow problems, but the producer was still banging his head against Lincoln Center. He must have understood the words of the put-upon king:

> What infinite heart's-ease
> Must kings neglect, that private men enjoy!

To Meryl, he seemed undaunted. "He's going to fly right into it: let the critics compare us to the British and tear us to bits," she told Fox, beaming. "He's going to have the whole stage open up and shoot flaming arrows into the lake." As the French princess Katherine, she would be offstage for the extravagant fight sequences. "I just wish I were in those scenes," she said hungrily.

They got the bill and headed for the door. She took her bicycle from the checkroom, threw on her backpack, and wheeled down to Rockefeller Center to see about that passport. The twenty-six-year-old actress seemed to Fox like a character from a movie: the starlet on the rise, the fresh face. Still, he would write, "There is something in Meryl Streep of the killer."

FROM HER APARTMENT on Sixty-ninth Street it was less than a block to Central Park. A quick bike ride got her to the Delacorte, the open-air oasis Joe Papp had built. A few steps more, and she was onstage, the Belvedere Castle towering in the background like expensive scenery, the midsummer sky wide and hot above her. Then the battles would begin.

Papp had assembled a massive cast—sixty actors, many of them recent drama school grads looking for a break. Most had auditioned down at the Public, in the theater where *A Chorus Line* had originated before its move to Broadway. The white line where the chorus members had stood still ran across the stage.

"They had a whole group of us come in and stand on that white line," an auditioner named Tony Simotes recalled. "All of a sudden, Joe started to talk about the show and what he saw in the show. Just kind of getting the background on it. And he says, 'Oh, by the way, you're all cast.' He kept talking and we're all like, 'What?' We all started screaming and cheering and hugging each other."

A cigar perpetually hanging from the side of his mouth, Papp wielded his power like a king's scepter. "Build me a tower," he would say, and a swarm of carpenters would rush onstage with hammers and lumber. At one point, he took to skipping rope in front of the cast to show that he hadn't lost his vitality.

A few days in, he fired the guy delivering the prologue ("O, for a muse of fire that would ascend / The brightest heaven of invention!") and replaced him with Michael Moriarty. By now, Moriarty was a Tony-winning Broadway actor. From offstage, Meryl would delight at his menacing take on the prologue. It was, she said later, "the first time I realized you can pull out anything, absolutely anything, from Shakespeare. Michael found every ribald line and pulled them out for our delectation, and it was wicked and wise."

The two actors had something in common, besides their onstage tryst in *The Playboy of Seville* five years earlier. They were the only members of the company who didn't seem terrified of the director.

"Michael Moriarty couldn't give two shits about Joseph Papp, which was pretty cool," one ensemble member recalled. "He just said, 'Yeah, you want me to play that? Alright, I'll do it.' A lot of the people on the set were really intimidated by him. But what I was struck by was how Meryl Streep would come and wrap her arm around him, treating him like she was his old friend."

She even started sounding like him in interviews. When the *Times* visited the Delacorte and asked her whether she envied the Shakespearean training enjoyed by the British, she shrugged and said, "I envy the wealth of experience they can call on, but we have a different tradition in America that is just as strong. It has to do with heart and guts." Heart and guts: a Papp specialty.

As Katherine, she had just two scenes, but they were minor coups de théâtre. One was entirely in French, as the princess learns the English words for body parts, mangling "the elbow" as "de bilbow." Later, she returns in a ridiculous headdress and charms the English king. "It was just one light, delicious cameo, and she floated through it," Rosemarie Tichler recalled. "You watch this poor, befuddled king being turned around and fall in love. And as he fell in love, the audience fell in love."

Working in Central Park had its own peculiar magic. By three in the afternoon, masses of New Yorkers would line up outside the Delacorte for free tickets. (Papp never wavered on the price, even when the city begged him to charge even a dollar.) Snaking counterclockwise toward the softball fields on the Great Lawn, the line became its own sort of Shakespearean scene, where the freaky energy of the city came out to play. One July afternoon, a conservatively dressed woman with law books stood behind a guy in a Hobie's Surfing Shop T-shirt, as a troubadour in Elizabethan dress sang madrigals in a midwestern accent for dimes and quarters. Nearby, a hot-dog vendor competed with a falafel cart, while a man in a purple shirt and purple jeans with a purple bike told anyone who would listen, "You do not really see me. You are hallucinating. You think you are seeing purple because that is the color of the magic mushroom."

Around five, the staff would hand out cards to be redeemed for tickets, and the luckiest 1,800 would file into the amphitheater for the eight-o'clock show. When Michael Moriarty came out invoking the muse of fire, the sun was still blazing overhead. By Act V, when Henry kissed Katherine, the scene was lit by moonlight. At night, the park turned into a den of muggers and gropers, and the small army of actors knew to walk out together in a self-protecting horde. Then Meryl was back in her lobby, back in her elevator, and back in the apartment she had all to herself.

FOUR DAYS AFTER *Henry V* closed at the Delacorte, *Measure for Measure* opened at the Delacorte. Ten minutes before the first show, a man in the audience had a heart attack. An ambulance rushed him to Roosevelt Hospital, but he was dead on arrival. At eight o'clock, the rain began, and the stage manager held the show for twenty minutes. They got through Act I before the downpour intensified. The performance was finally canceled, and everyone went home soaked.

Even in dry weather, the play was challenging. Neither tragedy nor comedy, *Measure for Measure* is one of Shakespeare's ambiguous "problem plays." The plot rests on a moral quandary: Vienna has become a den of brothels, syphilis, and sin. The Duke (played by the thirty-five-year-old Sam Waterston) leaves his austere deputy, Angelo, to clean up the mess. To instill fear of the rule of law, Angelo condemns a young man named Claudio to death for fornication. Claudio's sister, Isabella, is entering a nunnery when she hears the news. She begs for mercy from Angelo, who is knocked senseless by lust. He comes back with an indecent proposal: Sleep with me and I'll spare your brother's life. Despite her brother's pleas, Isabella refuses, telling herself:

Then, Isabel, live chaste, and, brother, die:
More than our brother is our chastity.

The line usually draws gasps.

"The role is so beautiful, but there are so many problems in it," Meryl said at the time. "One is that it's so hard for a 1976 audience to sit back and believe that purity of the soul is all that matters to Isabella. That's really hard for them to buy." *Sure, Angelo's a pig*, most people think. *But, come on, it's your brother's life! Just sleep with the guy!*

Meryl was determined to find Isabella's truth, to make her dilemma real even if the audience was rooting against her—the same hurdle she would face in *Kramer vs. Kramer*. Could she get people to side with a fanatic nun? "Men have *always* rejected Isabella, right through its history," she said during rehearsals, with anticipatory relish. From his retirement in Connecticut, her father dug up all the reading material he could find on the play. "He's really quite a scholar," Meryl would brag.

A plum role for Meryl Streep was one reason Papp had booked *Measure for Measure*, but the timeliness of the plot was likely another.

Shakespeare's Vienna is rife with corruption and perversity and grit, and the New Yorkers who had lived through the city's near bankruptcy could relate. Meanwhile, the whole country had gotten a lesson in official pardons, like the one Isabella seeks for Claudio. Two years earlier, President Gerald Ford had pardoned Richard Nixon for his Watergate crimes and now was paying a heavy toll in his electoral run against Jimmy Carter. Everywhere you turned, someone in the halls of power was making a shady backroom deal, or a city was crumbling under the weight of its own filth.

The director, John Pasquin, envisioned a Vienna that would reflect New York back to New Yorkers. Santo Loquasto's set looked like a subway station, or like the men's room right outside the theater: all sickly white tiles, practically reeking of urine, against a skyline of painted demons. While Angelo and his officials sneered from a raised walkway, the bawds and whores of Vienna rose up from a trapdoor, as if ascending from the underworld. It was Park Avenue society meeting the drifters of Times Square, the bifurcated city Papp had tried to unite in his theaters.

Meryl read the long and churning play over and over again. Cloaked in a white habit, she had only her face and her voice to work with. And in the park, exposed to the elements, her meticulous characterization could get easily thrown off course. One night, during the climax of her big soliloquy—"I'll tell him yet of Angelo's request, / And fit his mind to death, for his soul's rest"—what sounded like a Concorde blasted overhead, and she had to scream "his soul's rest." "It's ludicrous," she said soon after, "but it costs me my heart's blood, because I carefully put together a person and a motive, and then something comes along that's not even in the book, and ruins it."

But something else was happening to Meryl Streep, something she had even less control over than jumbo jets roaring over Manhattan. In her scenes with the forty-one-year-old actor playing Angelo, it was there for everyone to see: the push and pull of wills, the saint and the sinner locked in a battle of sex and death. It gave off heat. She stared into her leading man's coal-like eyes, his sallow face betraying a whimpering sadness. He gave her fire, she answered with icicles:

ANGELO

Plainly conceive, I love you.

ISABELLA

My brother did love Juliet,
And you tell me that he shall die for't.

ANGELO

He shall not, Isabel, if you give me love.

Meryl's understudy, Judith Light, would watch the Isabella and Angelo scenes every night, memorizing the contours of Meryl's performance in case she ever had to go on. (She didn't.) "It was their dynamic that carried the production along, and watching the two of them develop something together was incredibly electric," Light recalled. "You could see that something was developing, and that she was allowing herself to also be lifted by him."

Michael Feingold, Meryl's old friend from Yale, saw it, too. "The physical attraction between them was very real," he said. "And the idea of starting an Isabella-Angelo relationship with that present, not only in the actors' lines but in their lives . . . It puts an extra charge on everything, and she had that even inside the nun's habit."

Even the *Times* critic Mel Gussow picked up on it: "Miss Streep," he wrote, "who has frequently been cast as sturdier, more mature women, does not play Isabella for sweetness and innocence. There is a knowingness behind her apparent naïveté. We sense the sexual give-and-take between her and Angelo, and she also makes us aware of the character's awakening feelings of self-importance and power."

If he only knew the half of it.

When *Measure for Measure* is about a nun putting her principles over her brother's life, it's a problem play. But this *Measure for Measure* was about a man and a woman battling their unquenched sexuality, making pronouncements and questioning them at the same time, their ideals betrayed by their irrepressible desire. It is Isabella's purity that lights Angelo aflame, as the whores of Vienna could not. The two actors were nearly as preposterous a couple as their characters: the ice princess and the oddball. And yet everyone, onstage and off, seemed to feel their spark.

On opening night, Meryl and her Angelo slipped away from the cast party. They wound up at the Empire Diner in Chelsea, a greasy spoon tricked out in Art Deco silver and black, with a miniature Empire State Building on its roof. They ate and talked, and by the time she got home it was five in the morning. She couldn't sleep.

She woke up the next morning to let a reporter up to her apartment. As they talked over orange juice and croissants, her eyes were bloodshot, her face devoid of makeup. Even as she fielded questions about her extraordinary first year out of drama school, her mind kept returning to John Cazale. There was something about this guy. Something.

She heard herself say, "I've been shot through with luck since I came to the city . . ."

Fredo

❧

TIME MOVED DIFFERENTLY for John Cazale. Everything went slower. He wasn't dim, not by a long shot. But he was meticulous, sometimes maddeningly so. Even simple tasks could take hours. All of his friends knew about the slowness. It would drive them crazy.

His friend Marvin Starkman: "We had a house up in the country, and John would come up quite a bit. If his car was ahead of mine and we got to a tollbooth, he'd pull up and he'd look to see if the guy had a name or a number listed outside. He'd look at the guy, make sure he knew who he was talking to, take out a quarter or whatever it was: 'Here you go.' I mean, you would die in the car behind him."

Robyn Goodman, who was married to his friend Walter McGinn: "We got a color television. It was a brand-new thing, and we were all excited. Walter called John and said, 'Come up and help me, we're going to put it together.' And John said, 'Well, let's get the color all right.' That was around ten o'clock at night. I went to sleep about midnight, and they were still working. I think they were up most of the night tuning that thing."

The playwright Israel Horovitz: "We had to give him a key to the theater, because he was so slow taking off his makeup. We'd go to the restaurant around Astor Place, and he was supposed to meet us. We

135

were all going to eat, and we'd be finished before he got there. He was just the slowest person I knew."

His friend Al Pacino: "You eat a meal with him, I mean, you'd be done—washed, finished, and in bed—before he got halfway through his meal. Then the cigar would come out. He'd light it, look at it, taste it. Then *finally* smoke it."

John moved like he had all the time in the world.

He was like that with characters, too. Directors called him "Twenty Questions," because he wouldn't stop interrogating them in rehearsal. Before he could do anything, he had to know everything. He would try one thing a million different ways—there were so many possibilities. Marvin Starkman used to kid him: "Jesus, I bet your foreplay takes five hours."

He looked like no one else in the movies: spindly frame, honking nose, forehead as high as a boulder, bisected by a throbbing vein. When John set his sunken eyes on something, he could look as wounded and desperate as a dying dog.

"He was like from another planet," Robyn Goodman said. "He had such depth and truthfulness. There wasn't a false bone in his body, as a person or as an actor. And he experienced the world in a profound way."

John was slow because everything fascinated him. He loved his Datsun. He loved *The Bicycle Thief.* He loved Cuban cigars, which he smoked like crazy. "With John, he had a childlike curiosity and it wasn't put on," Starkman said. "If you didn't know him, you'd say, 'What's this bullshit?' It was no bullshit."

One time, he and Walter McGinn (John called him Speedy) found a parking meter lying on the sidewalk. They decided to bring it back to John's place and take it apart so they could see how it worked. Somebody must have reported them, because the police showed up and arrested him. He spent the night in jail.

"God, what was that like?" Starkman asked when he got out.

"Well, I made some friends there," John said. "And I found out how to get two lights off one match."

His characters shared his childlike innocence, but there was always melancholy pulsing underneath. "There was an undercurrent of sadness about him," his brother, Stephen, said. "I don't know how you'd explain it." He and Walter would talk for hours about acting, as Robyn Goodman watched. "They both had a very profound understanding that at the center of every character was a kind of pain," she recalled. "You could see that there was a little bit of damage in both of them that they were turning into art."

It was pain that defined his most vivid character, Fredo Corleone, in *The Godfather* and *The Godfather: Part II*. It's there when he's drunkenly hitting on his brother's girlfriend, Kay, at their sister's wedding. It's there when he's in his mustard-yellow suit and aviator sunglasses, playing big shot with girls and booze in Las Vegas. And it's there in the boathouse in Tahoe, when it all comes roaring to the surface.

MICHAEL

I've always taken care of you, Fredo.

FREDO

Taken care of me? You're my kid brother and you take care of *me*? Did you ever think about that? Did you ever *once* think about that? Send Fredo off to do this, send Fredo off to do that. Let Fredo take care of some Mickey Mouse nightclub somewhere. Send Fredo to pick somebody up at the airport. I'm your older brother, Mike, and I was stepped over!

Most actors would kill to play Sonny or Michael Corleone, the macho brothers who run the family racket. What young man doesn't want to play brave or cocky or strong? But John was like the B-side of American masculinity. Without flinching or showboating, he could play weakness, cowardice, shame, or fear. John could make the runt of the litter the best part in the film—that is, if you were paying attention. Most people walked out of his movies talking about Al Pacino or Robert De Niro or Gene Hackman, the guys who played the troubled heroes. But if you cared to notice him, John Cazale could break your heart.

IT STARTED WITH MUSIC. As children, John and his little brother idolized Toscanini. They spent hours listening to the wind-up Victrola: Bach's Second and Third Brandenburg Concertos, Debussy's Nocturnes, Wagner's overtures to *Meistersinger* and *Parsifal*. They wore out their albums of Haydn's Symphony No. 99—until Stephen, who was two years younger, sat on the fourth movement and broke it. "He was mad as hell," Stephen said. "He used to slug me a lot. My arms would be black and blue sometimes from his slugs."

They inherited the music bug from their Aunt Kitty, who took them to concerts and museums in New York City. She got it from their grandmother, Nonna, who sang snatches of Italian opera around the house. In her youth, Nonna had worked in a textile factory producing jute, and she proudly re-created the arm motions she had repeated at the loom. Her grandsons imitated the gesture behind her back and snickered.

Despite starring in the defining film saga of Italian-American immigration, John showed little interest in his heritage. Stephen would later unravel the family history, a real-life version of *The Godfather: Part II*, minus the mob. Their grandfather, Giovanni Casale, was born in Genoa and sailed to New York City on September 27, 1868—sixteen years old, dirt poor, and largely illiterate. Sixteen years later, for reasons lost to history, he signed his naturalization papers "Giovanni Cazale," with a "z"—the name that his children and grandchildren would bear. By then, he was working as a fruit vendor and an itinerant knife sharpener. With his wife, Annie, he moved to Revere, a seaside city near Boston, and he and two partners opened its first hotel. As Revere became a bustling resort, Giovanni bought up more property. Like Vito Corleone, he had built a new life in a new land, running his own business. Only this one didn't involve dumping bodies in the river.

Giovanni and Annie had a daughter, Catherine, whom John and Stephen knew as Aunt Kitty. Another daughter, Elvira, died young. Then there were the twins, John and Charles, born premature. Annie covered them with olive oil and warmed them in the oven; they survived. The brothers both became coal salesmen, and they loved betting on horses at the Suffolk Downs racetrack. John, the elder twin, married an Irish Catholic girl, and they had three children. Born in 1935, John Cazale was their middle child, a shy kid who worshiped the Red Sox and Ted Williams.

When John was five and Stephen was three, the family moved to Winchester. Their parents sent them to separate boarding schools: John to Buxton, in Williamstown, Massachusetts, and Stephen to Woodstock Country School, in Vermont. John was quiet and withdrawn, and no one could foresee his announcement that he had joined the school's drama club. "I was as surprised as anyone else when he realized he wanted to go into the theater," Stephen said. "It was the most unlikely thing for him to do."

As a teenager, John worked as a messenger for Standard Oil. One of his fellow messengers was Al Pacino, five years his junior. John went on to study drama at Boston University, where he met Marvin Starkman and Walter McGinn. They all revered their acting teacher, Peter Kass, who pushed his students to mine their own darkness, not to shy away from pain but to locate it in a character. (It was the same lesson Meryl resisted her first year at Yale.) John stayed in Boston and acted at the Charles Playhouse, part-timing as a cabdriver. Again, the slowness. "He didn't leave people off in the middle of the street," Starkman said. "He came right to the curb. He would open the door for people, he would come out. He was the perfect guy to be a cabdriver."

He moved to New York and found a walkup apartment in the West Sixties. "His housekeeping was abominable," Stephen recalled. The brothers spoke in nonsense Latin, and a pigpen was a "porcus pennus."

When John first showed Stephen his apartment, he proclaimed, "Welcome to the Porcus Hilton." Part of the mess was from his makeshift darkroom; he made money shooting sculptures for gallery brochures and headshots for actor friends. Photography suited his compulsive nature: he would painstakingly adjust the lighting on the sculptures, making sure they looked fully three-dimensional instead of flat. Some of the photos were just for him: landscapes in the Berkshires, or studies of Aunt Kitty at her piano.

Acting jobs were sparse. Starkman, who was producing commercials, tried to get him work, but the answer was always some version of "too ethnic." The best he could do was a TV spot for New York Telephone, in which John played an Indian chief. So he and Marvin made their own movies. In 1962, they shot an antic short film called *The American Way*, in which John plays an anarchist who can't manage to blow anything up. There were already glimmers of his contradictory screen presence: comedic but sorrowful, dangerous but feckless. Offscreen, the danger was absent, but his innocence was so genuine it could get him out of a jam. One Sunday morning, he was headed over to Starkman's place to start the day's shoot, carrying a fake TNT box under his arm. A policeman stopped him and said, "Hey, come here. Where are you going?"

John looked at him blankly and replied, "I'm going to Marvin's house."

"Oh, okay," the cop said, and sent him on his way.

His breakthrough came in the form of two plays by Israel Horovitz. While Horovitz was in drama school in England, he saw some hooligans harassing an Indian student in a turban. The incident inspired *The Indian Wants the Bronx*, which he staged back in New York. As the main hooligan, he cast Al Pacino, an unknown actor he had seen in a play in somebody's living room. As his victim—now Gupta, a frightened father lost in New York, trying to reach his son on a pay phone—he cast an Indian actor. But the man didn't have much acting experience and would inexplicably raise his hand whenever he had a line. "It became a play about this guy's hand," Horovitz recalled.

Pacino, who was intensely Method-oriented, couldn't focus. They had to replace the Indian, and Israel already knew John Cazale, having grown up in a neighboring town. Gupta's dialogue was all in Hindi, and John and Israel wrestled with whether an Italian actor should play the role. In the end, John agreed. The play was going up in Provincetown, and when Pacino got to the house on Cape Cod where everyone was staying, his costar poked his head out of the bedroom. Pacino recognized the face from years earlier, when he was working for Standard Oil.

"You again," Pacino said. "I know you."

The play moved to New York, to the Astor Place Theatre, in January, 1968. It won instant acclaim, typifying the raw, live-wire, from-the-streets aggression that was electrifying the downtown theater scene. Horovitz, Pacino, and Cazale all won Obie Awards. That summer, they brought the play to the Spoleto Festival in Italy. Between shows, John would gather the company in the main piazza and lead them in six-part harmony. They didn't know Italian, so they'd sing the words off the tourist maps: "Piazza del Duomo! Spoleto! Spoleto!"

It was another Horovitz play that gave John the boost he was so anxious for. *Line* was the kind of late-sixties minimalist experiment that was upending received notions of what constituted a play. There was no set, and barely a plot. All you needed was five actors to stand in a line, four men and one woman. What they're waiting for is never explained. Over the course of the play, they fight, fornicate, and fool each other into losing their place in line: a Hobbesian state of nature for cultured New Yorkers, who never see a line without wondering if they should be on it.

John played Dolan, a self-described "Mr. Nice Guy" who nonetheless almost chokes another character to death. At one point, Dolan describes his "Under*dog* philosophy," which could double as John's approach to acting, or at least his effect:

"Everybody wants to be first, right? . . . Now you can be obvious about it. Just jump in like the kid and yell and brag about being first. Or about deserving to be first. What I mean is you got to stand back a little . . . The easiest way to kick a dog in the balls is to be underneath him. Let him walk on top of you for a while. Take good aim. And . . ."

Line opened at the East Village theater La MaMa in the fall of 1967. Four years later, it was revived at the Theater de Lys, on Christopher Street, starring Cazale and Richard Dreyfuss, in his Off Broadway debut. One night, Dreyfuss invited Francis Ford Coppola and his casting director, Fred Roos, who were in preparation for *The Godfather*. When they saw Cazale onstage, Roos said instantly, "That's Fredo."

"THE SECOND SON, Frederico, called Fred or Fredo, was a child every Italian prayed to the saints for," Mario Puzo wrote in his novel *The Godfather*. "Dutiful, loyal, always at the service of his father, living with his parents at age thirty. He was short and burly, not handsome but with the same Cupid head of the family, the curly helmet of hair over the round face and sensual bow-shaped lips."

John Cazale wasn't short or burly, and he certainly didn't have a curly helmet of hair. But to Coppola and Roos, he had the look of someone who had always been passed over. Coppola, who had accomplished siblings (the author August Coppola and the actress Talia Shire, who played Connie Corleone), had a soft spot for Fredo. "In an Italian family, or at least in my family, there are always those brothers who are considered, you know, not as talented as the others," the director said. "They are made fun of. Maybe I was in that category some of the time, I don't know. I certainly had uncles that were put down. I think Italians that come from that little-town mentality are very hard on their own and very cruel unto those who don't quite cut the mustard at the same level that the star brothers or the star uncles do."

John was reunited with Al Pacino, as Michael Corleone. But the real thrill was acting alongside Marlon Brando, as his father, Vito. Brando was the undisputed giant of American film acting, and the younger actors—Pacino, Cazale, James Caan, Robert Duvall—revered him just as the Corleone brothers do their capo father. "Brando was our hero," Marvin Starkman said. "We would go to see *On the Waterfront, Streetcar*, all those early films, like you were going to a master class. We worshiped him. John gets to work with Brando, and it just lit him."

It came time to film the scene when Vito is shot in the street outside the fruit market, while Fredo fumbles with his gun as the would-be assassins get away. With the Godfather bleeding in the gutter, Fredo leans over him in hysterics, having failed his father in the worst way. Coppola filmed Brando playing near-dead on the curb, then turned the camera around for John's reaction shot. "Brando thought enough of John to get back and lie down in the gutter, so that John could work off him," Starkman said. "It was, like, the highest compliment."

The Godfather was released in March, 1972, while Meryl Streep was still performing in ski lodges in Vermont. It was nominated for eleven Academy Awards, and won Best Picture and Best Actor, for Marlon Brando, who sent the Native-American activist Sacheen Littlefeather to decline the prize. Al Pacino, James Caan, and Robert Duvall crowded the Best Supporting Actor category. John wasn't nominated.

Buoyed by the success of *The Godfather*, Coppola shot a drama about surveillance called *The Conversation*, starring Gene Hackman as "the best bugger on the West Coast." John played his assistant, Stan, an inquisitive technician in headphones and thick glasses. Once again, John tapped into the character's weaknesses—his immaturity, his nosiness—and infused them with childlike sweetness. The movie was nominated for three Oscars, including Best Picture. John wasn't nominated.

In *The Godfather: Part II*, Coppola brought Fredo's self-loathing to a crescendo. In his plaid suit and pencil mustache, Fredo was gregarious and impotent, unable to control even his drunken wife on the dance floor. After Fredo colludes on a failed attempt against his brother's life, guilt and fear devour him. In John's most iconic film moment, Michael clutches Fredo on the cheeks and tells him: "I know it was you, Fredo. You broke my heart. You broke my heart."

Fredo's betrayal of Michael, and Michael's decision to murder him, are at the heart of the film, giving John more to do onscreen than he'd ever had. *The Godfather: Part II* was nominated for eleven Academy Awards, including Best Picture, which it won. Al Pacino was nominated for Best Actor. Robert De Niro, Michael V. Gazzo, and Lee Strasberg competed for Best Supporting Actor, which De Niro won. John wasn't nominated.

Despite his Fredo-like knack for being passed over, John's gift grew more complex with each film, his capacity for exposing a character's psychic wounds more heartrending. At the same time, his appearance became increasingly sickly, his vitality receding along with his hairline. One summer, he was at Starkman's house in the Catskills when he took ill at the county fair. "We gotta get back to the city," he pleaded. Marvin and his wife drove him back, every bump and bang bringing John fresh agony.

They rushed to Roosevelt Hospital, where John was diagnosed with chronic pancreatitis. When Marvin came back to visit him, he was hooked up to tubes and could barely talk. Against the wall was a glass jar filling up with watery green bile from his stomach. "It was just awful," Starkman recalled. "I left there feeling, What can we do for this guy?" The doctors told John to quit drinking immediately, or else the alcohol would eat up his pancreas.

Somehow, his pallor only added to his singular onscreen presence. "There is a kind of moral decay in Fredo that's entirely borne out by the fact that, from the first picture to the second, Cazale has become more ghost-like," the critic David Thomson has observed. "He's thinner, his eyes are more exaggerated, his forehead is sticking out further."

By then, the filmmaking boom of the late sixties and seventies had opened the door for actors who were eccentric, ethnic, or just plain odd. Warren Beatty and Robert Redford aside, leading men were now olive-skinned like Al Pacino, or nebbishy like Dustin Hoffman, or black like Sidney Poitier, or devil-eyed like Jack Nicholson. Movie stars looked less and less like matinee idols and more and more like the people you might see on the street. Even Robert De Niro, the new standard-bearer of big-screen virility, was Italian. John's ashen face and off-kilter energy, which had once precluded him from TV commercials, were now his currency.

Not that he didn't possess a strange kind of sex appeal. John exemplified the French notion of *jolie laide*, or "ugly-beautiful." It was a concept that Hollywood was just beginning to grasp (at least when it came to men). As Horovitz liked to say, he looked like St. Francis of Assisi, but he never seemed to lack for beautiful dates, among them the actresses Verna Bloom and Ann Wedgeworth, his costar in *Line*. None of his friends knew how he did it. "He always had girlfriends," Starkman said. "He had some of the most beautiful girlfriends to be found, and eventually many of them broke up [with him] because of his slow snail pace about things."

As his career took off, he began dating a redheaded actress from Texas named Patricia. Patricia was a chilly beauty who hadn't had her big break. Some of John's friends detected an opportunistic streak, but he was smitten. Perhaps at her urging, he left his cluttered Upper West Side apartment, which had scared away previous girlfriends, and put down a chunk of his *Godfather* money on a loft downtown on Franklin Street. It was in a former storage building, with a fire escape, an elevator, and a diamond-plate loading platform facing the street. The traditionally industrial neighborhood was just on the cusp of transformation, as artists and experimental theater troupes took over buildings formerly owned by ship chandlers. New Yorkers would soon know it as Tribeca. For now, it was No Man's Land.

When John first saw the place, stacked floor to ceiling with tomato cans, he couldn't believe it. *Those floors must be strong*, he thought.

"You know what a No. 10 can is?" he told Marvin. "You've seen those big tomato cans? I mean a real can, about this big—they're heavy!"

Once the cans were gone, it was all bare brick and open space. John brought in wood planks and hammers. He and Patricia would be pioneers, building a nest in a stockroom.

But it didn't last. Patricia took off for California, leaving John with the apartment to himself.

Meanwhile, Pacino had signed on to Sidney Lumet's new film, *Dog Day Afternoon*. It was based on a real incident, in which a hapless criminal had held up a Brooklyn bank to pay for his lover's sex-change surgery. As the guy and his sidekick try to keep the hostages in line, cops and gawkers swarm outside, a kind of perverse street theater. Pacino begged Lumet to see John for the part of Sal, the sidekick, even though he looked nothing like the real guy. Reluctantly, Lumet agreed. John read about two sentences before the director said, "It's yours."

John's appearance as Sal was his most bizarre yet. With his oily hair now starting halfway up his cranium and slinking down to his shoulders, he looked like a beatnik vulture. Wielding his machine gun, he seemed, unlike Pacino's Sonny, like someone who might actually resort to using it. And yet his performance was still shot through with sorrow, as if even Sal, the bank-robbing thug, was once a neglected little boy.

Pacino marveled at how John would amp himself up, ad-libbing wildly until the cameras started rolling. At one point, they were shooting a scene in which the two crooks plan their escape. Everything's going to hell fast: the hostages need to pee, the cops are outside, and the whole operation has become a three-ring circus. Sonny tells Sal that if they ever get out of this mess, they'll have to leave town. Is there any special country he'd like to flee to?

Sal thinks for a moment and answers, "Wyoming."

On set, Lumet had to choke back his laughter, or else he'd ruin the take. Same with Pacino. In the script, John didn't have a line there. Naturally, "Wyoming" made the final cut.

Dog Day Afternoon was nominated for six Academy Awards, including Best Picture, and won for its screenplay. Al Pacino was nominated for Best Actor, and Chris Sarandon, as Sonny's lover, was nominated for Best Supporting Actor. John wasn't nominated.

As they shot *Dog Day Afternoon*, Pacino was acting in a workshop of a play, Brecht's *The Resistible Rise of Alberto Ui*. He gathered a cast together, including John, and found a place to rehearse: Joseph Papp's Public Theater. Papp had met Pacino in 1968, when he fired him from a play for mumbling. Now, he was happy to underwrite the actor's passion project, paying the cast of thirty to rehearse for weeks on end, with no guarantee of a final production. Papp didn't mind; it was enough to give Pacino a testing ground.

But he did notice John Cazale, who might have just the right menace for *Measure for Measure*, which he was casting for Shakespeare in the Park that summer. Papp had given Sam Waterston the choice to play Angelo or the Duke, and Waterston chose the Duke. So the producer invited John to audition for Angelo.

The night before the audition, John went to Walter McGinn and Robyn Goodman's place, at Eighty-sixth and Riverside. He was nervous; he hadn't done much Shakespeare. To make matters worse, he would be auditioning opposite the leading lady, a young drama school graduate who came with the project—Papp adored her. If he wanted the part, he'd have to impress Meryl Streep.

Walter, who was in *Henry V,* knew her a bit. John peppered him with questions—about the play, about the role, and, most of all, about the actress playing Isabella. "Walter assured him that Meryl would react well to a real actor's actor," Goodman said. "That's what John was."

The next day, John went in and read his scene from *Measure for Measure*. "I remember how intense John was," Goodman said, "and how scared he was, and how he called right after to say that he thought it went okay. You know, it could have gone better . . . He was never satisfied with his work."

But he had satisfied Joe Papp, and, just as important, Meryl Streep. He got the part.

In the rehearsal room, John kept mostly to himself, puffing on cigars by the window during breaks. "These are Cubans that I have brought in," he'd tell his castmates. "Do you smoke?"

Shakespeare's Angelo was a prudish, domineering creep—nothing like the weaklings John had played—Fredo, or Stan, or even gun-toting Sal. Or was he? Once again, John looked for the pain, and found it.

"He brought menacing. He brought the pain," Rosemarie Tichler said. "But the pain, instead of being weakness, was anger. There was anger under it. If you poked at it, he wouldn't fall apart. He would become dangerous."

As a casting director, she knew that the right mix of actors could give a play a startling new subtext. In the clash of wills that was *Measure for Measure*, John brought something that wasn't quite on the page. His Angelo was the guy who never got the girl, the loser who sat in the corner while everyone else partied on the dance floor. That's why he was clamping down on the brothels of Vienna. That's why he condemned Claudio to death for fornication. That's why he lusted so feverishly for pure-as-snow Isabella. She was every beautiful woman who never gave him the time of day.

> ... Never could the strumpet
> With all her double vigor, art and nature,
> Once stir my temper, but this virtuous maid
> Subdues me quite. Ever till now,
> When men were fond, I smiled and wondered how.

And so, on opening night, John Cazale and Meryl Streep sat at the Empire Diner, having ditched their own cast party, talking and laughing until five in the morning, the rising sun just beginning to glint on the mirrored walls and coffee cups and bar stools and her lemon hair. John had discovered something absolutely extraordinary. She was better than a Datsun. She was better than a Cuban cigar. She was better than getting two lights off of one match. She was someone worth staying up all night for, like a color TV—only better, because her colors were so infinite you couldn't possibly tune them all.

He told his friend Al Pacino, "Oh, man, I have met the greatest actress in the history of the world."

He's just in love, Pacino thought. *How good can she be?*

ALL THAT AUGUST, the subways in New York City were plastered with illustrated posters of John Cazale and Meryl Streep: Meryl in her white nun's habit, lips parted and eyes cast down, as if in mid-thought; John gazing at her from behind, with a yearning look and a cocked eyebrow. The thought bubbles coming out of their heads converge into a single cloud, bearing the words "Measure for Measure."

John was besotted. "Once he was in that play, the only thing he talked about was her," Marvin Starkman said.

"Walter said to me, 'I think he's falling in love with Meryl,'" Robyn Goodman recalled. "And I said, 'I hope she's falling in love with him.' By the time the show opened they were madly in love." Watching them, Robyn wondered if she was making out with her own husband enough—that's how explosive John and Meryl were. Arriving at the theater, Goodman said, "Her whole mouth was chapped from kissing."

Meryl was transfixed by this odd, tender, hawklike creature, whose hold over her was something she couldn't quite explain. "He wasn't like anybody I'd ever met," she said later. "It was the specificity of him, and his sort of humanity and his curiosity about people, his compassion."

Acting was their lingua franca. "We would talk about the process endlessly, and he was monomaniacal about the work," Meryl recalled. John would think and rethink his characters, opening them up and studying them like a parking meter, never content with the obvious or easy choice. "I think probably I was more glib and ready to pick the first idea that came to me," she said. "And he would say, 'There's a lot of other possibilities.'"

One night after the show, John introduced Meryl to his brother, Stephen, who had become a musicologist. For reasons neither brother could remember, they had always called each other by nicknames: Stephen was Jake, John was Bobo.

"Meryl," John said proudly, "talk to Jake! He knows Italian."

Stephen and Meryl stumbled through some conversation in Italian, until she broke down and laughed, "I can't! I can't!" Stephen was charmed.

Onstage at the Delacorte night after night, they enacted a forbidden attraction by moonlight. Offstage, their attraction wasn't forbidden, but it was certainly offbeat. Never had Meryl fallen for someone so peculiar. Side by side, they somehow accentuated each other's imperfections: her forked nose, his bulbous forehead. His pale skin, her close-set eyes. They looked like two exotic birds, or like Piero della Francesca's portraits of the Duke and Duchess of Urbino.

"They were great to look at, because they were kind of funny-looking, both of them," Israel Horovitz said. "They were lovely in their way, but it was a really quirky couple. They were head-turners, but not because 'Wow, is she a beauty!'" He was nothing like her previous boyfriends: hunky Bruce or strapping Bob or pretty Phil or even brooding Mike Booth. Perhaps she no longer needed a Prince Charming to reassure her of her beauty. She and John didn't "look good" together, but you couldn't take your eyes off them.

Everywhere they went, people would roll down their windows and scream, "Hey, Fredo!" "He was absolutely conflicted about the whole idea of fame," his brother said. "I don't think he really knew how to deal with it or wanted to." The *Godfather* films had made him recognizable, but they hadn't made him rich. When he and Meryl went to Little Italy, the restaurant owners would refuse to let them pay. So they went to Little Italy all the time, dining out on free pasta and caprese, their nights and bellies filled with "Hey, Fredo"s.

"The jerk made everything mean something," she said later. "Such good judgment, such uncluttered thought. For me particularly, who is moored to all sorts of human weaknesses. 'You don't need this,' he'd say, 'you don't need that.'" And yet John was Meryl's gateway to the elite of the acting world; in November, she accompanied him to the legendary acting teacher Lee Strasberg's seventy-fifth birthday bash at the Pierre, where the guest list included Al Pacino, Celeste Holm, and Ellen Burstyn.

The romance moved as fast as John moved slow, and before long Meryl moved into the loft on Franklin Street. Now they would be pioneers together, discovering a downtown that had barely discovered itself. She soon learned what John's past girlfriends had learned before her. "He took his time with stuff," she recalled. "It took him a really long time to leave the house, to lock the car." One time John decided to wallpaper a room. It took him three weeks.

But she didn't mind. Let time move as slow as molasses. They were happy.

A FEW WEEKS after Meryl's audition for *Julia*, Fred Zinnemann gave the title role to Vanessa Redgrave—hardly an unknown. He offered Meryl a small part as Lillian Hellman's gossipy friend Anne Marie. But he had too many blondes in the movie already: Would she consider wearing a wig? Of course, Meryl told him. She'd do anything.

In the fall, she flew to London to film her scenes. It was her first time acting in a movie—in the company of Jane Fonda and Vanessa Redgrave, no less. As on that first plane ride out of Bernardsville, her world was getting bigger.

Her first day on the set, she broke out in hives. For one thing, she looked awful: the curly black wig she'd been given made her look harsh, and her costumes were all absurd hats and furs and red period dresses. The scene was a party for Lillian Hellman thrown at Sardi's, the theater-district restaurant that had been replicated in London. Meryl prepared dutifully, as she would for Shakespeare, but when she showed up she was handed a rewrite. Her panic was evident in the red splotches below her neck, which the makeup people frantically pancaked over.

Most intimidating: her scenes were all with Jane Fonda. At thirty-eight, no film actress was more prominent or more controversial. Her sex-kitten *Barbarella* days were behind her. So was "Hanoi Jane." With *Fun with Dick and Jane*, she had reclaimed her stature as a mainstream star, and now used her clout to foster socially conscious projects like *Julia*, which featured her bravely outwitting Nazis.

Meryl was brought over to meet Fonda. "She had an almost feral alertness," Meryl recalled, "like this bright blue attentiveness to everything around her that was completely intimidating, and made me feel like I was lumpy and from New Jersey, which I am."

They rehearsed once through, and Fonda encouraged her to improvise. On the first take, Meryl embellished a bit. It seemed to work well. On the second take, feeling bold, she thought: *I'll try something else!*

Fonda leaned in and told her, "Look down."

"What?"

"Over there." Fonda pointed down. "That green tape on the floor. That's you. That's your mark. And if you land on it, you will be in the light, and you will be in the movie."

She was grateful for the help—she needed it—but she also observed the way Fonda carried her stardom. It seemed as if half of what Jane Fonda did was maintain the machinery of being Jane Fonda, as opposed to acting. "I admire Jane Fonda," Meryl said not long after. "But I also don't want to spend all my time immersing myself . . . in the business of myself . . ."

She was similarly awed by Vanessa Redgrave. They didn't share any scenes, but they shared a car ride. Meryl worried about being tongue-tied, but luckily Redgrave talked the whole time about politics and Leon Trotsky. Meryl didn't know much about Trotsky, but she knew something about Redgrave: this was the kind of screen actress worth revering, someone who led with her convictions and never cowed to expectations.

On days off, she would hang out with John Glover, who played her brother. Neither of them had much to do, so they'd kill time in the bar below her hotel, in South Kensington. (Meryl kept her per-diem money in a suitcase in her room, until one day she returned to find it had all been stolen.) Or they'd go to Harrods, where Meryl would study the shopgirls' accents. She was determined to nail the English pronunciation of "actually."

Other days, she would visit Glover at the house where he was staying. Over lavish homemade dinners, the actors and their hosts would play a game called Adverbs: whoever was up had to act in the manner of a word, and the other players would guess what it was. When it was Meryl's turn, she pretended to wake up in the morning and look out the window.

Everyone yelled out the word at once: "Beautifully!"

Midway through, Cazale flew over to visit. Her socializing with the other actors abruptly ended: she and John were back in their own all-consuming universe. When they returned to New York, John found out his agent had been trying to reach him. There was an offer to do a TV movie about the blacklist. No one could find him, and the part had slipped away. "What do you mean, you couldn't find me?" John said, uncharacteristically furious. They knew he was going to England, and he and Meryl needed the money.

When *Julia* came out the following fall, Meryl was equally vexed. Not only did she look ghastly in her marcelled black wig; half of her part had been cut, and the lines from one vanished scene had been transported to her mouth in another. Fred Zinnemann sent her a note of apology.

I've made a terrible mistake, Meryl thought. *No more movies.*

JOE PAPP WAS flailing at Lincoln Center. Like a losing baseball coach, he kept changing his strategy, but nothing stuck: challenging new plays, well-mannered chestnuts. Finally, he hit on a hybrid idea: matching classic plays with experimental directors, who could radically rethink them on a grand scale. "You can't do the classics conventionally anymore," he said. "They lay on you like bagels."

He hired Richard Foreman, the outré founder of the Ontological-

Hysteric Theater, to direct *Threepenny Opera*. The production, which opened in the spring of 1976, was a controversial success. As *Measure for Measure* ran at the Delacorte, Papp was juggling a trio of hits: *Threepenny* at the Vivian Beaumont, the Broadway-bound *for colored girls*, and *A Chorus Line*, which was grossing more than $140,000 a week at the Shubert. But somehow it wasn't enough. Despite playing to capacity, Lincoln Center was running a $1.2 million deficit.

Amid the turmoil, there were at least two people Papp wanted to keep busy: John Cazale and Meryl Streep. John and Al Pacino were anxious to work together again, and they talked about doing a double bill of Strindberg's *Creditors* and Heathcote Williams's *The Local Stigmatic* down at the Public. Meryl, meanwhile, would help ring in 1977 at the Beaumont, in a new production of Chekhov's *The Cherry Orchard* directed by Andrei Serban.

The Romanian-born, thirty-three-year-old Serban had been working at La MaMa when Papp discovered him. Serban found the Off Off Broadway world amateurish, preferring the discipline of the Eastern European avant-garde. Meryl saw his rigidity as an incentive. "That's when you can really work," she said before rehearsals began, "when a director knows exactly the construct he wants. I hate 'laid back' directors. I'd probably fare very badly in California."

Serban's *Cherry Orchard* would do away with the solemn psychological realism of most Chekhov productions and look for, in his words, "something much lighter and closer to the fluidity of real life." Chekhov had, tantalizingly, called *The Cherry Orchard* a comedy, a description that Stanislavsky had ignored when he directed the 1904 premiere, enraging the playwright. Serban wanted to defy Stanislavsky and restore *The Cherry Orchard* as a rip-roaring farce.

He would be aided by Elizabeth Swados, a moody twenty-six-year-old composer and Serban's frequent collaborator at La MaMa. Serban, Swados, and Foreman were key to Papp's last-ditch plan to solve the riddle of the Vivian Beaumont. For the role of Madame Ranevskaya, Papp secured the sixty-year-old stage star Irene Worth. Meryl had seen her the previous season, in a Broadway revival of Tennessee Williams's *Sweet Bird of Youth*, and gushed soon after that "you could have taken away all the other characters in the play, the sets, everything, and still have understood every theme in the play."

In the lead-up to the Tony Awards, Meryl and Mary Beth Hurt had attended an awards breakfast at the Regency Hotel. When the young actresses arrived, Arvin Brown offered to introduce Meryl to Miss Worth, who was nominated for Best Actress in a Play. Starstruck, she and Mary Beth decamped to the ladies' room to smoke cigarettes, until Arvin knocked on the door: "Come out of there—I've got Irene."

Meryl slinked back out and was delivered to Miss Worth.

The great actress looked Meryl up and down and asked her, "What do you plan to do in December?"

"Unemployment, I guess," she stammered.

"Fine," Worth said. "Think about *The Cherry Orchard*."

She did. Her regard for Worth—or, more to the point, Papp—was enough that she took the role of Dunyasha, the chambermaid. It was a small part, one that she might have otherwise turned down. "Everybody was talking about this fantastic young actress, and many were surprised she accepted to play such a small part in *The Cherry Orchard*, when she could have already been offered a Broadway lead," Serban recalled. "But she decided she still wanted to learn from watching the elders, in this case from the great Irene Worth playing Ranevskaya. I remember Meryl coming to rehearsals even when she was not called, quietly sitting and knitting on the side, watching every detail of Irene's unique technique and being fascinated."

Papp had assembled a powerhouse cast, including Mary Beth Hurt as Anya and the high-spirited Puerto Rican actor Raúl Juliá (one of Papp's notable finds) as Lopakhin. He envisioned the *Cherry Orchard* ensemble forming the nucleus of an American classical acting company, the kind Tony Randall dreamed of as well. Meryl and Mary Beth shared Dressing Room No. 18. J. Roy Helland was back doing the wigs, and he fashioned Meryl a wacky, nimbus-like updo.

Rehearsals got off to an awkward start. Serban knew Meryl only from *27 Wagons Full of Cotton*, and when she walked in the first day, he looked at her and balked. "You're not fat!" he growled in his thick Romanian accent. "*No fat, no funny!*" Things got tenser from there. Serban hated the concept of "style" and told the cast he wanted the acting to be "simple." But what did that mean? Meryl questioned him: Wasn't "simple" a style in itself?

More frustrating were the improvisation exercises that Serban led in rehearsal. In one, he had the stage managers read out the text as the actors mimed the action. In another, he had them invent a nonexistent fifth act after the play ends. Irene Worth embraced Serban's methods, at one point impersonating a swan on the attack. But Meryl was impatient. Perhaps she was unhappy playing the servant, or maybe the improv games reminded her of those dread early days at Yale. Her irritation boiled over during one exercise, in which she acted out Dunyasha's resentment, which by that point seemed to have fused with her own.

"I've never seen an angrier improvisation come out of anyone than the one that Meryl did when she was asked to improvise how this person, this servant, viewed her life," Mary Beth recalled. "She was crawling on the floor and spitting and hocking. That girl was really angry at Andrei Serban."

But Serban was pleased. "She was fearless," he recalled. "One is usually afraid to throw oneself outside the norm of what is accepted as the standard heavy method of acting the 'Russians': an artificial, sentimental way of feeling for the character, but Meryl was only concerned with what was valid and alive in the moment. No methods were of any help to her except the pure discovery that came to life in improvisation."

Serban encouraged Meryl's "Lucille Ball tendencies." In return, she developed a dead-on Serban imitation, bellowing, "Falling down *verrry verrry* funny." By the time the play opened, on February 17, 1977, she had found a singular take on Dunyasha: a sexy, frantic, pratfalling Matryoshka doll who tumbled to the floor whenever she made an entrance. As in *27 Wagons*, her knack for physical comedy was evident, but even more so in *The Cherry Orchard*, which she played for pure slapstick. When Yasha the butler kissed her in Act I, she fainted and broke a teacup. When he left her in Act IV, she tackled him to the ground. She spent much of Act II with her bloomers around her ankles.

Naturally, Serban's clownish take on *The Cherry Orchard* polarized critics. In *The New Leader*, John Simon called it "coarse" and "vulgar," adding, "We are not interested in the truth as a Romanian parvenu pipsqueak sees it. We're interested in the truth as the great master Chekhov saw it." But Clive Barnes, in the *Times*, delivered a rhapsody: "It is a celebration of genius, like the cleaning of a great painting, a fresh exposition of an old philosophy. . . . The State Department should send it instantly to its spiritual home—the Moscow Art Theater."

Audiences were similarly divided. One spectator wrote to Papp and Serban, "I think that if this horrifying production had been done in Russia, the two of you and perhaps Mr. Julia would have to face a firing squad." Another suggested, in a letter to the *Times*, that the play be retitled "The Wild Cherry Orchard." Some believed Meryl was shamelessly hogging the spotlight. When Papp wrote to subscribers about his "respect and admiration" for Serban, one recipient sent back the letter with blue scrawl in the margins: "Are you kidding?! Impossible! Can you understand a production in which the maid is the outstanding performer?"

A MONTH INTO performances of *The Cherry Orchard*, Meryl hit a quiet milestone: her debut as a screen actress. With *Julia* not yet released, the occasion was a television movie called *The Deadliest Season*, about the rough-and-tumble world of professional ice hockey.

Michael Moriarty played a Wisconsin hockey player under pressure to rev up his aggression on the ice. He checks a buddy on the opposing team during a game, and the guy is carted off to the hospital with a ruptured spleen. When the friend dies, Moriarty is tried for manslaughter. John's friend Walter McGinn played the district attorney. Meryl was

Moriarty's wife, who desperately wants to believe her husband is innocent. The role was a variation on Adrian from *Rocky*, which was released in November, 1976, the same month *The Deadliest Season* was shot.

Meryl had gotten the part on the suggestion of the casting director Cis Corman. When the director, Robert Markowitz, saw her audition, he went back to the screenwriter and told him to beef up her scenes. Much of the dialogue was between the hockey player and his lawyer, but Markowitz wanted to shift some of that action to the husband and wife. "She was like a centrifugal force," Markowitz recalled.

On set in Hartford, Meryl was jumpy. Moriarty noticed her continually twirling her hair or biting her nails. She gave her character a similar set of nervous tics—biting her lip, chewing her hand, rolling her eyes. She adopted a flat Wisconsin accent ("Maybe I'll take some *cawffee* out") and a low-grade uneasiness that matched Moriarty's disassociated gentle giant. In one scene, she sank on a hotel bed and told him, "When I watched you in a game, hittin', checkin', it would turn me on. I couldn't wait to get home in bed with you. I don't know, there was something different tonight."

It wasn't exactly Tennessee Williams, and Meryl was usually hesitant to play somebody's wife or girlfriend. But the character had her own kind of dignity, confronting her husband about the violence on the ice. As the director saw it, "She was not a subjugated wife, because she was confronting him at the heart of what he does."

Word of her talents was spreading. While *The Deadliest Season* was still being edited, three notable filmmakers came to look at the footage: Miloš Forman, who had just made *One Flew Over the Cuckoo's Nest*; Louis Malle, who would soon direct *Pretty Baby*; and the Czech-born director Karel Reisz, who was four years away from *The French Lieutenant's Woman*. Meryl's performance also impressed the special's producer, Herbert Brodkin, who was preparing for the miniseries *Holocaust*.

The Deadliest Season got a warm response when it aired on CBS, on March 16, 1977. Two weeks later, Walter McGinn was driving in

Hollywood before dawn and plunged off a cliff near Mulholland Drive. He was forty years old. Robyn Goodman had lost a husband, and John Cazale had lost one of his closest friends. A black cloud had formed over their little world, but, for Meryl and John, the worst was yet to come.

THREE DAYS AFTER *The Cherry Orchard* closed at Lincoln Center, Meryl was announced as Shirley Knight's replacement in *Happy End*. Nothing could be less appropriately titled than the Chelsea Theater's production. The show was, in a word, cursed.

The trouble started early on. Michael Posnick, who had directed the Brecht-Weill musical at the Yale Rep, was restaging it at the Brooklyn Academy of Music, where the Chelsea was in residence. Christopher Lloyd played the Chicago gangster Bill Cracker. Shirley Knight, who had beaten Meryl and Mary Beth for the Tony the previous year, was playing Hallelujah Lil, the Salvation Army girl who tries to convert him—the part that Meryl had taken over in New Haven on an afternoon's notice.

Posnick was relatively inexperienced, and the temperamental Knight was walking all over him. To make matters worse, she wasn't much of a singer, and the conductor never knew when she'd come in. "The songs went west, the cues went north," said Michael Feingold, who had adapted the script. One night after her first song, Knight turned to the orchestra and said, "I didn't like how I did that. I think I'll do it again." The second go-round wasn't much better.

Chaos broke out. One actress stomped out center stage moments before the first preview, raging that there was a mistake in her bio. Another actor pushed a castmate off of a four-foot riser during the song "Brother, Give Yourself a Shove." Two of the gangsters who were constantly fighting got locked in a dressing room together. And Christopher Lloyd was having an extreme case of nerves. "In my gut," he recalled, "I felt this production was a disaster."

With the show bound for Broadway, he expressed his concerns to the Chelsea's artistic director, Robert Kalfin. Overwhelmed by his leading lady, Posnick quit at the same moment that he was fired. Then Kalfin took over as the director and promptly fired Shirley Knight. It was then that Joe Grifasi, who was playing Brother Hannibal Jackson, made a suggestion. Meryl Streep already knew the part from Yale. Why not ask her?

Once again, Meryl learned the part of Hallelujah Lil under duress. With her kohl eyes, bowler hat, and curly yellow wig, she looked like a demented Kewpie doll, or an extra from *A Clockwork Orange*. "She saved the show," Christopher Lloyd said.

But the *Happy End* curse continued. Two days before it opened at BAM, Lloyd fell onstage during a fight scene and dislocated his knee. He was told he would need major surgery. The Broadway opening was postponed, and Lloyd was replaced by his understudy, Bob Gunton. At the same time, Kalfin retooled the script, infuriating Feingold and antagonizing the Brecht estate.

As if that wasn't enough, Bob Gunton came down with rubella, a.k.a. the German measles. On a Tuesday at one p.m., the cast lined up to receive gamma globulin injections to prevent further infection. That night, Christopher Lloyd returned in a hip-to-ankle cast and a painkiller haze, becoming the understudy to his understudy. "When I opened my mouth to sing my first song, I was an octave too high," he recalled. "It was kind of torture. But Meryl was there, and she had a wonderful way of teasing and fun."

Meanwhile, John Cazale's plans to share a double bill with Al Pacino had fallen apart, now that Al was starring on Broadway in *The Basic Training of Pavlo Hummel*. Still mourning over Walter McGinn, John had found a suitable alternative: Andrei Serban's production of Aeschylus's *Agamemnon*, with music by Elizabeth Swados. John would play Agamemnon and Aegisthus. It would start at the Vivian Beaumont two weeks after *The Cherry Orchard* closed, continuing the Serban streak.

By the end of April, 1977, Meryl and John were both in rehearsals for separate Broadway shows. Come May, she'd be starring in *Happy End* as it limped to the Martin Beck, while he played the title role in *Agamemnon* twenty blocks north. By day, they'd have the cobblestones of Franklin Street. At night, they'd have the lights of Broadway.

There was just one problem: John Cazale was coughing up blood.

Linda

❦

THE MOURNERS ARE gathered at a hilltop cemetery. It's November: bare trees, gray skies pumped with smoke from the nearby steel mills. A priest swings a censer and sings a dirge. Meryl Streep turns to her left and, through a thick black veil, sees Robert De Niro. She searches his face—he seems utterly lost. She looks down at her feet in the withered grass. The grief in the air is lacquered by disbelief. Nobody thought it would turn out like this, least of all her.

One by one, they approach the coffin. Meryl lays down a white flower with a long stem, looking like a woman whose innocence has been torn asunder, her great love scythed down before it ever got to blossom. She crosses herself and follows De Niro to the cars. She does not turn around, and therefore does not see the pale, mustachioed face of John Cazale. He is the last one to lay down a flower, and the last to leave.

Pull the frame out a few inches, and the trees are resplendent, the grass green. A vast stretch of summer surrounding a patch of brown fall, like an oasis in reverse. It's the set of The Deer Hunter. *The coffin is empty.*

HAPPY END was finally getting to Broadway, curse or no curse. Despite its haunted house's worth of calamities, it had one unassailable asset: Meryl, who had relearned the part of Hallelujah Lil in three afternoons. Still, time was short, and on the day the scenery loaded into the Martin Beck, everyone was on edge. The cast had one chance to run through the show. And Meryl was nowhere to be found.

Uptown, *Agamemnon* was wrapping up its first week of previews, and it, too, was missing its star. On May 3, 1977, the stage manager wrote in his daily report: "John Cazale was out most of the day for medical tests, so Jamil played Agamemnon."

It had become clear that something was seriously wrong with John. Meryl had noticed "disturbing symptoms," and at her urging he agreed to see a doctor—previews be damned. But the two actors knew nothing about navigating the Manhattan medical world, where the doctors' offices on Park Avenue could be booked up for weeks. Luckily, they knew someone with clout, maybe the one person in the downtown theater who could get anything he wanted with a phone call: Joseph Papp.

Beleaguered as he was by his bloated theatrical empire, Papp would throw everything aside to help an actor or a playwright in an hour of need. Mary Beth Hurt had learned this firsthand, when he salvaged her from the psych ward at Roosevelt Hospital. For Meryl and John, he would do no less. He arranged for them to see his doctor, William Hitzig, at his practice on the Upper East Side.

An Austrian-born septuagenarian, Dr. Hitzig had a warm bedside manner that belied his vast influence. Aside from Papp, his patients included Emperor Haile Selassie of Ethiopia and the Indian statesman V. K. Krishna Menon. He had been given the key to the City of Hiroshima after treating two dozen women disfigured by the atomic bomb, and later flew to Poland to care for survivors of Nazi medical experiments. Despite his global humanitarian efforts, he was also one of the few New York doctors who made house calls.

If Dr. Hitzig had an extravagance, it was his vintage Rolls-Royce, painted, Gail Papp recalled, in "some outrageous color like citron." At Papp's request, Hitzig agreed to have his chauffeur pick up John and Meryl, and they spent the day being driven to what seemed like every cancer specialist in the city. It was grimly ironic: here they were, like two movie stars arriving at a premiere, but with any sense of luxury erased by the hovering dread.

John called in sick to *Agamemnon* the next night. And the next. That first week of May was a blur of medical tests, hopping in and out of Dr. Hitzig's Rolls-Royce, with Joe Papp on hand to make sure they were treated like royalty. "He checked us in at the hospital, sat in the chair for hours and waited for the results of the tests," Meryl would recall. "He asked the questions we were too freaked out or too ignorant to ask." After this, Papp would no longer be the man who gave Meryl her first job in New York City. He would be Papa Joe, the only boss she ever loved.

After several exhausting days, Meryl and John sat in Dr. Hitzig's office with Joe and Gail Papp. Nothing in the doctor's kindly demeanor betrayed the horror of the diagnosis: John had advanced lung cancer, and would need to start radiation immediately. "He broke the news to him in his way, holding out a branch of hope for the future, although there was in fact none," Gail Papp recalled. "His cancer had spread all throughout." It was the kind of news, she said, that makes you feel "like you've been struck dead on the spot."

John fell silent. For a moment, so did Meryl. But she was never one to give up, and certainly not the kind to succumb to despair. Maybe it was just the uncanny sense of confidence that she was always able to trick herself into having, or at least showing. But right then, Meryl dug into some great well of perseverance and decided that, as far as she was concerned, John was going to live.

She looked up and said, "So, where should we go to dinner?"

LIKE AGAMEMNON, WHO returns home from the Trojan War only to be killed by Queen Clytemnestra, John Cazale had been dealt a terrible fate. With Meryl on his arm, he sulked into the Vivian Beaumont on May 6th and took aside the director, Andrei Serban. He would no longer be able to continue with the production. That evening, the stage manager's report simply read: "After tonight, Jamil Zakkai will play Agamemnon and Aegisthus."

Meryl returned to *Happy End*, in some sense the latest victim of the curse. If she was roiled by the backstage chaos or the unfolding tragedy at home, she didn't show it: her fellow actors saw nothing but dogged professionalism. One time, she took John and the cast to Manganaro's, the old-school Italian eatery on Ninth Avenue, famed for its hanging salamis and meatballs in marinara sauce. It was John's favorite restaurant, Meryl told her castmates, a steely grin on her face.

When John showed up backstage, everyone who knew what was going on was staggered to find him still smoking Cuban cigars. Meryl had declared her own dressing room smoke-free, so John would go down to her costar Grayson Hall's quarters, which had become the company's unofficial smoking lounge. Christopher Lloyd, still in his hip-to-ankle cast, took note of Meryl's fortitude. "She had a kind of a tough love about it," he said. "She didn't let him malinger."

But the reality was becoming hard to ignore, especially for John. When his brother, Stephen, showed up at the loft and heard the words "They found a spot on my lung," he knew instinctively that it was a lost cause. He went out onto John's fire escape and broke down into heaving sobs. All John could say was, "Did you ever think of quitting smoking?" Not long after, the three of them went out to lunch in Chinatown. Stephen was horrified when John stopped on the curb, hunched over, and spit blood into the gutter.

Their friends were hopeful, or tried to be. Robyn Goodman, still adjusting to life as a young widow, thought to herself, *John always looks sick. How bad can this be?* Al Pacino sat in the waiting room as John went in for treatment, but the patient's attitude was always some variation of "We're gonna get this thing!" John repeated the sentiment, like an incantation, to Israel Horovitz, interrupting his optimism only to wonder aloud, "Will they let me work?"

Night after night at the Martin Beck, Meryl sang her weary solo,

"Surabaya Johnny," Hallelujah Lil's account of a distant love affair with a pipe-smoking scoundrel from the East. In the song, she follows him down the Punjab, from the river to the sea, until he leaves her flat. With her own stage-door Johnny lying in her dressing-room cot, Meryl gave each lyric a rueful sting:

> *Surabaya Johnny, why'm I feeling so blue?*
> *You have no heart, Johnny, and I still love you so . . .*

That June, *Happy End* was up for a Tony Award for Best Musical. The producers asked Meryl to perform "Surabaya Johnny" live at the broadcast. She looked at them and said, "No, I don't have enough confidence to do that," in a manner so confident that the answer seemed to contradict itself. In any case, Christopher Lloyd performed another song, on crutches, and the show lost to *Annie*.

By then, Meryl and John were planning their next move, one that had little to do with doctors and radiation and everything to do with what brought them together in the first place: acting. While John had the strength, they would give a piece of themselves to the only thing they considered sacred, which was make-believe. They would star together in a movie.

A CERTAIN MYTHIC miasma would forever cloud *The Deer Hunter*. Even as it marched to the Academy Awards, a Writers Guild arbitration would have to sort out its byzantine list of screenwriters. The murkiness of its origins was indicative of the deeper mysteries that came to haunt the film, among them: Was Russian roulette really played in Vietnam? Does it matter? Is it even a Vietnam movie, or a meditation on grand themes of friendship and manhood? Is it antiwar—or fascist—propaganda? A masterpiece, or a mess?

At the center of the fog, and most often its source, was the director, Michael Cimino, a man later prone to such gnomic statements as "When I'm kidding, I'm serious, and when I'm serious, I'm kidding" and "I am not who I am, and I am who I am not." Short and soft-spoken, with a bulbous nose, thick jowls, and puffy hair, Cimino looked nothing like a debonair movie director. If his appearance was modest, his ego was boundless—he once claimed that he had been an artistic child prodigy, "like Michelangelo, who could draw a perfect circle at age five." Of his family, he said little. He grew up in New York and started his career making commercials for L'eggs and United Airlines, before directing Clint Eastwood in *Thunderbolt and Lightfoot*, in 1974.

Two years later, Cimino was approached by the British producer Michael Deeley, of EMI Films. Deeley wanted him to take a look at a screenplay he had lying around, by Quinn Redeker and Lou Garfinkle. Redeker had based it on a photo spread he had seen in a magazine two decades earlier, showing a man playing Russian roulette with a Smith & Wesson revolver. He and Garfinkle spun the image into an adventure story about two guys who join a Russian-roulette circuit. Over the course of a year and some twenty-one drafts, they kept changing the setting: South Dakota, the Bahamas. By the time the script reached Deeley, who bought it for $19,000, it was set in Vietnam and titled *The Man Who Came to Play*.

America had only begun to reckon with the catastrophe of the Vietnam War, but Michael Deeley was undeterred, even after five major studios told him different versions of "It's too soon." Besides, the real hook was not Vietnam but the harrowing scenes of Russian roulette played by American POWs. Still, Deeley thought the story needed character development, and he set out in search of a writer-director who could flesh out the script. Enter Michael Cimino. When Deeley met him, he thought he had a "muted" quality, or at least had shown one with Clint Eastwood, with whom one does not mess.

Whether Cimino saw himself that way is another matter. After the moderate success of *Thunderbolt and Lightfoot*, he was poised to join the crop of pioneering directors who were shaping the New Hollywood: rambunctious auteurs like Martin Scorsese, Peter Bogdanovich, and Francis Ford Coppola, who had jolted American movies by importing the racy inventiveness of European art-house cinema. Films like *Bonnie and Clyde*, *Easy Rider*, and *Midnight Cowboy* had ushered in a creative revolution that belonged squarely in the hands of directors, who wielded more and more control over budgets and tone.

Deeley and Cimino met for lunches at EMI's rooftop garden in Beverly Hills, agreeing that some character background was called for, maybe twenty minutes at the beginning. Some time after Cimino had gone on his way, Deeley discovered that the director had sub-contracted a writer named Deric Washburn, without mentioning it to Deeley. It was a red flag—a minor one, but the first in a series that led Deeley to doubt everything he had thought about Cimino. "All I can possibly say," the producer said later, "is that from my point of view he appeared to be quite peculiar in lots of different ways, and one of them was in difficulty telling the truth sometimes."

Washburn, whom the Writers Guild would deem sole screenwriter (Redeker and Garfinkle, along with Washburn and Cimino, got story credit), remembered Cimino as "very guarded." The exception was the three days they spent at Cimino's house in Los Angeles, transform-ing *The Man Who Came to Play* into something decisively their own, namely *The Deer Hunter*.

"The thing just flowed out," Washburn said. "It was like a tag-team thing. We had an outline and dialogue and characters. We had the whole damn thing in three days. Never happened to me again. So I sat down and started writing. I think it took three weeks. And every night Cimino would send an assistant in to take the pages away. Of course, I had no copies of them, which came up later, because when the script was finished my name wasn't on it."

Washburn worked twenty-hour days. When he was done, Cimino took him out to a cheap restaurant off the Sunset Strip, along with his associate producer and sidekick, Joann Carelli. When they finished dinner, according to Washburn, Carelli looked at him and said, "Well, Deric, it's fuck-off time." The next day, Washburn got on a plane and resumed his life in Manhattan as a carpenter.

The script that Cimino then delivered to EMI retained almost nothing of *The Man Who Came to Play*. It was set in the industrial town of Clairton, Pennsylvania. The original protagonist had been split into three, all steelworkers of Russian extraction. The movie would have a triptych structure. In Act I, the carefree young men of Clairton prepare to go off to war. In Act II, they face the verdant hell of Vietnam, where prison guards force them to play Russian roulette. Act III, back in Clairton, shows the devastating aftermath. Michael, the noble sufferer, returns alive but alienated. Steven comes back without his legs. And Nick becomes a shell-shocked zombie, doomed to play Russian roulette in a Saigon betting ring, until a bullet finally ends the pain.

Deeley's business partner Barry Spikings recalled being on a plane with Cimino, who turned to him and said, "You know what that Russian roulette thing is? It's really a metaphor for what we're doing with our young men, sending them off to Vietnam." Ultimately, the script had less to do with the politics of the war than with the profundity of male friendship. Critics would later observe that the director and his protagonist shared a first name, Michael. More revealing was the character's last name, Vronsky, borrowed from *Anna Karenina*—a clue, perhaps, to Cimino's Tolstoyan sense of scale. He had solved the problem of character development with a raucous Act I wedding party for Steven and his girlfriend, Angela. In the screenplay, it took up seven and a half pages.

"Michael, this could really eat us up a bit," Spikings would say.

"Oh, no, it's going to be a flickering candle," Cimino assured him. "We can knock it out in a couple of days."

In the midst of the men's camaraderie, Cimino and Washburn placed a woman: Linda, a supermarket checkout girl, torn between her engagement to Nick and the deeper allure of Michael. Described in the screenplay as "a fragile slip of a thing with a hauntingly lovely face," she was less a fully realized character than the archetypal girl back home, the Penelope waiting at the end of a modern-day Odyssey.

Knowing that a movie about Vietnam would be a hard sell, EMI needed a star to play Michael Vronsky. Aside from being noticeably non-Russian, Robert De Niro couldn't have been more tempting. His roles in *Mean Streets*, *The Godfather: Part II*, and *Taxi Driver* had solidified him as the rough-and-tumble hero of the New Hollywood. EMI paid the asking price of $1.5 million, then placed a full-page ad in *Variety* announcing its coup, showing De Niro in sunglasses, holding a rifle.

Cimino and De Niro began scouting for actors to round out the cast. At a steel mill in Gary, Indiana, they got a tour from the burly fore-man, Chuck Aspegren, and then enlisted him to play Axel, the group's hard-drinking rascal. Back in New York, De Niro nabbed the thirty-four-year-old Christopher Walken, who had recently starred opposite Irene Worth in *Sweet Bird of Youth* on Broadway, to play Nick. He saw John Savage in *American Buffalo* and thought he would be perfect for Steven, the bridegroom turned amputee. And at the Vivian Beaumont, he saw Meryl Streep as the pratfalling Dunyasha in *The Cherry Orchard*. The role was nothing like the demure Linda, but when Cimino caught her a few weeks later, singing "Surabaya Johnny" in *Happy End* at BAM, she got the offer.

Movies didn't rank high among her ambitions, and she had told herself she wasn't an ingénue. Linda, she would say, was "the forgotten person in the screenplay and also in the other characters' lives." The girlfriend part, the blonde in the love triangle—that was someone else's job, someone else's dream. Rather than "hitting it big as some starlet," Meryl had planned her burgeoning stage career to achieve the opposite. In less than two years she'd been a nun, a French princess, a Southern floozy, a Manhattan secretary, a Civil War belle, a clumsy Russian maid, and a Salvation Army crusader—not to mention the menagerie of parts she'd played at Yale. Linda the checkout girl could erase all that.

"They needed a girl between two guys," she said later, "and I was it."

But there was another pull to *The Deer Hunter*, one that super-seded her typecasting concerns: it had a role for John Cazale. Stanley the steelworker was the jester of the group, the "failed alpha male" (in Cimino's summation) who rankles his buddies with cheap jabs and gossip. He was the guy who preens in the mirror despite his receding hairline, who wagers twenty bucks that the Eagles quarterback is wearing a dress. Like Fredo Corleone, he was the weakling in a band of brothers, quick to overcompensate with a trashy date or a defensive barb, always fighting a comic brawl with his lagging masculinity.

John, according to Cimino, wanted the chance to act alongside De Niro. But he was hesitant to take the role, for reasons he didn't initially make clear. Finally, he came to Cimino and told him he was undergoing radiation for lung cancer. If the director didn't want to take the risk, he would understand. Stunned, Cimino told him they would go ahead as planned. The actors were required to take medical exams before the shoot—what should I say? John wondered. Tell the truth, Cimino told him. They would all hold their breath and wait.

The Deer Hunter was set to begin filming in late June, just as Meryl was wrapping up her run in *Happy End*. Weeks went by without a word about the physical, until, the day before shooting, Cimino got a frantic call from an executive at EMI, most likely Michael Deeley. The studio had to insure the film, and suddenly the awful reality of John's health was a matter of dollars and cents. According to Cimino, "the morons at EMI" told him to fire John. The director exploded. "I told him he was crazy," Cimino said later. "I told him we were going to shoot in the morning and that this would wreck the company. I was told that unless I got rid of John, he would shut down the picture. It was awful. I spent hours on the phone, yelling and screaming and fighting."

Barry Spikings and Michael Deeley both deny that EMI ever demanded that John be fired. "There was no question of letting him go," Deeley said. "He was Meryl Streep's lover and had been introduced to us by Robert De Niro, and both of them would have been very upset." The medical advice they received indicated that John would not reach a "crisis-point" until his work on the film had been completed. They would shoot out of order to get his scenes in the can first. Still, Deeley thought it sensible to have some kind of Plan B. He asked Cimino to devise a backup scene explaining Stan's disappearance, so that any completed footage would not be compromised in the event of John's death.

This set off another explosion. In Cimino's telling, the director found the request so unseemly that he consulted a psychiatrist. This was beyond moviemaking. *I'm getting out*, he thought. *I can't do this. It is not worth it, talking about life and death like this.* Finally, he agreed to write the alternative scene, some "absolute dreadful piece of shit" that he had no intention of using. He slammed down the phone in disgust.

But there was still the matter of insurance. In later years, the story got out that Robert De Niro secured the bond on John's participation with his own money. It was a real-life analogue to the loyalty portrayed in *The Deer Hunter*, in which Michael vows not to leave Nick in the wilds of Vietnam. Publicly, De Niro would play coy about the insurance, with vague assertions like "He was sicker than we thought, but I wanted him to be in it."

But Deeley and Spikings both insist this never happened. "Who was going to be the beneficiary?" Deeley said. "EMI wasn't, because EMI had no involvement in insuring him. We couldn't get insurance. What makes anybody think that Robert De Niro has any special edge in the insurance business?" Nevertheless, Meryl was so convinced of De Niro's magnanimity that she repeated the story decades later. Like almost everything about *The Deer Hunter*, it acquired the ring of legend.

If John were to go uninsured, as the producers claim he did, everyone would simply have to pray that his health held out long enough to complete his scenes. According to Savage, the actors were asked to sign an agreement, promising that if John were to pass away during filming they would take no legal action.

Time was now everything. The longer the shoot went on, the more complicated it would be to edit around his scenes if the unspeakable occurred. The making of *The Deer Hunter* was turning into its own game of Russian roulette, with each round of dailies a fresh bullet in the chamber.

TWO FIGURES WALK *along the main street of Clairton, Pennsylvania, arm in arm. The man is a Green Beret in uniform, the woman in a crisp blue coat. To the townsfolk passing by, they look like a happy couple promenading down the dusty boulevard. But their faces are tense, and they rarely make eye contact. When someone stops to greet the man on the street, the woman furtively glances at a shop window to fix her hair.*

"Cut!"

Meryl removed her arm from Robert De Niro's. It was the first day of shooting on *The Deer Hunter*, and everything was out of order. The scene of Michael and Linda stepping out together in Clairton was from the story's post-Vietnam third act. They would have to imagine all that came before: the flirtatious glances across the wedding hall, the tentative homecoming. All that they'd film later.

Also, this wasn't Clairton. The real town hadn't fit Michael Cimino's vision for *his* mythic middle-American hamlet. Instead, he had cobbled together bits and pieces of seven different towns in the corner of the heartland where Ohio, Pennsylvania, and West Virginia converge. The movie's Clairton would be a compendium of places like Weirton, Duquesne, Steubenville, and Follansbee. In Cleveland, he had handpicked St. Theodosius, a historic Russian Orthodox cathedral, for the wedding ceremony. In Mingo Junction, Ohio, he remodeled Welsh's Lounge, a dive bar down the street from the steel mill, to serve as the local watering hole.

Wherever the cast and crew descended like a traveling circus, the local papers rushed to the scene, printing headlines like "Mingo Citizens Elated by Film" and "Movie Makers Leave Cash, Not Pollution, Here." Only Lloyd Fuge, the mayor of the real Clairton, Pennsylvania, seemed wary, telling Steubenville's *Herald-Star*, "They say the nature of the scenes down there would not be beneficial to our town." He was probably right. The Clairton of Cimino's imagination was a gray place, with dusty shop signs and furnaces choking the sky with smoke.

The screenplay called for drab November: deer-hunting season. But when the crew set up in the Rust Belt, it was one of the hottest summers on record. Once the cast and the financing had come together, the filmmakers knew they had to move fast, and the ticking time bomb of John Cazale's health made waiting for autumn even more dangerous. Instead, they would tear the foliage off the trees, spray the green grass brown, and scatter the ground with dead leaves. The citizens of Mingo Junction could be forgiven for wondering why the trees outside the Slovak Citizens Club had gone bare in late June.

The heat was punishing on the actors, too. Even in scorching ninety-degree weather, the actors wore flannel shirts and wool caps, while the crew was in shorts. After each take, they would trade their sweat-drenched clothes for a dry set. George Dzundza, who played the barkeep, wore fake sideburns that continually slid off his face. Meryl kept a blow dryer handy, to make sure her hair wasn't limp on camera.

Few people around Mingo Junction took notice of her—unlike De Niro, who couldn't walk down Commercial Street without his picture landing in the Steubenville *Herald-Star*. She filled the dead hours between shots knitting sweaters, just like her character. When she could, she explored the town. At Weisberger's clothing store, she bought a scarf and made small talk with the owner. The shopkeeper delighted in conversing with a movie actress, unaware that she was working, absorbing the pace and the particulars of life on the Ohio River.

She still had her doubts about Linda, and she wasn't keeping them quiet. When the *New York Times* came to town to report on the "Vietnam Movie That Does Not Knock America," she was astonishingly forthright.

"Linda is essentially a man's view of a woman," she said. "She's extremely passive, she's very quiet, she's someone who's constantly vulnerable. She's someone who always has a tear in her eye but an unbreakable spirit, someone who cares a lot but who is never depressed.

Someone who's beaten down a lot by everybody, but who never gets angry about that."

Driving the point home, she continued, "In other words, she's really far from my own instincts. I'm very much of a fighter myself. So this is very hard for me. I want to break her out of her straitjacket, but of course I can't even let that possibility show. I tend to think she's someone who will grow up into one of the millions of neurotic housewives. But this is a man's movie, it isn't about Linda's problems. I think the point of view of the story is that she's a lovely person."

For a no-name actress filming her first big movie role, airing such grievances to the *Times* was beyond bold.

Her main concern wasn't Linda, though; it was John. On set, she watched him carefully, making sure he didn't overextend himself. He was weak, and it showed. Beneath his flannel shirt was a small tattooed mark on his chest made by the radiation techs, like the crosshairs in a hunting rifle's scope. Most of the cast knew what he was up against, though nobody really talked about it. Perhaps Meryl had finally convinced him to quit smoking, and now he would chastise anyone who lit a cigarette. "One look and he'd come up behind us and grab it and put it out, scream at us," John Savage recalled. "He put people at ease by slamming them with criticism, with humor. Basically, 'If you're gonna smoke, you're gonna die. Don't screw around with that!'"

Those first few weeks, Cimino knocked out the movie's final third, the downcast post-Vietnam scenes. In Duquesne, Pennsylvania, he converted a small field into a cemetery, where they shot the funeral for Christopher Walken's character. When they were done, they gave it to local kids to use as a ball field. In Welsh's bar, they filmed the indelible finale, in which the mourners sing a doleful rendition of "God Bless America." Meryl and John sat side by side, singing of mountains and prairies and oceans white with foam.

Having shot the movie's tragic end, Cimino then backtracked to its raucous beginning. By then, the cast had developed an easy camaraderie, which would serve the freewheeling tone. Cimino wanted these scenes to feel like home movies, as if the audience were watching snatches of its own past. He had gone to great lengths to imbue the actors with a sense of authenticity, even mocking up Pennsylvania driver's licenses that the guys kept in their pockets.

The centerpiece of the first act was the wedding party, which Cimino envisioned as a richly detailed set piece—far from the quick scene-setter Michael Deeley had in mind. Cimino had been the best man at a Russian Orthodox wedding just like it, and his aim was to shoot the sequence like a documentary, with as many real-life elements as possible. In that spirit, the location would be Cleveland's Lemko Hall, a ballroom where the neighborhood's Slavic community held celebrations.

For three days, an instructor named Olga Gaydos taught the actors Russian folk dances like the korobushka and the troika, the dance of the three stallions. Meryl and her fellow bridesmaid Mary Ann Haenel would twirl on either side of John, laughing at his two left feet. "That's enough," he'd say, a little peeved. Suddenly, everyone would flood him with concern: "Are you okay?" "Do you need to take a break?"

When they could, the couple would steal some private moments. "They talked quietly together," Mary Ann Haenel recalled. "They had their heads together. They walked together. They looked happy. But every now and then, you would see that look that they would give each other—it was a deep look."

The world of Clairton was just background noise to John's health problems. "Being in a movie was like the smallest part of the tricky part of that landscape of our lives," Meryl would recall. "I mean, it was really tough, and nobody really knew whether these protocols would work. And we were always really hopeful that everything would work out well."

Finally, on August 3rd, with the schedule already delayed by weeks, Cimino began shooting one of the craziest, drunkest, *longest* wedding parties in movie history. Outside Lemko Hall, the street was closed to traffic and crammed with trucks and generators.

Inside, the windows were cloaked in black, so that the hall remained in perpetual night. Giant high school portraits of Savage, Walken, and De Niro hung on the walls, along with banners wishing the boys well in Vietnam. The barroom in back was kept open all day long, so that everyone could pass the time playing gin rummy, maybe guzzle a bottle of Rolling Rock. Of course, Cimino didn't mind if the actors were soused. All the better.

The filmmakers had advertised for extras from the community, hiring some two hundred wedding guests from three different parishes. They were paid twenty-five dollars a day—two bucks extra if they showed up with a wrapped gift box. They were told to leave the presents at the back of the hall, where the boxes towered to the ceiling. Right before filming, the assistant director went up to Cimino and said disbelievingly, "Michael, everybody brought a gift!"

"Well, we told them to," the director said.

"You don't understand." Inside the boxes were toasters and appliances and silverware and china. The parishioners had bought actual gifts, as if they were attending a real wedding.

The party began each morning at seven-thirty and raged until nine or ten at night. Everyone was tired and confused and happy. Cimino captured the chaos with anthropological curiosity, intervening only to choreograph a moment here or there. At one point, John's character is dancing with a bridesmaid, and the bandleader, played by Joe Grifasi, cuts in. When John notices him grabbing her behind, he leaps up and pulls them apart, then turns to the girl and slugs her on the cheek. Cimino said that his uncle did the same thing at a family wedding.

Other moments of carousal came organically. An old man gorging himself on stuffed cabbage. Christopher Walken leaping over a mug of beer. Chuck Aspegren hauling a bridesmaid to the coatroom as she pummels him with an umbrella. During one take, De Niro was so exhausted as he carried John over to take a group photo that he lost his balance, and both men collapsed to the floor. Cimino kept the take: he was looking for accidents, not grace.

Meryl got caught up in the revelry, at least when the camera was pointed at her. When De Niro spun her on the dance floor, she erupted into dizzy laughter. When she caught the bouquet, she screamed with joy. She may not have thought much of her character, but she had found a way to play her. "I thought of all the girls in my high school who *waited* for things to happen to them," she said later. "Linda waits for a man to come and take care of her. If not this man, then another man: she waits for a man to make her life happen."

In essence, she was playing the character she'd perfected in high school: the giggling, pliable, boy-snatching cheerleader. In her poofy pink gown and bow, she channeled that forgotten girl, who knew that the best way to land a second date with a Bernards High football player was to forgo all opinions; when Michael Vronsky asks Linda what beer she prefers, she shrugs and says, "Any kind." Meryl found that she had "stockpiled" that character and could revive her at will. Only now, of course, she was self-assured enough to banish her once the cameras stopped rolling.

In place of the cheerleading squad, she had her fellow bridesmaids, Mary Ann Haenel, Mindy Kaplan, and Amy Wright. One day, the four of them were getting restless during a break. Meryl went out to see what the holdup was and returned to say that they had run out of film stock. (Cimino, trying to capture every moment, was burning through miles of it.) On the bright side, a guy had shown her how to kill a fly—there had been one buzzing around the dressing room all day. Meryl showed the girls what to do: clap your hands just *above* the fly, and it'll zip up so you can kill it. When she tried it, the fly swooped up and escaped, finding shelter in Amy Wright's cleavage. The girls squealed and guffawed as she frantically lifted her petticoat to let it out.

At long last, Cimino called it a wrap, and the wedding that seemed to go on for eternity finally ended. The banners came down. The stuffed cabbage went in the trash. The extras were paid their day rates and dispersed. So did Meryl and John and Christopher Walken and Robert De Niro. With the hall eerily empty, Cimino saw a local man sitting on the stage, holding a half-empty glass of beer. He was weeping quietly.

"What's wrong?" the director asked him.

Through his tears, the man said, "It was such a beautiful wedding."

BY THE TIME *The Deer Hunter* rolled out of the Rust Belt, Meryl's scenes as Linda were done. But Cazale still had the hunting scenes, in which the hungover bachelors head to the mountains in the morning light. Cimino treated these scenes with a mythopoetic reverence, scoring De Niro's trek through the mist to the sound of an angelic choir. Of course, Meryl might have pointed out that this celestial hunting trip was boys only, a girl like Linda having no place in the sacred union between man and nature.

It was late summer, and none of the mountains in the Northeast were snowcapped. So Cimino flew the actors across the country, to the Cascade range in Washington State. As Stan, Cazale's job was once again to play the fool, and the foil, amid all the bravado. On a mountain road, he emerges from the Cadillac in a rumpled tuxedo and a ridiculous fur hat. He has forgotten his hunting boots—as *always*—and De Niro's Michael Vronsky refuses to let him borrow his own. "This is this," Michael explains.

"What the hell's that supposed to mean?" Stan snarls back. " 'This is this.' I mean, is that some faggot-sounding bullshit or is that some faggot-sounding . . ."

Stan grabs the boots anyway, and Michael glares, holding his rifle. "What?" Stan retorts. "Are you gonna shoot me? Huh? Here."

With that last word, John Cazale opened part of his tuxedo shirt, exposing a small wedge of skin. He had chosen the spot of the crosshairs tattooed on his chest during radiation. It was, Cimino said later, "some strange prefiguration of his own death."

The crew built a cottage between two peaks, where the guys gathered to shoot a scene from the second hunting trip, after Michael has returned from Vietnam. Stan is now carrying a dinky little revolver everywhere, and, after some mild provocation, Michael grabs it and threatens to shoot Stan in the head. We see then how truly far away he is, how the inferno of war has sundered him from the old gang. At the last moment, he points the gun heavenward and shoots the ceiling.

De Niro, who had studied everything from POW testimonials to hunting guides in preparation, thought the scene would play better if there was a live round in the gun. "Are you crazy?" Cimino said. De Niro insisted that they ask John.

"John, Bob would like to play this with a live round in the gun," the director said.

Cazale looked at him and blinked.

"Okay," he said. "But I have to check the gun first."

Before each take, John would spend a half an hour checking the gun to make certain the bullet wasn't in the wrong place, driving everyone crazy: again, the slowness. Why had he agreed to this? He had spent months looking his own mortality in the face. And yet nothing thrilled him like the electric charge between two actors.

Those days in the mountains were majestic but harried. Whenever the fog cleared, Cimino would sound the alarm and everyone would rush into position, knowing the sun might disappear again at any moment. But time worked differently for John Cazale. Cimino would catch him between takes, smelling the mountain flowers.

ALL MERYL WANTED to do was be with John, but fate was pulling her in two directions. One: the hard-fought road to his recovery. The other: show business, where she was increasingly in demand.

Herbert Brodkin, the producer of *The Deadliest Season*, had hired her for his next project, the nine-hour television miniseries *Holocaust*. The series would tell the story of a single German family scattered to the winds by the rise of the Nazis. In scope and seriousness, it would follow the mold of *Roots*, the epic ABC miniseries about the African-American experience, which had aired the previous January to unprecedented ratings. Hoping to give NBC its own prestige blockbuster,

Brodkin hired Marvin Chomsky, one of the directors of *Roots*, to film the entirety of *Holocaust*.

Meryl took the job for one reason: money. She had been quietly helping to pay John's medical bills, and after *The Deer Hunter*, neither of them knew when he'd be able to work again. She expected John would go with her to Austria, but when the time came he was just too weak.

In late August, she flew to Vienna alone. Austria was "unrelentingly Austrian," she said later. "The material was unrelentingly grim. My character was unrelentingly noble." She was playing Inga Helms Weiss, a gentile German woman who marries into a Jewish family, not expecting the calamity that would follow. Her husband, Karl, played by James Woods, is a painter and the son of a prominent Berlin doctor. Seized for "routine questioning," Karl is sent to Theresienstadt, which the Nazis presented as a "model" camp for propaganda purposes. There, he joins a band of artists plotting to smuggle drawings of their true conditions to the world.

Like Linda, Inga represented an ideal: the "good Aryan" bystander who stands with the Jews in the face of Nazi treachery. In one sickening sequence, she allows an SS officer to defile her in exchange for taking Karl off quarry duty and delivering her letters. ("I've had to do things to get these letters to you," she writes, "but my love for you is undying.") Finally, she materializes at his art studio in Theresienstadt, having sacrificed her freedom to be with her husband.

Vienna was "extraordinarily beautiful and oppressive," Meryl wrote in a postcard to Joe Papp on August 29, 1977. She was entranced by the city's artistic legacy but appalled by its lingering Nazi presence. The city would shut down at nine; sometimes, there would be two separate movie houses showing films on Hitler on the same night. It was not lost on her, either, that Vienna was the setting of *Measure for Measure*. It had been only a year since she and John had played those scenes. She told Joe that she missed the "hurly burly" of New York.

In *Holocaust*, Meryl was reunited with Michael Moriarty, who played the über-Nazi Erik Dorf with sociopathic relish. She didn't do much research, apart from reading Erich Fromm's *The Anatomy of Human Destructiveness*. But the wrenching history she was enacting was evident all around her. Filming on location at the Mauthausen concentration camp was "too much for me," she recalled. "Around the corner there was a *hofbrau*, and when the old soldiers got drunk enough, and it was late enough, they would pull out their souvenirs of the war; it was very weird and kinky. I was going crazy—and John was sick and I wanted to be with him."

The shoot kept extending; she felt like she was in prison for two and a half months. Marvin Chomsky saw how badly Meryl wanted to be somewhere else, and he knew why. "She may have made associations between the potential of losing John and the character of her husband," he said. "How she used it was how she used it. I didn't ask, I didn't suggest. I did not want to take advantage of the passion that she had privately. She wanted to rely on professional passion. That was more than enough." Stunned by her abilities, he asked her between takes, "Meryl, tell me: where does it come from?" She replied coyly, "Oh, Marvin . . ."

Her cheery professionalism, though it masked an internal restiveness, was a relief, given the subject matter. On their days at the gas chambers in Mauthausen, the set would erupt in squabbling. "The reason was that we felt so awful in a place like that, and we tended to take it out on the people we were working with, when in fact, we were feeling this rage against the Nazis," James Woods observed soon after. "In a situation like that—and there were many of them—Meryl was the one who could always say just the right thing to defuse the tension."

Blanche Baker, the twenty-year-old playing Meryl's sister-in-law, was in awe of the older actress, who at twenty-eight seemed like the most sophisticated person in the world. Despite being the daughter of an Auschwitz survivor (the director Jack Garfein), Blanche was less interested in atrocities than in flirting with Joseph Bottoms, who played her brother. On days off, she and Meryl went out to Viennese bakeries and ordered pastries *mit Schlag* (with whipped cream). Meryl confided in Blanche about her ailing boyfriend back home—to her, it all seemed very grown-up.

Blanche was raised in show business; her godfather was Lee Strasberg and her mother was the actress Carroll Baker, who had immortalized Tennessee Williams's Baby Doll on screen. Still, the impressionable Blanche saw Meryl as the model of serious acting, and did her best to imitate her. Before "Action," Meryl would take a quiet moment to turn away and collect herself; Blanche started doing the same. Meryl's script was scrawled with notes in the margins; Blanche started writing notes in her script, too. She had studied sculpture as a girl, and Meryl's meticulous scribbles reminded her of a sculptor's sketches.

Meryl spent her last three weeks on set counting the hours, sleeplessly waiting for dawn under "that damn eiderdown" covering her bed. She didn't stay in Austria a moment longer than she had to. "She was very anxious to do her very last scene and then zip back and out," Chomsky recalled. "I mean, I don't even think we had a moment to say goodbye." When she returned to New York, John was limping. He was in worse shape than ever.

NO ONE SAW Meryl for a while. No one saw John, either. Offers for parts came and went. Friends called the loft for John, and Meryl would pick up.

"He's really ready to go to sleep at the moment. Maybe another time . . ."

Click.

They went out sparingly, and with great effort. One time, Meryl's old Yale classmate Albert Innaurato spotted them at a diner on Barrow Street, and was startled to find Meryl supporting John as they made their way to the table. "It was not a side of her I ever expected to see," he said.

On trips to Memorial Sloan Kettering Cancer Center, the doctors took note of John's undaunted companion. When one surgeon remarked on her distinctive beauty, John said that it was an example of nature at its finest: "One that I hope to keep seeing as long as possible."

Her resolve convinced everyone—couldn't they tell she was acting her heart out? As she wrote her Yale acting teacher Bobby Lewis, "My beau is terribly ill and sometimes, as now, in the hospital. He has very wonderful care and I try not to stand around wringing my hands but I am worried all the time and pretending to be cheery all the time which is more exhausting mentally physically emotionally than any *work* I've ever done. I have *not* worked, thank God, since October, or I don't know how I'd have survived."

John's lung cancer had metastasized to the bone, and he got weaker by the day, which Meryl attributed to the chemotherapy. The accoutrements of her old life now seemed trivial; the only role she had time for was nurse. Despite their troubles, Meryl valued that time, with the distractions of show business far away and the two of them alone together, sharing the intimacy of close quarters. "I was so close," she said, "that I didn't notice the deterioration."

The months went by: 1977 turned to 1978. In January, freezing snow and rain covered the city, and hundreds of thousands of people lost power. Two weeks later, thirteen inches of snow came down—the biggest blizzard of the decade. The metropolis that had just weathered a blackout and Son of Sam now found itself unable to clear the mountains of drifted snow and trash in the streets. Every few days, the city would declare a "snow emergency," a phrase used so often that it became meaningless.

On Valentine's Day, four more inches fell. From their fire escape, John and Meryl could see Franklin Street paved with white. It couldn't have been a romantic image. Buried beneath the snow were muck and garbage bags and potholes. The city was sick in its guts.

NOW WITHOUT MERYL, production of *The Deer Hunter* moved to Thailand, Cimino's stand-in for Vietnam. The movie was over budget, and the schedule had gone out the window. The wedding scene, far from being a "flickering candle," had eaten up considerable time and money, worrying EMI executives. Barry Spikings took the director on a walk by a lake.

"Michael," he asked, "are you doing your best?"

Cimino assured him he was.

Shooting in Thailand was not only costly but dangerous. The State Department had warned the filmmakers away from the country, which was controlled by a right-wing junta. On the Burmese border, where armed insurgents were rampant, Cimino and his cast stayed in thatched huts and ate green cobra, said to increase virility.

Cimino wanted the Vietnam sequence to have the same vérité style as the Clairton scenes. He hired local nonactors to play the boys' Vietnamese captors. As POWs, De Niro, Walken, and Savage wore the same clothes every day. They didn't shave or shower. They slept in their uniforms. They "smelled to high heaven," Cimino would brag. During a scene in a submerged tiger cage, a rat began nibbling at Savage's face. Cimino put it in the movie.

There was a strict military curfew in effect, so the film crew would set up in secret locations at two in the morning, as CIA officers supervised. (Cimino put them in the movie, too.) They were allowed to export negatives but not to reimport the prints, so they were shooting blind, without the benefit of dailies. Spikings had flown in to oversee production, and his point man was General Kriangsak Chomanan, the Supreme Commander of the Royal Thai Armed Forces. Midshoot, he summoned Spikings to Bangkok and kindly asked for the weapons, helicopters, and armored personnel carriers they had borrowed, since he was staging a military coup that weekend. He promised Spikings they would have everything back by Tuesday.

The most treacherous scene was the helicopter escape, shot on the River Kwai. (Cimino relished the David Lean connection.) The water was ice-cold and full of snakes and saltwater crocodiles, and riverboat traffic had clipped the underwater bamboo into deadly spears. The scene called for De Niro and Savage to plunge almost a hundred feet from the helicopter into the current. The stunt doubles refused.

"We'll do it," De Niro said. "The actors."

"Understand, you won't be insured," Spikings told him.

"Who's gonna tell the insurance people?"

Savage and De Niro climbed onto a temporary steel crossing, which the crew had made to look like a rickety rope bridge. As the helicopter pulled in, one of its skids got stuck under the thirty-ton cable holding up the bridge. The copter tilted and roared, as De Niro frantically tried to free the skid. While the pilot screamed into a radio in dialect, Cimino, dressed in fatigues in the helicopter, reached out his hand for De Niro's, knowing that the spinning rotors might very well tip over and kill him, his stars, and half his crew.

The copter broke free, flipping the bridge upside down. The cameras were still rolling as it flew off, with De Niro and Savage dangling above the river.

"Michael, should we drop?" Savage screamed to his scene partner, still using his character name.

"Savage, for Christ's sake," De Niro howled, "we're not in character anymore! We're not in the fucking movie!"

They dropped, one after the other, into the spiky, crocodile-infested, freezing river. After a moment, they emerged—still in the scene and, like their characters, astounded that they were still alive.

"MERYL! HI!"

She would have recognized that voice anywhere: the bubbly, high-pitched warble of Wendy Wasserstein. At twenty-seven, she was still the warm, unkempt, insecure woman Meryl remembered from the costume crew. Now she was calling for a favor.

Two and a half years after graduation, Meryl's Yale classmates were making inroads in the theater world. Christopher Durang and Sigourney Weaver had continued their madcap collaboration with *Das*

Lusitania Songspiel, a Brecht-Weill parody that played on Vandam Street. Albert Innaurato's *Gemini* was produced at Playwrights Horizons, also with Weaver. And William Ivey Long was about to design costumes for his first Broadway show, kicking off what would be a multi-Tony Award–winning career.

Now, it was Wasserstein's turn. In the summer of 1977, she had gone to the O'Neill to workshop *Uncommon Women and Others*, the play she'd begun at Yale. The Phoenix produced it that fall on the Upper East Side. The all-female cast, whose characters were based on Wendy's classmates at Mount Holyoke, included rising talents like Jill Eikenberry and Swoosie Kurtz. The thirty-year-old actress Glenn Close played Leilah, the restless wallflower who longs to graduate and study anthropology in Iraq.

With *Uncommon Women*, Wendy had dramatized her generation's ambivalence about second-wave feminism and the sky-high promises it failed to keep. In the college-flashback scenes, the girls gab about Nietzsche and penis envy and how they'll be "pretty fucking amazing" by the time they're thirty. When they reunite six years later, they're in therapy or working at an insurance company or pregnant, certain they'll be pretty fucking amazing when they're forty. Maybe forty-five.

The three-week run garnered good reviews and Wasserstein's first taste of public validation. By the time the play closed, on December 4, 1977, TV's Thirteen/WNET had selected it to air on PBS, as part of its "Great Performances" series. (*Secret Service*, the Civil War drama starring Meryl and John Lithgow, had aired the previous winter.) The Off Broadway cast would reunite for the filming, with one exception: Glenn Close was due at a Buffalo tryout of *The Crucifer of Blood*, a Broadway-bound Sherlock Holmes drama. Wendy needed a fast replacement. She called Meryl.

Leilah was one of the smallest parts in the play, and it certainly wouldn't do anything for Meryl's career. But Wendy was asking for a favor, and it would be only a few days. She said yes. But she would have to bring John.

A few weeks into 1978, Meryl took the trip to Hartford, Connecticut, where the play was being shot in a television studio. (For PBS, "pretty fucking amazing" became "pretty amazing.") John mostly stayed at the hotel. Steven Robman, who directed the play and codirected the taping, remembered Meryl from her first year at Yale, when she was in his production of *The Lower Depths.* Her air of confidence had always struck him, but now it was accompanied by camera experience that outpaced his own. Filming a scene with Ellen Parker, she stopped and said, "Steve, do we have a camera on Ellen's face right now? It's a really great reaction, and I think you might want to have it in the can." It was like a replay of *Julia,* with Meryl now the knowing scene partner Jane Fonda had been to her.

Meryl's take on the part was appropriately lost and languorous. Her interpretation didn't diverge widely from Close's: both were angular beauties who managed to tap into Leilah's yearning solitude. But Robman saw the gap in their upbringings leak through. Close had grown up in a stone cottage in Greenwich, Connecticut, the daughter of a surgeon. "That was the difference to me," Robman said. "How does an aristocratic girl feel about being isolated like this, versus a girl who wishes she was homecoming queen?" It was the first of many times the actresses would be compared to each other.

As February turned into March, the snow kept pummeling New York City, and layers of sludge coated the streets. With its broken-down fleet of mechanical sweepers, the city was powerless against the onslaught. When the snow finally began to thaw, it revealed sidewalks covered in slimy debris that had been buried for two months. Tribeca reeked of rotting trash.

Meryl's brother Third had been calling the loft, hoping for good news about John, who was now too ill to leave the house. Usually Meryl averted his concern with an upbeat deflection: "We're doing great!"

Then, one day, her answer was different. "He's not doing so good."

It was the first time she had betrayed any lack of hope. It was the day John Cazale moved into Memorial Sloan Kettering for the last time.

Meryl kept watch in the hospital at all hours, as John seemed to shrink into his neat white bed. She kept his spirits up with the only elixir she had: performance. She filled the room with comic voices, reading him the sports pages with the whiz-bang delivery of Warner "Let's go to the videotape!" Wolf.

When friends visited, they saw not Meryl's weariness but her fortitude. "She took care of him like there was nobody else on earth," Joe Papp said. "She never betrayed him in his presence or out of his presence. Never betrayed any notion that he would not survive. He knew he was dying, the way a dying man knows it." Nevertheless, "She gave him tremendous hope."

Decades later, Al Pacino would say, "When I saw that girl there with him like that I thought, There's nothing like that. I mean, that's it for me. As great as she is in all her work, that's what I think of when I think of her."

Around three in the morning on March 12, 1978, John closed his eyes. "He's gone," the doctor said. But Meryl wasn't ready to hear it, much less believe it. What happened next, by some accounts, was the culmination of all the tenacious hope Meryl had kept alive for the past ten months. She pounded on his chest, sobbing, and for a brief, alarming moment, John opened his eyes.

"It's all right, Meryl," he said weakly. "It's all right . . ."

What was it that brought him back? A final rush of blood to the brain? Her sheer force of will? Whatever it was, it lasted only for a second or two. After that, John Cazale closed his eyes again. He was forty-two.

Meryl called his brother, waking him up.

"John is gone," she told him.

"Oh, God," Stephen said.

She burst into tears. "I tried."

She returned to the loft, shell-shocked. In the days that followed, she found herself unable to help plan a memorial or even "negotiate the stairs." She meandered from room to room in John's apartment, the one with the floor so strong it could hold stacks of tomato cans. Suddenly, that didn't seem strong enough.

She sleepwalked through the memorial service, where luminaries of theater and film paid homage to their perpetually undersung collaborator. Israel Horovitz wrote in his eulogy:

> John Cazale happens once in a lifetime. He was an invention, a small perfection. It is no wonder his friends feel such anger upon waking from their sleep to discover that Cazale sleeps on with kings and counselors, with Booth and Kean, with Jimmy Dean, with Bernhardt, Guitry, and Duse, with Stanislavsky, with Groucho, Benny, and Allen. He will make fast friends in his new place. He is easy to love.
>
> John Cazale's body betrayed him. His spirit will not. His whole life plays and replays as film, in our picture houses, in our dreams. He leaves us, his loving audience, a memory of his great calm, his quiet waiting, his love of high music, his love of low jokes, the absurd edge of the forest that was his hairline, the slice of watermelon that was his smile.
>
> He is unforgettable.

Meryl was "emotionally blitzed." "It was a selfish period, a period of healing for me, of trying to incorporate what had happened into my life," she recalled. "I wanted to find a place where I could carry it forever and still function."

After the memorial, she packed some things and went to Canada to stay at a friend's house in the country. Left alone, she drew sketches. The same images kept recurring, as if they were living things trying to break through. Sometimes she drew Joseph Papp, the man who had held her hand throughout this ordeal, and who now had her unconditional loyalty.

But mostly she drew John, over and over again, like the French lieu-tenant's woman sketching her faraway paramour. She just wanted to see his face.

IT TOOK MICHAEL CIMINO three months just to look at all the footage he had shot, working thirteen or fourteen hours a day. With the editor Peter Zinner, he began chipping away at it, carving out a movie. He fin-ished dubbing one night at three in the morning and delivered a rough cut to EMI. It was three and a half hours long.

By then, Michael Deeley, the president of EMI Films, had come to think of Cimino as "deceitful" and "selfish." The movie, budgeted at $8.5 million, had cost $13 million. The character development he had asked for had ballooned into an extra hour. A three-hour film would lose a quarter of the potential revenue, since it could only be shown in theaters so many times per day. Even so, Deeley and Barry Spikings were thrilled with the rough cut, sensing its raw power.

But when they screened the film for their American partners at Uni-versal, it got a decidedly lukewarm reaction. The suits were appalled by the movie's violence and, especially, by its length. Even Cimino con-ceded the screening was a "disaster," recalling one executive exclaim-ing, when De Niro shot the deer, "That's it! We lost the audience! It's all over!" Another, Sid Sheinberg, took to calling it "The Deer Hunter and the Hunter and the Hunter." They wanted an hour cut. Why not start with that wedding scene?

Cimino refused to shrink his epic, certain that the movie's dark magic lay in its "shadows." EMI threatened to take him off his own picture. "I told them I would do everything I could," he said. "I took things out of the movie and then put them back in. The thought that I would be removed and someone else would take over made me phys-ically ill." He went to bed every night with a headache, then woke up with his head still throbbing. He gained weight. "I was willing to do anything I could to prevent this picture from being taken away from me and ruined."

Universal agreed to test-run two different cuts: an abridged version, which they'd show in Cleveland, and Cimino's longer version, which they'd show in Chicago. According to Cimino, he was so worried that the Cleveland audience would like what they saw that he bribed the projectionist to jam the film halfway through. The three-hour version won.

Meryl watched the film over and over again at a screening room on Sixth Avenue, six times in all. She always shielded her eyes during the torture scenes, but somehow it wasn't quite as hard to watch John. As the screen flickered in front of her, she saw all the sly and silly human touches he had left behind in his final performance:

John crossing himself in the church.

John tapping his foot as the bride walks down the aisle.

John checking his fly as the wedding guests pose for a photo.

John running after the newlyweds, throwing rice like a boy hurling a baseball.

John's craggy profile, half in shadow, as the barkeep plays a Chopin nocturne.

John telling Meryl at Michael Vronsky's welcome-home party, "I know Nick'll be back soon. I know Nick. He'll be coming back, too."

John looking at his pale reflection in the Cadillac window, straightening his collar, and declaring: "Beautiful."

One Sunday morning, John's brother, Stephen, met Meryl at the screening room. They waited anxiously for the movie to roll. "When is it going to *staaart?*" Meryl groused with mock impatience. They sat back and watched. When he got home that night, Stephen went to bed with a bottle of vodka.

MERYL HAD BARELY worked during the five months she cared for John. Now her schedule was bleakly open. "I don't want to stop replaying the past—that's all you have of someone who is dead," she said at the time, "but I hope that working will offer some diversion." She was ready to dig out of the trenches and act again.

Fortunately, there was a movie offer: *The Senator*, a political fable written by Alan Alda, the amiable star of *M*A*S*H*. Alda would play the senator, Joe Tynan, a principled family man lured astray by backroom dealing and adultery. Meryl was offered the part of his mistress, a Louisiana labor lawyer with a breezy sexuality and an insider's grasp of the Washington game. "When I want something, I go git it," she tells Joe Tynan. "Just like you."

In other words, she was everything Linda the checkout girl was not: a brashly independent "modern woman," as Meryl described her. As a vocal feminist and advocate for the Equal Rights Amendment, Alda had observed the sleaze of politics close up. Campaigning for the ERA in Illinois, he saw a state legislator telling a female lobbyist he'd consider voting for it while offering her a key to his hotel room. Alda didn't have the blind spots Meryl had encountered in other male collaborators, who shoehorned female characters into broad archetypes. Had her heart not been so heavy, it would have been a thrilling opportunity.

The director, Jerry Schatzberg, visited her in John's loft. He could sense the sadness of the place, but they didn't discuss why. He told her he was looking for a pinch of Southernness, but not a strong accent. Meryl adopted the same Dinah Shore drawl she had used in *Trelawny of the "Wells."* Then, four disorienting weeks after John's death, she packed a bag and headed down to Baltimore.

As on *Holocaust*, her upbeat presence masked a dull pain. "I did that film on automatic pilot," she said soon after. Work was a distraction, not a comfort: "For some things, there is no comfort." In keeping with her character, she kept things light. Rip Torn, her former costar in *The Father* at the Yale Rep, had a supporting role as a skirt-chasing lawmaker. Schatzberg was working with Meryl on her costume and told her he was about to see Rip. "Oh," she responded, "tell him not to be such a pain in the ass!"

She was also reunited with Blanche Baker, her sister-in-law from *Holocaust*, who was playing Joe Tynan's teenage daughter. Baker had a big crying scene with Alda, and she made the mistake of bawling her eyes out during the master shot. Then everyone broke for lunch. When they came back for her close-up, she felt tapped out. Meryl saw that the young actress was panicking, and once again played the role of big sister. "It's there," she assured her. "You just have to trust it. Just be more specific."

She applied the same bedrock of technique to herself, and the results pleased Schatzberg. "The scenes with her were so great," he said, "that when the film was finished, I had a problem, because I felt that she was so good maybe Joe Tynan *should* have gone off with her. So I had to think of a way to diminish her character so that he goes back to his wife."

At the Maryland State House, in Annapolis, Schatzberg enlisted local politicians to play senators and congressmen. One delegate was under the impression that the movie was about a senator who has an affair with his secretary. "I'm actually his lawyer," Meryl said when she heard that, adding, "That really tells you something, doesn't it?"

As they shot, Schatzberg and Alda continually clashed over the script. Alda wanted the actors to stick to the dialogue he'd written, while he freely improvised. Barbara Harris, who was playing his wife, complained to Schatzberg, "Anytime he wants to change *his* dialogue, he does."

Meryl stayed out of the bickering and sailed through her scenes, the beauty of autopilot being that you don't get too involved. Alda, she said later, couldn't have been "a more lovely, more understanding person," given the timing. But she was nervous about their frisky bedroom scenes. Apart from the melancholy love scenes with De Niro in *The Deer Hunter*, she had never had to play sexy on camera. Dino De Laurentiis's "*che brutta*" comment may have still echoed in her mind. At any rate, she didn't feel so frolicsome.

"It's a scene that demands tremendous high spirits and a great deal of sexual energy," John Lithgow said soon after, "and at that time, right after John Cazale had died, Meryl was in no mood for either. And she was embarrassed by the scene. She said she would perspire until she was dripping wet from embarrassment."

Schatzberg called as few crew members as possible to the Baltimore hotel room where they were shooting, to avoid gawking. Meryl slipped under the sheets along with Alda. The cameras rolled. In their postcoital glow, she grabbed a beer, poured it on Joe Tynan's crotch, peeked under the covers, and drawled: "It's true, things *do* contract in the cold!"

Then it was over. "She looked at the movie as some kind of test, a test she had to pass," Alda said later. "She was determined not to buckle."

MIDWAY THROUGH THE SHOOT, *Holocaust* aired on NBC. The relentlessly hyped broadcast lasted four nights, from April 16th through 19th. Some 120 million Americans tuned in—more than half the U.S. population. For the first time, Meryl Streep's face was seen internationally, by families gathered around television sets.

The broadcast inevitably ignited controversy. On the first day of its airing, Elie Wiesel, who, since the publication of *Night*, had become the world's most recognized Holocaust survivor, published a scathing appraisal in the *Times*, calling the series "untrue, offensive, cheap." Next to a photo of Meryl struggling against SS officers, he wrote, "It tries to show what cannot even be imagined. It transforms an ontological event into soap-opera. Whatever the intentions, the result is shocking."

Among the scores of letters in response to Wiesel's was one from Joe Papp, who admitted to wincing at the series' "Errol Flynn heroics." Still, he argued, "The acting was first-rate. As hour by hour went by, the actors, many of whom I know personally, were no longer actors or my friends. They were Jews and Nazis."

In Germany, where the word "Holocaust" was not widely used, the impact was seismic. More than twenty million West Germans tuned in, many describing themselves in an official survey as "deeply shaken." In Meryl's fair-haired Inga, they saw a model of gentile righteousness worth emulating. The broadcast touched off a national debate that played out in newspapers, schools, call-in shows, and the halls of government. In Bonn, the Bundestag was readying to debate the statute of limitations for Nazi war criminals, many of whom were still in hiding. In the weeks following the broadcast, public support for continuing the prosecutions shot up from 15 to 39 percent. Six months later, the Bundestag voted 255 to 222 to suspend the statute of limitations, opening the door to more trials and a national reckoning.

For Meryl, who was entrenched in tiny tragedies rather than historic ones, all this must have felt unfathomably distant. But the change in her day-to-day existence was palpable. Wandering Annapolis one Wednesday in May, wearing baggy jeans and a badly matched tweed blazer, she was approached by fans wielding Kodak Instamatics. Before *Holocaust* aired, she had eaten in Maryland restaurants unnoticed—unless, perhaps, she was sitting next to Alan Alda. Now, people were coming up to *her*.

That first brush with fame was "something surreal," she said at the time. Back in New York, she was riding her bicycle through Chelsea and some guys in a Volkswagen called out, *"Hey, Holocaust!"* Meryl shuddered. "Can you imagine?" she said soon after. "It's absurd that that episode in history can be reduced to people screaming out of car windows at an actress."

In September, she won an Emmy Award for Outstanding Lead Actress in a Limited Series. She didn't attend the ceremony. The statuette arrived a few months later, in a box. She placed it in her study, "propped up like an object" amid pictures of friends: inert. "I wish I could assign some great importance to it," she said at the time, but the honor had "no lasting power."

The day after the Emmys, a woman came up to her at Bloomingdale's and said, "Did anyone ever tell you that you look exactly like Meryl what's-her-name?"

"No," she replied, "nobody ever did."

UNIVERSAL HAD A PLAN: they would open *The Deer Hunter* in single theaters in Los Angeles and New York, then pull it after a week. That way, it would qualify for the Academy Awards, attract some buzz during its sold-out run, and then open wide in February as public interest percolated.

The bid worked. On December 15th, Vincent Canby described the film as "a big, awkward, crazily ambitious, sometimes breathtaking motion picture that comes as close to being a popular epic as any movie about this country since 'The Godfather.'" *Time* echoed the praise: "Like the Viet Nam War itself, *The Deer Hunter* unleashes a multitude of passions but refuses to provide the catharsis that redeems the pain."

But a backlash was brewing. Leading the charge was *The New Yorker*'s Pauline Kael, who clucked at the film's treatment of "the mystic bond of male comradeship," echoing the "celibacy of football players before the big game." More damning was her assessment of the Vietnamese torturers, portrayed in "the standard inscrutable-evil-Oriental style of the Japanese in Second World War movies." She wrote, "The impression a viewer gets is that if we did some bad things over there we did them ruthlessly but impersonally; the Vietcong were cruel and sadistic. The film seems to be saying that the Americans had no choice, but the V. C. enjoyed it."

Few critics could deny the movie's psychological potency, or its agonizing depiction of war and its aftermath. But the more scrutiny it got, the more questions nagged. Did the Vietcong *really* force American soldiers to play Russian roulette? Was there not something homoerotic about those all-male hunting trips? And what about that final rendition of "God Bless America"? Was it meant to be ironic? Or deadly earnest?

Providing a direct counterpoint was another Vietnam film, Hal Ashby's *Coming Home*. Both featured a wheelchair-bound veteran and a woman caught between two military men. But the politics of *Coming Home* was explicitly antiwar, and its liberal credentials were synonymous with its star, Jane Fonda. After *Julia*, Fonda had been hyping Meryl around Hollywood, even trying to find her a part in *Coming Home*, but the scheduling didn't work out. Playing an army wife tapped on the shoulder by history, Fonda once again personified political conscience. With her tin-soldier husband (Bruce Dern) in action, she finds a deeper bond with Jon Voight's paraplegic pacifist, who ends the film lecturing to high school kids about the senselessness of war.

Whereas *The Deer Hunter* showed people losing their way, and one another, *Coming Home* was about finding connection and purpose—political kinship as opposed to spiritual discontent. Fonda's character, unlike Linda, doesn't wait around for a man to rescue her: she volunteers at a VA hospital, becomes radicalized, and, with Voight's help, achieves her first orgasm. The straightforward liberalism of *Coming Home* seemed to expose an unconscious conservatism in *The Deer Hunter*, though it lacked the latter's sweep and horror and ambiguity.

On February 20, 1979, the showdown was made official. *The Deer Hunter* was nominated for nine Academy Awards, *Coming Home* for eight. They would compete for Best Picture, along with *Heaven Can Wait*, *Midnight Express*, and *An Unmarried Woman*. Robert De Niro was up against Jon Voight for Best Actor, with Christopher Walken competing with Bruce Dern for Best Supporting Actor.

John Cazale wasn't nominated. But he had achieved a quiet landmark: of the five features he had acted in, all were nominated for Best Picture. And though he hadn't lived to see it, Meryl Streep was nominated for her first Academy Award, for Best Supporting Actress.

As the Oscars approached, the debate over *The Deer Hunter* intensified. In December, Cimino had given an interview to the *New York Times*, in which he insisted that anyone attacking the film on its facts was "fighting a phantom, because literal accuracy was never intended." The piece noted that Cimino, who gave his age as thirty-five, "joined the Army about the time of the Tet offensive in 1968 and was assigned as a medic to a Green Beret unit training in Texas, but was never sent to Vietnam."

Michael Deeley was among the first to raise an eyebrow: his insurance records indicated that Cimino was just short of forty. Thom Mount, the president of Universal, got a call from a studio publicist:

"We got a problem." The reporter couldn't corroborate what Cimino had said about his military service, and, as far as Mount was concerned, "He was no more a medic in the Green Berets than I'm a rutabaga." (The *Times* ran it anyway.) In April, the Vietnam correspondent Tom Buckley published a full accounting in *Harper's* of what he considered Cimino's distortions. The Pentagon had told him that Cimino enlisted in the Army Reserve in 1962—nowhere close to the Tet Offensive— and spent a placid six months in New Jersey and Texas.

What bothered Buckley was not the personal distortions (which Cimino vehemently denied) but the way they were "mirrored" in the film. His most pungent criticism, like Kael's, was of its portrayal of the Vietnamese. "The political and moral issues of the Vietnam war, for ten years and more this country's overriding concern, are entirely ig-nored," Buckley wrote. "By implication, at any rate, the truth is turned inside out. The North Vietnamese and the Vietcong become the mur-derers and torturers and the Americans their gallant victims."

But the legacy of *The Deer Hunter* was far from settled. Jan Scruggs, a former infantry corporal, saw the film one night in Mary-land. Back in his kitchen, he stayed up until three a.m. with a bottle of scotch, kept awake by a torrent of flashbacks. In the boys of Clairton, he saw the unspoken pain of a generation of soldiers, some who came back, some who didn't. The next morning, he told his wife that he'd had a vision: a memorial for Vietnam veterans, listing the names of the fallen. It was the beginning of a three-year journey that ended on the National Mall.

ONE VETERAN WHO agreed with the criticisms was Mike Booth. Five or six years had passed since he had seen Meryl, having lost himself in his studies in Mexico. After changing his major from art to philoso-phy to Latin American studies and, finally, to American literature, he finished up his degree in Santa Cruz, where he met a girl and got en-gaged. One day in 1977, he took her to see *Julia* and blanched midway through. "That's my old high school girlfriend!" he told her.

Now approaching thirty, Mike yearned to settle down, to "try to be a normal person instead of a vagabond." He brought his fiancée back east, to Newport, Rhode Island. He dreamed of being a writer, but he wanted to support a family, so he took a job at his father's pigment business, in Fall River, Massachusetts. It had a small office in an old mill building, and Mike took on various tasks: typing invoices, loading trucks, sometimes mixing batches of color in the factory. He would end his days in sweaty coveralls splotched with red and yellow pigment.

When he saw Meryl in magazines, he admired how she was pursuing the thing she loved, how accomplished she was. He had just gotten married when his sister told him not to see *The Deer Hunter*, because she thought it would "hit close to home." He went anyway. When he saw the Vietcong holding the Clairton boys in underwater tiger cages, he started feeling the old fire that had propelled him to Nixon's motorcade. "The Communists did plenty of nasty things," he said later, "but from what I recall *our* side used the tiger cages." And Russian roulette? He had never heard of anything like that in Vietnam.

But, as he sat in the Newport movie theater, he saw other things, too. He saw Robert De Niro, on his first night back in Clairton, seeing the "Welcome Home" sign hung in his honor and telling his driver to keep on driving. He saw Christopher Walken, at a military hospital in Saigon, staring at a photo of the girl back home. He saw verdant jungles rocked by explosions, and halting conversations with old friends, and some inkling of the way he felt when he got home to Bernardsville.

And he saw Meryl.

Meryl catching the bouquet.

Meryl tossing rice at the newlyweds.

Meryl giggling and twirling on the dance floor.

Meryl fixing her hair in the shop window.

Meryl breaking down in tears in the supermarket storeroom for reasons she can't possibly explain.

Meryl telling a distant Michael Vronsky, "Can't we just . . . comfort each other?"

Stepping out into the New England night, Mike was shaken. He had seen distortions, yes. But he'd also seen the girl to whom he'd once given that "JUNIOR PILOT" ring, now arm in arm with her man in uniform. For all the reasons his sister had warned him, the movie did hit home. But "it hit home, also," he recalled, "because she looked so beautiful."

ON APRIL 9, 1979, Meryl arrived at the Dorothy Chandler Pavilion in Los Angeles, wearing a black silk crêpe dress she had bought off the rack at Bonwit Teller and ironed herself the night before. ("I wanted something my mother would not be ashamed of," she said.) That week, she had passed through the Beverly Hills Hotel unrecognized. She even took a dip in the pool: a rookie move, as it was designed to be lounged beside, not swum in. But Meryl knew little of the etiquette of Hollywood, nor did she care. Apart from the palm trees swaying overhead, it might as well have been the community pool in Bernardsville.

Now, as the car pulled closer, Meryl heard demonstrators from Vietnam Veterans Against the War, protesting the movie for which she was nominated. Some, in fatigues and berets, waved placards that said "NO OSCARS FOR RACISM" and "THE DEER HUNTER IS A BLOODY LIE." There were reports of rocks being hurled at limos. By the end of the night, thirteen people had been arrested.

The case against *The Deer Hunter* had become increasingly rancorous. At the Berlin International Film Festival, the socialist states had protested in solidarity with the "heroic people of Vietnam." At a house party, a female war journalist went up to Barry Spikings and punched him in the chest, saying, "How *dare* you?" When confronted, Cimino would say that the characters "are not endorsing anything except their common humanity." Meryl was similarly apolitical. "It shows the value of people in towns like that," she said. "There is such a fabric of life to look at."

Inside the hall, the tensions were subdued. Neither Michael Deeley nor Deric Washburn was on speaking terms with Michael Cimino. As the awards began, Johnny Carson, hosting for the first time, welcomed the crowd with the immortal line, "I see a lot of new faces. Especially on the old faces."

Over the next three hours, *The Deer Hunter* went head to head with *Coming Home*, in what seemed like a battle for Hollywood's political soul. Jane Fonda won Best Actress and delivered part of her speech in sign language, because "over fourteen million people are deaf." Christopher Walken beat Bruce Dern for Best Supporting Actor. Robert De Niro, who had stayed home in New York, lost to Jon Voight for Best Actor. *Coming Home* won Best Screenplay, but then Francis Ford Coppola handed his "paisan" Michael Cimino the Oscar for Best Director. "At a moment like this," Cimino said in his speech, "it's difficult to leaven pride with humility."

And in the race between Meryl Streep and *Coming Home*'s Penelope Milford, the winner was . . . Maggie Smith, for *California Suite*. Meryl smiled and applauded gamely.

At the end of the night—an endless one; the East Coast broadcast lasted until 1:20 a.m.—John Wayne came onstage to present Best Picture. The Duke looked uncharacteristically feeble, ravaged by the stomach cancer that would kill him two months later. When he announced *The Deer Hunter* as the big winner, the applause, the *Los Angeles Times* reported, was "respectful but well short of thunderous," as if tinged with buyer's remorse.

On the way to the press area, Michael Cimino found himself in the elevator with Jane Fonda, who had blasted *The Deer Hunter* as a "racist, Pentagon version of the war," before admitting that she had not seen it. Both of them held their Oscar statuettes. Fonda refused to look him in the eye.

When the Oscars were over, Michael Cimino went back to work on his next film, *The Johnson County War*, which would be released the following year as *Heaven's Gate*. John Cazale slid into a posthumous obscurity, forever the ghost in the New Hollywood machine. And Meryl Streep, having begun what no one yet knew to be a record-breaking streak of Academy Award nominations, returned to New York City with her husband.

Joanna

※

SIX MONTHS.

That's how long it took. Six months and change. On March 12, 1978, the love of Meryl Streep's life died as she sat by his bedside. By late September, she was married to another man.

Six months in which Michael Cimino hacked away at the dailies. Six months in which *Holocaust* broadcast her face into living rooms from Hollywood to Hamburg. Six months in which the actress who was now turning twenty-nine would play three indelible roles at the exact same time. Six months in which, depending on whom you ask, she was either an emotional wreck or a virtuoso reaching the culmination of her craft.

Six months to pick up the pieces of her life without John and refashion them into something new and whole and lasting. How?

It started with a knock on the door. And not a welcome one.

SHE MUST HAVE been some combination of baffled and distraught when she opened the front door of the loft on Franklin Street and saw a wan, redheaded Texan she had never met. No doubt, John had told her about the girlfriend who had picked up and left for California. Or maybe not.

Only three weeks had passed since John died, and Meryl was still wandering the apartment like a blank-eyed zombie. Traces of him were in every corner, making the fact of his absence counterintuitive. When was he coming home? Because she was having trouble with everyday tasks, her brother Third had moved in with her. At least she wouldn't have to face the day alone. Automatic pilot.

As if to break the fog and force her back into the practicalities of living, the redheaded woman now stood before her, claiming that her name was on the deed with John's and that it was she, Patricia, who had rights to the apartment. Meryl would have to vacate at once.

Of all the things she wanted to think about, this was surely dead last. Not the apartment, exactly, but the claim this woman professed to have on John's home. *Their* home. He and Meryl had been together less than two years, but what they went through seemed to bear the weight of a lifetime. What had Patricia really meant to him? And why hadn't he handled this mess when he was alive? In a way, it was typical John, so spellbound by the present that he was blind to the future, which had now brought a ghost from his past.

Also, where was she going to live?

Her friends were shocked. "We just assumed that she could live there, or maybe Patricia would give up her rights," Robyn Goodman said. "I mean, honestly, if it was me I would have said, 'Meryl, it's your loft now.' We all thought, Oh, it'll be fine. Because what person would kick Meryl out?"

Robyn called Patricia and pleaded with her. Was it money she wanted? Then ask for money.

When pleading didn't work, Robyn tried intimidation: "You're going to get a terrible reputation, because everybody knows about this."

"Everybody" was their community of actors, the people who loved John and loved Meryl and couldn't believe what was happening. One night, Robyn was at a bar called Charlie's when an Italian actor they both knew came up to her.

"I hear Meryl's having trouble with this Patricia about the loft."

"I'm trying to make it not happen," Robyn said. "I'm trying to help."

The actor leaned in. "You know, I know guys in New Jersey who can take care of this girl."

Robyn blinked. Was she being offered a hit man? This was getting into *Godfather* territory. "No," she said, a little reassured but slightly terrified. "I don't think we want to be responsible for something like that."

Patricia wouldn't budge.

"My brother says it's valuable and I should have it," she said. Her brother was right: the neighborhood increasingly known as Tribeca (though the name was in contention with Lo Cal, Washington Market, and SoSo) was already being hyped as the "international art center" of the future, and property there could be a goldmine.

"Things are not going to go well for you," Robyn told Patricia, as if placing a curse.

It didn't do Meryl much good. She was grieving. She was tired. And now she was homeless.

NEW YORKERS MEASURE their lives in apartments. The two-bedroom on West End Avenue that first year in the city. The loft on Franklin Street. The rental on Sixty-ninth Street. What summer was that? How many apartments ago?

When Meryl got kicked out of John's loft, it was the end of her old life and the beginning of something she couldn't have anticipated. But sometimes apartments write the next chapters themselves.

She and Third began packing up their stuff: an overwhelming task, and not just physically. Each box was a talisman of her life with John, holding its own sad weight. Maybe the best thing was to put it all out of sight. Third had a friend in SoHo, a block or two away, who offered to help. He was a sculptor: brawny, curly-haired, with a sweet smile, like Sonny Corleone with more bulk and less temper. Meryl had met him two or three times, but she didn't remember him.

Even after the three of them had put everything they could into storage, there were still more boxes left over. They were like a force that couldn't be contained, a cumbersome reminder of how messy everything was. The sculptor offered to store the remaining posses-sions in his studio, on lower Broadway.

With all that sorted out, Meryl went off to Maryland to shoot *The Senator.* One day, Third came to visit her on set, along with the sculp-tor. Once she got back to New York, she wouldn't have a place to stay, so the sculptor said she could crash at his loft. He was about to go on a trip around the world on grant money, so she'd have the place all to herself. She accepted the offer.

Left alone, she started to wonder about her host. Once again, she was living among the detritus of an absent man, though this time the house was full of life, not death. She was intrigued by the sculptures spilling from his workspace: massive, gridlike hulks of wood and cable and Sheetrock.

She began writing him letters. Replies came from faraway places like Nara, Japan, where he was studying the patterns on folding screens and floor mats. In his second year of college, the master sculptor Robert Indiana had told him, "If you're going to be an artist, you should travel and see the world." Now he was heeding the advice, soaking in the ge-ometry of the Far East, which would linger in his mind before surfac-ing someday in his hands, just as Meryl absorbed people's gestures and cadences, knowing they might turn up one day in a character.

As she pored over his letters, surrounded by his handiwork, Meryl learned more about the man she had met only a handful of times. His name was Don Gummer, and he was thirty-one. He was born in Lou-isville, Kentucky, and grew up in Indiana with five brothers. Objects had always spoken to him. As a boy, he built tree houses and model airplanes and forts. There were new houses going up in his neighbor-hood all the time, and he would play for hours in the construction sites. Then he'd come home and make his own edifices with an Erector Set.

He was at art school in Indianapolis when Robert Indiana told him to see the world, so in 1966 he moved to Boston, with little more than $200 and a pair of pants. He was married to his college girlfriend, but she stayed back in Indiana and the relationship fell apart. While

Meryl was at Vassar, discovering *Miss Julie*, Don was at the Boston Museum School, discovering the hidden voice of objects. A lecture by the painter T. Lux Feininger planted the idea that abstract shapes could be expressive, a lesson reiterated by George Rickey's book *Constructivism*. He became obsessed with materials and space and what happened when you put the two together.

In 1969, he found a dark piece of stone that reminded him of Brancusi's *Fish*. He sawed it in half and suspended the two pieces above a concrete slab, placing a small patch of grass below the bisected stone. Between the two halves of rock, he kept a tiny sliver of empty space— like the space between two repelling magnets, or the schism within a soul. He called it *Separation*.

The next year, he went to Yale for his M.F.A., where he continued making large-scale installations. He covered an entire room with dry earth and rock, stretched a wire mesh over the expanse, and called it *Lake*. He got his degree in 1973, unaware of the drama student improvising her own death down the street. In New York, he took a job as a union carpenter at the Olympic Tower. The work trickled into his sculptures, which started resembling deconstructed tabletops. Gravity interested him. Shadow interested him. A year into his New York life, he was picked by Richard Serra to mount his first solo show, on Wooster Street. He filled the gallery with a huge, complicated structure he called *Hidden Clues*.

All this was new to Meryl, a language she didn't speak but could instinctively understand, as someone who was also constantly remixing the raw materials of life. Then again: What exactly was going on here? It had been only weeks since John died, and here she was in another man's apartment, her mind pulled between her grief and the vitality that seared through Don's letters.

Their epistolary flirtation came to a head with the alarming news that Don had been injured in a motorcycle accident in Thailand. He was laid up at the Lanna Hospital, in Chiang Mai, where he spent the hours making sketches for a new piece—a relief of painted wood, arranged in crisp rectangular patterns like the ones he had seen on Tatami floor mats. He would construct it when he got home to New York, which would now be sooner than expected.

Meryl sat with Robyn Goodman in the loft, a note from Don in her hand. It wasn't a love letter, exactly, but the tone had changed. He wanted to spend time with her when he got back, in some serious way that frightened her. As in her best roles, the conflict must have played out across her face. She was pulled between desire and guilt, past and future, loss and life. She had nursed John for so many months, putting his needs before her own with a single-minded devotion that rendered everything else irrelevant. Now the world beyond was coming back into focus, and her eyes hadn't quite adjusted. Was it too soon? Was she betraying John? Should she be chaste like Isabella? Surely not— but this was all happening so quickly.

She showed the letter to Robyn and said, "I think he's trying to say something that I'm not ready for."

Robyn knew how she felt. After Walter McGinn's car plunged over the Hollywood Hills the year before, she had found herself a widow at twenty-nine. For a while, she couldn't leave the house. "Nobody's ready to be a widow," she said later. "Nobody at that age—at our age— was ready. You don't know until it happens to you whether you're ready for it or whether you're any good at it."

Then Robyn got a call from Joe Papp, who, in his benevolent way of commanding people what to do, informed her that he had a role for her at the Public. Arguing was useless.

"Joe, I don't—"

"Here's the rehearsal date."

Robyn had forced herself to leave the house to do the play. And then life kicked back in. She met someone and had an affair, ignoring the concerned comments from friends who thought it was too soon. "It's been eight months!" she'd say. "I mean, can I sleep with someone, please?" It wasn't long after that that Joe told her she was meant to be a producer. In 1979, she would cofound the company Second Stage, which would make its home at an Upper West Side theater christened the McGinn/Cazale.

It had been eerie, John and Walter dying a year apart, leaving these two young women to sort out the pain. But with her running start at rejuvenation, Robyn knew the worst thing that Meryl could do was wait.

"Look," Robyn told her. "I had an affair. I'm not judgmental about that. You have to get on with your life. If you like Don, spend time with him."

It seemed so simple. But it wasn't. Any room she made for Don in her heart would have to coexist with the huge space she had carved out for John.

When Don got back, he built Meryl a little room of her own in his loft. Suddenly, she was home. She'd snapped out of automatic pilot, in more ways than one. She was now, as she recalled later, "greedy for work."

FORTUNATELY, THERE WAS someone just as greedy for Meryl's success: Sam Cohn, the show-business swami of ICM. Since Yale, her representatives at the agency had been Sheila Robinson and Milton Goldman, in the theater department. But now that her star was rising in movies, she'd caught the attention of Cohn, whose official title was "head of the New York motion-picture department." That didn't even begin to cover it.

Since negotiating the merger that created ICM, in 1974, Cohn presided over his own busy fiefdom, a boutique agency within the agency. His colleague Sue Mengers called him "agent-auteur." From his desk on West Fifty-seventh Street, he would cook up projects for the dozens of actors, writers, and directors he represented, from whom he expected—and received—bone-deep loyalty.

His deal-making prowess was legendary. "Sam gets away with more than anybody else I know can get away with," the Broadway producer Gerald Schoenfeld once said. "He does more what he wants to do when he wants to do it and in the way he wants to do it than anybody I know and gets away with it."

But he didn't look like a bigwig, his wardrobe consisting of baggy V-neck sweaters, ill-fitting khakis, and thick glasses through which he squinted enigmatically. At first glance, he seemed shy, until you got an earful of his speaking voice, which *The New Yorker* described as "a confident staccato, as unstoppable as a bunch of marbles rolling down a hill." By the end of a meeting at an associate's office, he'd somehow wind up in the host's chair, his feet perched on the other man's desk.

As notorious as his power-brokering—but connected to it by mysterious threads—were his habits, at once peculiar and rigidly consistent. Morning: arrive at work, fling his coat across the desk for an assistant to retrieve, and bark out the names of the four or five people he needed to get on the line. Sam Cohn and the telephone were a curious pair: by one estimate, the phones in his offices would ring about two hundred times per day, and he was never off of them. And yet he was one of the hardest people to reach in New York City.

"We had a rolling list every morning, called the Unreturned List," Susan Anderson, his executive assistant for twenty-eight years, recalled. "And the further you got down on the Unreturned List, the chances were likely you weren't going to be hearing from him. Because he was such a person who lived in the present that the top of the Unreturned List is pretty much what got done every day." Friends joked that his tombstone should read: "Here lies Sam Cohn. He'll get back to you."

Lunch, without fail, was at the Russian Tea Room, where Cohn had the first booth on the right. (The first booth on the left was reserved for Bernard B. Jacobs, the head of the Shubert Organization.) Cohn relished the fact that he was the only male patron not required to wear a blazer. "Oh, that guy's not wearing a jacket," the other diners would say. "It must be Sam Cohn."

Then it was back to the office until quarter to eight, when he would leave for the opera, or, more often, the theater, which he loved—he saw approximately seventy-five plays a year. After curtain call, he'd eat dinner, typically at Wally's, where he ordered the sirloin steak with peppers and onions. There, or at lunch, he met with his high-strung, high-powered cadre of friends, who were almost always his clients: Bob Fosse, Roy Scheider, Paddy Chayefsky, Paul Mazursky. "It was never one on one," recalled Arlene Donovan, who worked in the literary department. "It was like one on five."

The next morning, he'd start the crazy routine again: dodging calls, making deals. New York (midtown, specifically) was his universe. He loathed Los Angeles, which he considered a cultural desert, and spent as little time there as someone in the movie business possibly could. At the Oscars, which he attended grudgingly, he'd sit and read the *New York Times*. "I can't stay longer," he'd say, running to catch a redeye. "I'm afraid I'll like it." But he never did.

Of all Cohn's eccentricities, the strangest was his tendency to eat paper. Newspapers, matchbooks, screenplays: somehow they'd end up wadded into little balls in his mouth, before he deposited the remains in an ashtray. He would rent a car at the Los Angeles airport and eat the claim check before reaching the garage. "One time, he was supposed to meet me somewhere," Donovan recalled, "and he ate the paper about where he was supposed to meet me." Another time, a seven-figure check arrived for his client Mike Nichols, who had sold some fine art. It had to be reissued after Cohn unconsciously ingested the signature.

By 1978, one of the few people who could break through the bulwark of Cohn's telephone line was Meryl Streep. As a compulsive theater-goer, he knew what she was capable of before Hollywood did. Unlike his inner circle of nebbishy middle-aged men, she was like a daughter to be doted on. (Along with Robert Brustein and Joe Papp, she was lousy with Jewish father figures.) He didn't consider most people smart, but Meryl was smart.

"He was in awe of her," Donovan said. "And he was very careful in her selection of material." Cohn saw Meryl as she saw herself: as an actress, not a starlet. But he also knew how big a career she could have. It was just a matter of picking the right projects. No shlock.

"She wasn't making the kind of money that being in a blockbuster would have afforded her," Anderson said. "But that was never the plan. The plan for Sam was always quality first."

At the moment, there was a screenplay on his desk that hadn't yet been chewed up into spitballs. It was written by another client, Robert Benton, based on a novel by Avery Corman, and it was called *Kramer vs. Kramer.*

UNTIL AVERY CORMAN was eleven years old, he believed his father was dead. In the Bronx apartment where he lived with his mother and sister, the man was seldom discussed. When pressed, his mother said he'd been killed in the Canadian Army. Later, the story shifted to a car crash. Avery got suspicious.

One day around 1947, he was playing cards with his aunt and told her that some boys at school had teased him for being fatherless. This was a lie. "Do you want to know where your father is?" his aunt, who was deaf, said in sign language. She swore him to secrecy.

"California."

Avery fished out the truth by means of another lie. He told his mother brightly, "If your father is dead, you have to be bar mitzvah-ed at twelve and not thirteen because you have to become a man earlier in the Jewish religion." As the boy was about to turn twelve, she had no choice but to sit him down in the living room and confess that his father was alive.

The details spilled out: Avery's father had always struggled to hold down a job. He'd sold newspapers and been fired. He ran a shoe store, but it went under. As his debts mounted, he resorted to gambling—Avery's mother was still paying off a collection agency on his behalf. At one point, Avery learned later, he'd been caught robbing a candy store. He had filed divorce papers in 1944, making Avery's mother one of the only divorced women in the neighborhood. "I told you he was dead," she said, "because he's as good as dead."

Three decades later, Corman was living on East Eighty-eighth Street with his two small sons and his wife of ten years, Judy Corman.

His novel *Oh, God!* had brought him some acclaim, especially after it was made into a movie starring George Burns. His father had called him once, when Avery was twenty-six; the conversation was fruitless, and for years he did nothing. By the time he hired a private detective to learn more, his father had been dead for six years.

For now, Avery concentrated on being the husband and parent his father never was. When he met Judy, she was a music publicist, but now she stayed home with the kids, taking an occasional job as an interior decorator. She didn't mind not working full time, but it wasn't the fashion. In 1974, she joined a women's consciousness-raising group, one of many that were sprouting up in living rooms and church basements across the country. Each member would speak on a topic—anything from breast-feeding to orgasms—the idea being to organize women into a self-empowered political class. Judy did and didn't fit in. At one meeting, she asked the group, "If we met at a party and you asked me what I did, and I said I was home with two young children, what would you do?" One woman admitted she'd probably go talk to someone else across the room.

Inspired by what she heard at the group, Judy created a fixed schedule dividing domestic responsibilities between her and Avery. Whoever shopped for dinner also cooked and did the dishes, giving the other person an uninterrupted night off. The experiment fell apart after six months. Their older son, Matthew, had little concept of one parent being on duty or off, and would constantly disrupt Avery's writing. The bulk of the childcare fell back to Judy.

Avery began noticing something he didn't care for in the women's movement. "I could not reconcile some of the rhetoric I was hearing with my own personal experience as a father, as well as the personal experiences of many of the men I knew," he said later. "It seemed to me that the rhetoric from feminists was lumping all men together in one box as just a whole bunch of bad guys."

Avery felt that there was an entire precinct going unrecorded: good fathers. From what he could tell, the loudest voices of the feminist movement were those of unmarried women, who were more qualified to tackle workplace inequality than to dictate how married men and women should behave at home. Not only that: he had seen some seemingly happy relationships collapse after the woman aired her grievances at a consciousness-raising group. One friend's wife had even walked out on her marriage. "I saw a few examples of what we would call self-absorption and narcissism in the service of fulfilling one's personal destiny," he recalled.

In these disconcerting trends, Avery saw the makings of his next novel, one that would counteract the "toxic rhetoric" he was hearing and make the case for the good father. His protagonist was Ted Kramer, a thirtysomething workaholic New Yorker who sells ad space for men's magazines. He has a wife, Joanna, and a little boy named Billy. In the early chapters, their marriage is portrayed as superficially content, with wells of ennui underneath.

The problem is Joanna Kramer. Described as "a striking, slender woman with long, black hair, a thin elegant nose, large brown eyes, and somewhat chesty for her frame," she quickly finds that motherhood is, by and large, "boring." She tires of playing with blocks and of discussing potty training with other mothers. When she suggests to Ted that she might want to return to her job at an advertising firm, he balks—after the babysitting fees, they'd end up *losing* money. She starts taking tennis lessons. Sex with Ted is mechanical. Finally, about fifty pages in, Joanna informs Ted that she's "suffocating." She's leaving him, and she's leaving Billy.

"Feminists will applaud me," she says.

"What feminists? I don't see any feminists," he snarls back.

After that, Joanna more or less disappears. Ted gets over his shock, hires a nanny, and gets back into the swing of single life. More important, he learns how to be a good father. The turning point comes when Billy falls and slashes his face. Ted rushes him to the emergency room, standing close as the doctor stitches him up. The child, who once seemed alien to Ted, is now "linked to his nervous system."

It is at this revelatory moment that Joanna does the unthinkable: she returns and tells Ted she wants custody. Having undergone a journey of self-discovery in California, she is now fit to be a mother. The ensuing custody battle, which gives the novel its title, lays bare the ugliness of divorce proceedings and the wounds they allow people to inflict on each other. The judge awards custody to Joanna, but in the final pages she has a change of heart and leaves the boy in the care of his father.

As Avery wrote the climactic court scenes, Judy came down with pneumonia. Saddled again with the household chores, he struggled to get to the final page. When his wife read the manuscript, she was pleased to see that Joanna hadn't been demonized. "That was my main concern," she said when it was published, "how the woman was going to be portrayed." Still, in the wrenching last chapters, it's hard to see Joanna as anything but an obstacle between father and son, who now share a loving bond, and an exemplar of the "narcissism" Avery had observed in his social circle.

The novel was destined to hit a nerve. Divorce had become a staple of American life, with the trend line only going up. In 1975, divorces in the United States passed the million-per-year mark, more than double the number recorded a decade earlier. When *Kramer vs. Kramer* was published, many readers assumed that it was the story of Avery Corman's own awful divorce. In fact, he was happily married, and would be for thirty-seven years, until Judy's death. What almost no one realized—"the Rosebud," he said—was that the author was the child of divorce. He wasn't Ted Kramer. He was Billy Kramer.

Before *Kramer vs. Kramer* even hit the bookstores, the manuscript fell into the hands of Richard Fischoff, a young film executive who had just accepted a job with the producer Stanley Jaffe. Fischoff read the book overnight in Palm Springs. He thought it tapped into something new: the divorce phenomenon from a father's point of view, allowing that the man's side of the story had the same "range, depth, and complexity of feeling" as the woman's. It was the first property he brought to Jaffe's attention.

Ted Kramer reminded Fischoff of an older version of Benjamin Braddock, the character played by Dustin Hoffman in *The Graduate*. In perhaps the most indelible screen image of the sixties, Benjamin ends the film in the back of a bus with his beloved Elaine, having rescued her from her own wedding to someone else. Riding off into their future, their exhilarated faces melt into ambiguity and something like fear. Did they think this through? What really lies ahead? Ted and Joanna Kramer, Fischoff thought, were Benjamin and Elaine ten years later, after their impulsive union has collapsed from the inside. The movie would be a kind of generational marker, tracking the baby boomers from the heedlessness of young adulthood to the angst of middle adulthood. No one was yet calling people like the Kramers "yuppies," but their defining neuroses were already in place.

Jaffe had gone through a difficult divorce involving two young children, so Fischoff knew the book would resonate with him. It did. What they needed next was a director, and Jaffe went to Robert Benton. Kindhearted and approachable, with a rumpled white beard (his friend Liz Smith called him "Professor Bear"), Benton, as everyone called him, was best known for cowriting *Bonnie and Clyde*. Jaffe had produced his first directorial feature, *Bad Company*, and Benton was presently in Germany promoting his second, *The Late Show*. He had already read and rejected *Kramer vs. Kramer*, after getting the manuscript from Arlene Donovan, Avery's agent at ICM. Unlike his previous work, *Kramer* was completely character-driven. *How am I going to do this?* he thought. *Nobody carries a gun.*

Benton thought of writing the screenplay for his friend François Truffaut to direct, but the French auteur had other projects lined up. Jaffe wanted to move fast, and started talking to other directors. Benton, meanwhile, was working on a draft of an art-world whodunit called *Stab*, which would later become the Meryl Streep movie *Still of the Night*. When he showed the screenplay to Sam Cohn, the agent told him, "This is terrible." (It probably tasted bad, too.) Scrambling for a directing project, Benton asked Jaffe if *Kramer* was still available. The producer reached him in Berlin to tell him it was.

Everyone liked the idea of a spiritual sequel to *The Graduate*, which meant that the one and only choice for Ted Kramer was Dustin Hoffman. *Midnight Cowboy* and *All the President's Men* had made the forty-year-old actor the era's antsy everyman, but he was now at one of the lowest points of his life. Amid contentious experiences filming *Straight Time* and *Agatha*, he was mired in lawsuits and countersuits and had decided to quit movies and go back to the theater, where he'd have more creative control. He was in the middle of an emotional separation from his wife, Anne Byrne, with whom he had two daughters. She wanted to pursue her acting and dancing career; Dustin objected. "I was getting divorced, I'd been partying with drugs, and it depleted me in every way," he said later. Instead of endearing him to *Kramer*, as with Stanley Jaffe, the familiarity of the material repelled him. He sent word to Jaffe and Benton that the character didn't ring true: "not active enough."

Taking the criticism to heart, Benton rewrote the script. In the winter of 1977, he and Jaffe flew to London, where Dustin was still filming *Agatha*. At four in the afternoon, they went to the Inn on the Park and found the actor alone in the lobby. Benton knew immediately he was going to say no—otherwise, he would have invited them up to his room. When they went to sit for tea, the maître d' apologized that there were no free tables. They had no choice but to go up to Dustin's suite, where the three men talked for more than two hours. Benton laid out the case, dad to dad: "This is a movie about being a father." (His son went to preschool with Dustin's oldest daughter.) By the end of dinner the next night, Dustin had agreed to play Ted.

Back in New York, the trio met at a suite at the Carlyle Hotel, where they spent a week hashing out the script, working twelve-hour days. "It was almost like group therapy: talking, talking, knowing that no one would repeat outside what was being said," Jaffe recalled. With a tape recorder on, Benton and Dustin would spiral off into "what if"s, until Jaffe reeled them back in. Benton's aim was to tailor the script to Dustin, "like fitting a suit." Minor characters from the novel—the grandparents, the nanny—fell away, leaving a taut chamber drama in which every moment throbbed with emotion. The "spine" they agreed on, Dustin would recall, is that "what makes divorce so painful is that the love doesn't end."

The men wrote as fathers and as husbands, as people who had loved and failed and picked up the pieces. But, as they refashioned the script in their own image, the thing they were missing was the voice of Joanna Kramer, the woman who abandons her child and then reclaims him for reasons she is barely able to articulate. In the case of *Kramer vs. Kramer*, the scales of dramatic justice were weighed decidedly toward Ted. "We didn't do that much work on Joanna," Benton recalled. "Now that I think back on it, probably because Joanna wasn't in the room."

JOE PAPP HAD once again coaxed a traumatized actor from the brink, offering a renewed life on the stage. This time the actor was Meryl Streep, and the play was *The Taming of the Shrew*, which he announced for the 1978 summer season at Shakespeare in the Park. Meryl was playing the shrew.

It was a bold choice: an all-out war of the sexes in which a man turns a headstrong woman into an obedient wife. In Shakespeare's plot, the demure Bianca cannot wed until a husband is found for her older sister, Katherina, known throughout Padua as an "irksome, brawling scold." In comes Petruchio to woo the unruly Kate, whom he starves, deprives of sleep, and practically abducts in his quest to domesticate her.

Clearly, the play was at odds with the consciousness-raised New York City of 1978. In modern times, directors had undercut the play in every which way, trying to make sense of what seemed like a sexist broadside. How could any self-respecting actress deliver the final monologue, a paean to feminine submission?

I am ashamed that women are so simple
To offer war where they should kneel for peace,
Or seek for rule, supremacy and sway,
When they are bound to serve, love and obey.

One day, Meryl sat in a rehearsal room at the Public, her skirt hiked up to reveal two red kneepads—protection for Act II, Scene i, Kate's first knockout brawl with Petruchio. Beside her was her leading man, Raúl Juliá.

With his flamenco dancer's physique and peacock's flair, Juliá seasoned Shakespeare's blank verse with piquant Latin cadences. "She swings as sweetly as the nightingale," he said, reciting a line. Then he caught himself—"Jesu Christ!"—and leaped out of his chair. "*Sings*. She *sings* as sweetly as the nightingale."

Picking up on his flub, Meryl snapped her fingers and swing-danced in her chair. When she first met Raúl, she was "terrified" by the sheer size of his eyes, his gestures, his smile. As she came to discover, he was an engine of combustible joy. At one point, he stopped a rehearsal mid-scene to declare, "The girl is an *acting factory*!" If anyone could match his live-wire machismo, zinger for zinger, it was Meryl.

To her, the play was perfectly compatible with the women's movement, if you saw it—and acted it—with the right slant. In preparation, she was reading Germaine Greer's *The Female Eunuch*, one of the sharpest polemics of second-wave feminism, which argued that women are victims of their own enforced passivity, muzzled by a male-supremacist society that seeks to repress the female sexual instinct. Greer wrote of Kate and Petruchio, "He wants her spirit and her energy because he wants a wife worth keeping. He tames her as he might a hawk or a high-mettled horse, and she rewards him with strong sexual love and fierce loyalty." Imagine a woman like Greer succumbing to the charms of Petruchio, who calls his conquest "my goods, my chattels." What contortion of the will would it take?

Meryl found the answer between the verses. "Feminists tend to see this play as a one-way ticket for the man, but Petruchio really gives a great deal," she told a reporter. "It's a vile distortion of the play to ever have *him* striking *her*. Shakespeare doesn't do it, so why impose it? This is not a sadomasochistic show. What Petruchio does is bring a sense of verve and love to somebody who is mean and angry. He's one of those Shakespearean men who walk in from another town. They always know more, see through things. He helps her take all that passion and put it in a more lovely place."

A year ago, her answer might have been different, her judgment of Kate harsher. But in talking about "giving," she was talking about her months at John Cazale's bedside. "I've learned something about that," she continued. "If you're really giving, you're totally fulfilled." She had put a man's needs before her own and come out more fully human—a counterintuitive feminist principle if there ever was one. Now she would have to stand in front of a crowd of Manhattanites and exhort the women to "place your hands below your husband's foot."

"What I'm saying is, I'll do *anything* for this man," she reasoned. "Look, would there be any hang-up if this were a mother talking about her son? So why is selflessness here wrong? Service is the only thing that's important about love. Everybody is worrying about 'losing yourself'—all this narcissism. Duty. We can't stand that idea now either. It has the real ugly slave-driving connotation. But duty might be a suit of armor you put on to fight for your love."

In a way, Petruchio reminded her of John, the way he had stripped her down to the essentials: "you don't need this," "you don't need that." In their darkest hours, only the life she gave him remained, and "losing yourself" hadn't been a question. That truth still guided her like a torch, not just through Shakespeare but through her breakneck romance with Don Gummer. On afternoons, they would go to museums; he'd see shapes, she'd see characters. Or vice versa. "She's learned how to look at objects and I've learned how to look at people," as Don put it soon after. Theirs was a bond built on "a very deep-rooted feeling of trust," he said, as sturdy and foundational as the concrete base of one of his sculptures.

It was this Meryl Streep—simultaneously grieving and infatuated—who got word from Sam Cohn about a possible role in *Kramer vs. Kramer*. The part of Joanna had been given to someone else: Kate Jackson, the "smart one" on *Charlie's Angels*. Jackson had the name recognition and the crystalline beauty that Columbia Pictures required. But the negotiations had hit a snag when Aaron Spelling asked for a firm stop date, so that Jackson could get back to production on *Angels*. The *Kramer* team knew they couldn't guarantee one, and Spelling wouldn't bend his schedule. Jackson was forced to pull out of the film, kicking and screaming.

According to Richard Fischoff, who was billed as associate producer, the studio sent over a list of possible replacements, essentially a catalog of the bankable female stars of the day: Ali MacGraw, Faye Dunaway, even Jane Fonda. Katharine Ross, who had played Elaine in *The Graduate*, was a natural contender. With *The Deer Hunter* still in postproduction, the name Meryl Streep meant nothing to the West Coast, apart from sounding like a Dutch pastry. But she and Benton shared an agent, and if anyone knew how to get someone into an audition room, it was Sam Cohn.

Meryl had met Dustin Hoffman before, and it hadn't gone well. During drama school, she auditioned for *All Over Town*, a Broadway play he was directing. "I'm Dustin"—*burp*—"Hoffman," he said, before putting his hand on her breast, according to her. *What an obnoxious pig*, she thought.

Now surer of herself, she marched into the hotel suite where Hoffman, Benton, and Jaffe sat side by side. She had read Avery's novel and found Joanna to be "an ogre, a princess, an ass." When Dustin asked her what she thought of the story, she told him in no uncertain terms. They had the character all wrong, she insisted. Her reasons for leaving Ted are too hazy. We should understand why she comes back for custody. When she gives up Billy in the final scene, it should be for the boy's sake, not hers. Joanna isn't a villain; she's a reflection of a real struggle that women are going through across the country, and the audience should feel some sympathy for her. If they wanted Meryl, they'd need to do rewrites.

The trio was taken aback, mostly because they hadn't called her in for Joanna in the first place. They were thinking of her for the minor role of Phyllis, the one-night stand. Somehow she'd gotten the wrong message. Still, she seemed to understand the character instinctively. Maybe this was their Joanna after all?

That, at least, was Meryl's version. The story the men told was completely different. "It was, for all intents and purposes, the worst meeting anybody ever had with anybody," Benton recalled. "She said a few things, not much. And she just listened. She was polite and nice, but it was—she was just barely there." Dustin said, "She never opened her mouth. She never said a word. She just sat there."

When Meryl left the room, Stanley Jaffe was dumbfounded. "What is her name—Merle?" he said, thinking box office.

Benton turned to Dustin. Dustin turned to Benton. "That's Joanna," Dustin said. The reason was John Cazale. He knew that Meryl had lost him months earlier, and from what he saw, she was still shaken to the core. That's what would fix the Joanna problem: an actress who could draw on a still fresh pain, who was herself in the thick of emotional turmoil. It was Meryl's weakness, not her strength, that convinced him.

Benton agreed. "There was a fragile quality she had that made us think that this was Joanna, without making her neurotic," he said. "Meryl's Joanna wasn't neurotic, but she was vulnerable, frail." According to the director, she had never been considered for Phyllis. It was always for the role of Joanna.

Clearly, there was a discrepancy between what they saw and how Meryl saw herself. Was she a fearless advocate, telling three powerful men exactly what their script was missing? Or was she a basket case whose raw grief was written all over her face? Was she Germaine Greer or "barely there"? Whichever Meryl Streep walked out of that hotel room, she got the part.

THE WOMAN IS *in profile, eyes cast down on her child's bed. Her chin rests on her hand, which sports a gold wedding band. Lit by the glow of a lamp covered by a red handkerchief, her face is all cheekbones and shadows, an ambivalent chiaroscuro. She could pass for a Vermeer.*

"I love you, Billy," she says.

She leans down and kisses the boy, then packs a bag.

It was the first day of principal photography on *Kramer vs. Kramer*, and everything was hushed in the 20th Century Fox soundstage at Fifty-fourth Street and Tenth Avenue. Robert Benton was so anxious he could hear his stomach grumbling, which only made him more anxious, since he worried the sound might wind up in the shot.

The little boy under the covers was Justin Henry, a sweet-faced seven-year-old from Rye, New York. In her search for a kid who could play Dustin Hoffman's son, the casting director, Shirley Rich, had looked at hundreds of boys. The blond, cherubic Justin Henry hadn't seemed right to Dustin, who wanted a "funny-looking kid" who looked like him. But Justin's tender, familial way with Dustin in screen tests changed his mind, along with the realization that Billy Kramer shouldn't look like Dustin. He should look like Meryl: a constant reminder of the absent Joanna.

Getting Meryl past the studio hadn't been easy. Some of the marketing executives at Columbia thought she wasn't pretty enough. "They didn't think that she was a movie star. They thought that she was a character actress," Richard Fischoff said, describing exactly how Meryl saw herself. But she had her advocates, including Dustin Hoffman and Robert Benton, and that was enough to twist some arms.

In preparation, Meryl flipped through magazines like *Cosmopolitan* and *Glamour*, the kind Joanna might read. (Meryl hadn't bothered with beauty magazines since high school.) They all featured profiles of working mothers, brilliant judges who were raising five adorable children. The assumption now was that any woman could do both: the dreaded cliché of "having it all." But what about the Joanna Kramers, who couldn't manage either? Meryl called her mother, Mary Wolf, who told her: "All my friends at one point or another wanted to throw up their hands and leave and see if there was another way of doing their lives."

She sat in a playground in Central Park and watched the Upper East Side mothers with their perambulators, trying to outdo one another. As she soaked in the atmosphere—muted traffic noises, chirping birds—she thought about the "dilemma of how to be a woman, how to be a mother, all the gobbledygook about 'finding yourself.'" Most of her friends were actors in their late twenties who didn't have children, women at their peak career potential, which, paradoxically, was the height of their baby-making potential. Part of her wished she'd had kids when she was twenty-two. By now, she'd have a seven-year-old.

She thought about Joanna Kramer, who *did* have a seven-year-old, who looked at those same super-women in the magazines and felt she couldn't hack it. "The more I thought about it," Meryl said, "the more I felt the sensual reason for Joanna's leaving, the emotional reasons, the ones that aren't attached to logic. Joanna's daddy took care of her. Her college took care of her. Then Ted took care of her. Suddenly she just felt incapable of caring for herself." In other words, she was nothing like Meryl Streep, who had always felt supremely capable.

While brushing her teeth one morning, she thought about Margaret Mead, the famed anthropologist who had journeyed to Samoa and New Guinea. Meryl was reading her memoir, *Blackberry Winter*. It occurred to her that people outside an experience often have greater insight than the ones living it. Mead had wed her own instincts with the power of observation and gotten at something very deep. Unlike Joanna Kramer, Meryl wasn't a mother or a wife, and she didn't live on the Upper East Side. But she could travel there in her imagination, just as Mead had traveled to the South Pacific.

"I did *Kramer vs. Kramer* before I had children," she said later.

"But the mother I would be was already inside me. People say, 'When you have children, everything changes.' But maybe things are awakened that were already there. I think actors can awaken things that are in all of us: our evil, our cruelty, our grace. Actors can call these things up more easily than other people."

Before shooting, Dustin, Meryl, and Justin had gone to Central Park with a photographer to pose for blissful group portraits. These were the photos that would decorate the Kramer household, snapshots of a once happy family. Benton had wisely cut the first part of the novel, showing the buildup to Joanna's departure. The movie would start on the night she leaves—the night the bomb goes off in Ted Kramer's life.

When he first saw the set, Dustin said, "My character wouldn't live in this apartment." The whole thing was quickly redesigned to fit whatever was in his head. Unlike with most films, they would shoot the scenes in order, the reason being their seven-year-old costar. To make the story real to Justin, they would tell him only what was happening that day, so he could *experience* it instead of *acting* it, which would inevitably come off as phony. His direction would be communicated solely through Dustin, as a way of bonding onscreen father and son.

On the second day, they continued shooting the opening scene, when Ted follows the hysterical Joanna into the hallway. They shot the bulk of it in the morning, and then after lunch set up for some reaction shots. Dustin and Meryl took their positions on the other side of the apartment door. Then something happened that shocked not just Meryl but everyone on set. Right before their entrance, Dustin slapped her hard across the cheek, leaving a red mark in the shape of his hand.

Benton heard the slap and saw Meryl charge into the hallway. *We're dead*, he thought. *The picture's dead. She's going to bring us up with the Screen Actors Guild.*

Instead, Meryl went on and acted the scene.

Clutching Joanna's trench coat, she pleaded with Ted, "Don't make me go in there!" As far as she was concerned, she could conjure

Joanna's distress without taking a smack to the face, but Dustin had taken extra measures. And he wasn't done.

In her last tearful moments, Joanna tells Ted that she doesn't love him anymore, and that she's not taking Billy with her. The cameras set up on Meryl in the elevator, with Dustin acting his part offscreen.

Improvising his lines, Dustin delivered a slap of a different sort: outside the elevator, he started taunting Meryl about John Cazale, jabbing her with remarks about his cancer and his death. "He was goading her and provoking her," Fischoff recalled, "using stuff that he knew about her personal life and about John to get the response that he *thought* she should be giving in the performance."

Meryl, Fischoff said, went "absolutely white." She had done her work and thought through the part—she didn't need Dustin throwing shit at her. This was just like Allan Miller in her first year at Yale, pushing her to mine her own pain for *Major Barbara*. She wasn't that kind of actress. Like Margaret Mead, she could get where she needed to go with imagination and empathy. And if Dustin wanted to use Method techniques like emotional recall, he should use them on himself. Not her.

They wrapped, and Meryl left the studio in a rage. Day 2, and *Kramer vs. Kramer* was already turning into Streep vs. Hoffman.

WOODY ALLEN WAS making his next picture in luminous black and white, which is how he saw his subject, Manhattan. Coming off of *Annie Hall* and *Interiors*, he'd established himself as the chronicler of the modern urban neurotic: the squash players and the therapy-seekers and the name-droppers he met at Elaine's, where he ate dinner nearly every night for ten years.

Meryl arrived one morning at Washington Mews, a gated row of houses just north of Washington Square Park. She was there to film two short scenes for *Manhattan*, playing Woody's ex-wife, Jill. For a comedy, the mood on set was dead serious: no joking around. The director sat in a corner, reading Chekhov. He said very little, even to the actress he had hired to belittle him.

It was a small part, requiring only three days' work. That's all she had anyway, given that she was also acting in *Kramer vs. Kramer* and *The Taming of the Shrew*. Woody's longtime casting director, Juliet Taylor, recalled feeling "very, very lucky" to get her—so white-hot was the buzz that had attached itself to her name, even with *The Deer Hunter* still six months from release.

Of the film's constellation of women, Jill was easily the least developed: "more of an authors' idea than a character," according to Woody's cowriter, Marshall Brickman. Unlike Diane Keaton's pretentious journalist or Mariel Hemingway's underaged ingénue, or even the oblivious hausfrau played by Anne Byrne—Dustin Hoffman's real-life estranged wife—Jill is more talked about (derisively) than seen. Having left Woody's character, Isaac, for another woman, she is now penning a devastating memoir of their relationship, *Marriage, Divorce, and Selfhood*, which reveals not only Isaac's sexual foibles but the fact that he cries during *Gone With the Wind*. For Allen, who had been divorced twice, she was clearly the manifestation of some Freudian anxiety: a woman who castrates her husband not just once, with lesbianism, but again, with public humiliation. "I think he just hated my character," Meryl said later.

Taylor, who had done casting for *Julia*, needed someone with "dimension," who could bring fullness to a part that was "maybe even slightly underwritten." There wasn't much chance to dig deeper. As was Woody's custom, Meryl got her six pages shortly before filming; only a select few got to read the whole script. Over at *Kramer vs. Kramer*, Benton encouraged the actors to improvise, treating his own screenplay as a mere blueprint. At *Manhattan*, the script was more like scripture. "Woody would say, 'Um, there's a comma in the middle of that sentence,'" Meryl would recall. "'It's there for a reason, and maybe you should just do it the way it's written.'"

When she got to the set, she introduced herself to Karen Ludwig, the woman playing her lover. In the scene they were about to shoot, Isaac shows up at their door to pick up his son and pleads with Jill not to publish the memoir. (This is after he stalks her on the street, begging her not to write about their marriage.) Jill accuses him of trying to run her lover over with his car. Upon meeting, the two actresses had only moments to establish their screen relationship.

"Let's pretend that we've just made passionate love on the kitchen table," Meryl told Ludwig.

"Okay," Ludwig said. She took off her chunky turquoise necklace and gave it to Meryl—a secret token of their intimacy.

Woody got up from his chair and called "Action." Then he was "Isaac," the bumbling television writer, in love with Groucho Marx and Swedish movies and the second movement of the *Jupiter* Symphony, and a mess when it came to everything else, especially women. As in all her scenes, Meryl's job was to keep moving—clearing the table, gliding from room to room—like a morose firefly Isaac can never quite catch in his net. None of the three actors made eye contact. But the erotic secret Meryl had concocted with Ludwig made Isaac seem like even more of an intruder, a man always chasing after a woman's turned back.

Despite her short screen time, Meryl would leave a memorable mark on the film, her silk hair and darting frame more a compositional element than a person. "I don't think Woody Allen even remembers me," she said two years later. "I went to see *Manhattan* and I felt like I wasn't even in it. I was pleased with the film because I looked pretty in it and I thought it was entertaining. But I only worked on the film for three days, and I didn't get to know Woody. Who gets to know Woody? He's very much of a womanizer, very self-involved."

The urbane world that Woody had created didn't impress her, either—more of the "narcissism" that she, like Avery Corman, saw pervading the culture. "On a certain level, the film offends me because it's about all these people whose sole concern is discussing their emotional states or their neuroses," she remarked at the time. "It's sad, because Woody has the potential to be America's Chekhov, but instead, he's still caught up in the jet-set crowd type of life and trivializing his talent."

*　　*　　*

ACROSS A SMALL table covered in a checkerboard cloth, Dustin Hoffman glared at Meryl Streep. The crew had taken over J. G. Melon, a burger joint on Third Avenue and Seventy-fourth Street. Today's pages: a pivotal scene in *Kramer vs. Kramer*, in which Joanna informs Ted that she plans to take back their son.

The weeks had been fraught, and Benton was panicking. "I was in unfamiliar territory," he said: no guns, no outlaws. "The suspense had simply to do with emotion, not anything physical." Benton and his wife had planned to take their son skiing in Europe after the shoot. But two-thirds of the way through, convinced he was never going to work again, he came home and told his wife, "Cancel the trip. We need to save all the money we have."

Dustin, meanwhile, had been driving everyone nuts. In his effort to fill every screen moment with tension, he would locate the particular vulnerability of his scene partner and exploit it. For little Justin Henry, who experienced the story day by day, Dustin's methods elicited a child performance of uncommon nuance. Before playing a serious scene, Dustin would tell him to imagine his dog dying. For the harrowing sequence in which Billy falls from the monkey bars at the playground, Justin had to lie on the pavement and cry through fake blood. Knowing how Justin had befriended the crew, Dustin crouched over and explained that film families are temporary, and he would probably never see his pals again.

"You know Eddie?" Dustin said, pointing to a crew guy. "You may not see him."

Justin burst into tears. Even after the scene was done, he couldn't stop sobbing.

"Did it feel like you did a good job?" Dustin asked him.

"Y-yeah."

"How do you feel about that—when you do a scene you really cry?"

"T-terrific."

"You're an actor, then."

With his grown-up costars, Dustin's tactics had more mixed success. Gail Strickland, the actress hired to play Ted's neighbor Margaret, was so rattled by the intensity of their scenes that she developed a nervous stammer within the first few days. When it became clear that most of her dialogue would be unusable, she was replaced by Jane Alexander. (The papers reported "artistic differences.") Alexander had acted with Dustin in *All the President's Men* and enjoyed his "febrile" way of working. She was taken aback, though, when she told Dustin she didn't care to watch the dailies and he responded, "You're a fucking fool if you don't."

Then there was Meryl. Unlike Strickland, she hadn't buckled when Dustin identified her vulnerability. When asked, she'd say she regarded him like one of her kid brothers, always seeing how far he could push. "I never saw one moment of emotion leak out of her except in performance," Benton said. She thought of the movie as work, not as a psychological minefield.

At the moment, she had a question. The way the restaurant scene was written, Joanna starts off by telling Ted that she wants custody of Billy. Then, as Ted berates her, she explains that all her life she's felt like "somebody's wife or somebody's mother or somebody's daughter." Only now, after going to California and finding a therapist and a job, does she have the wherewithal to take care of her son.

Wouldn't it be better, Meryl asked on set, if Joanna made the "somebody's wife" speech *before* revealing her intention to take Billy? That way, Joanna could present her quest for selfhood as a legitimate pursuit, at least as the character saw it. She could say it calmly, not in a defensive crouch. Benton agreed that restructuring the scene gave it more of a dramatic build.

But Dustin was pissed. "Meryl, why don't you stop carrying the flag for feminism and just *act the scene*," he said. Just like Joanna, she was butting in and mucking everything up. Reality and fiction had become blurry. When Dustin looked across the table, he saw not just an actress making a scene suggestion but shades of Anne Byrne, his soon-to-be ex-wife. In Joanna Kramer, and by extension Meryl Streep, he saw the woman making his life hell.

In any case, Dustin had a scene suggestion of his own, one he kept secret from Meryl. Between takes, he approached the cameraman and leaned in, as if they were plotting a jailbreak. "See that glass there on the table?" he said, nodding toward his white wine. "If I whack that before I leave"—he promised to be careful—"have you got it in the shot?"

"Just move it a little bit to the left," the guy said out of the corner of his mouth.

Dustin sat back down. "Action!"

In the next take, Dustin's agitation was palpable. *"Don't talk to me that way,"* Ted says at the end of the scene, wagging his finger in Joanna's face. Then, as he stood up, Dustin smacked the wineglass and shattered it on the restaurant wall, its contents bursting in a deafening splat. Meryl jumped in her chair, authentically startled. "Next time you do that, I'd appreciate you letting me know," she said.

There were shards of glass in her hair. The camera caught the whole thing.

"DEAR MR. PAPP," wrote a resident of 5 Jane Street:

> *Last week I saw the Festival's production of the Taming of the*
> *Shrew in Central Park and found it so offensive that I feel obliged*
> *to protest both your choice of the play and the interpretation it*
> *was given.*
>
> *At best, it can only be called insensitive to put on a play that*
> *celebrates the subjugation of women. But to play it straight,*
> *without any acknowledgment of the dehumanization and*
> *suffering inflicted on women by the canon of male dominance, is*
> *an act of aggression against women.*
>
> *It is particularly ironic that you should choose to celebrate*

*the oppression of women this year. Just a month or two ago,
the New York Police Department, under pressure of a lawsuit
brought by battered women, agreed for the first time to start
enforcing the laws against assault, battery, and attempted
murder where women have been attacked by their husbands.
Right now, after six years of politicking and back room deals,
this country is still denying women the constitutional right to
equal protection of the law.*

*If discrimination, rape, exploitation, and myths of the
inferiority of women were mere antiquities, I too could laugh
at the Taming of the Shrew. But I still have to get home from
the theater by public transportation and be on my guard
against the male criminals who think I'm an easy or deserving
target because I'm a woman. I still have to earn my living in
competition with men who are never held back by the notion that
their true vocation is raising children. I still have to pay taxes
to support programs like yours, which ennoble my oppression
and call it culture.*

*I have urged all my friends to boycott this production, but the
more I think about it, I think we really should be picketing it.*

August, 1978. Onstage at the Delacorte, Meryl Streep and Raúl
Juliá came at each other like poet gladiators, unleashing a nightly ar-
senal of wit and wordplay and physical force. Meryl, in her unkempt
strawberry curls, would come on doing chin-ups, hike up her skirt,
stomp on some shrubbery, then wail and slap and spit in Petruchio's
face. Raúl, strutting in his black boots, would throw her over his knees,
grab her ankles and tickle her feet, wrestle her to the ground and then
sit on her like a stool. And that was just Act II, Scene i.

It was love as blood sport, and the riled-up spectators were willing participants. When a sweaty, snarling Petruchio called Kate "my
horse, my ox, my ass, my anything," in Act III, he'd get an eruption

of applause, followed by a smattering of boos, then a few whistles and, finally, some nervous laughter. One night, Raúl threw a piece of "mutton" and accidentally hit a woman in the audience ("but she was not injured," the stage manager reported).

At intermission, the battle of the sexes continued. "I can't believe how many people were applauding when he did that 'my horse, my ass' bit!" a young woman in the audience said one night.

"That scene is a good representation of what our relationship strives to be," her boyfriend quipped, as the woman rolled her eyes.

During one performance, a documentary crew followed Meryl into her dressing room, where she opined on Kate the Shrew. "She lives in a very—a highly conventional society where brides are bought and sold. This is a society that *constricts her*," she said, choking on the words as a dresser laced up her corset. "Don't you think the corset's a little tight, girls?"

By Act V, the shrew was tamed, or at least that's how it looked. Kate's closing monologue was the hardest part to sell. How to convince a 1978 audience that wives should "serve, love and obey" their husbands? Was Kate just another brainwashed version of "the female eunuch"? If Meryl was "playing it straight," as the woman from Jane Street had it, you could certainly see it that way. But there was something else at work. When Kate advised the ladies to "place your hands below your husband's foot," Meryl would kneel at Petruchio's boot. But then Raúl would grab her palm and kiss it, lowering himself beside her as they shared a knowing gaze. Was this subjugation or an alliance?

"I feel very ambiguous," a thirtyish woman said one night after curtain call. "Yes! I feel sick. But I also say, 'Oh, isn't she lucky,' you know? And I feel sick of myself for feeling that. And it's that whole ambiguity that makes it such a fabulous play—and such a disgusting play."

Backstage, Meryl and Raúl put on a play of their own for the cameras.

MERYL:

When you give, it's the greatest happiness you can feel.

RAÚL:

The ultimate satisfaction is service, believe it or not. Man or woman.

MERYL:

That's it! Why is it so hard for someone to say, just because it's a man, that "I'd—I'd do anything for you"? Why is it so hard?

As a stagehand mended their torn costumes, she continued, "That's *love*. That's absolute selflessness. It's where the self disappears into the love that you're giving to this person."

"Exactly."

"Absolute selflessness" was what she had learned that terrible winter at John's bedside. Five months later, her life was like a one-woman repertory theater. Uptown, she was Joanna, the mother who leaves her son. Downtown, she was Jill, the wife who humiliates her husband. By night, in Central Park, she was Kate, the shrew to be tamed. Joanna, Jill, and Kate: three women who break the rules, leaving the men around them befuddled, cowed, and furious.

At *Kramer vs. Kramer*, Stanley Jaffe didn't understand how she could possibly do his movie *and* a play, not to mention *Manhattan*. But it didn't bother Meryl in the least. At Yale, she'd been trained to switch from part to part, slipping characters on and off like masks. Do it right, and they begin to speak to each other, a repertory of the mind. If anyone understood that, it was Joe Papp.

"Joe had no problem with that schedule as long as I showed up for work and chewed up the scenery nightly in the park," Meryl told his biographer. "The movie producers, on the other hand, were very nervous about whether or not I'd be able to maintain the concentration and physical stamina necessary to the part of Joanna Kramer. Joe looked at actors as dray horses, muscular and fearsome, while the movies were more prone to mollycoddling. Even now when I see Joanna Kramer in television showings of the movie, I think of her red-haired alter ego, Katherine the Shrew, spitting and sweating all over the first four rows of spectators at the Delacorte."

SHE SHOWED UP at the appointed time at Tweed Courthouse, the massive stone edifice at 52 Chambers Street. It was named after William M. Tweed, the Tammany Hall boss who embezzled funds from the construction budget, then was tried and convicted in 1873, in an unfinished courtroom of the very same building. By the time Meryl Streep arrived, 105 years later, it had long been converted into municipal offices. Now, there would be one more hearing, in the matter of *Kramer vs. Kramer*.

"We were all wrecked and tired," Robert Benton recalled. Dustin was getting sick. Everyone else was sick of Dustin. And the courtroom scene would be particularly onerous. For every shot of a witness giving testimony, Benton would need three or four reaction shots: Ted, Joanna, the judge, the opposing counsel. The whole thing would take several days.

First on the stand: Joanna Kramer. Benton had been struggling with her testimony, which he saw as absolutely crucial. It is the one chance she has to make her case—not just for custody of Billy, but for her personal dignity and, by extension, womankind. For most of the movie, she has been a phantom, with phantom motives. Then her lawyer asks, "Mrs. Kramer, can you tell the court why you are asking for custody?"

Benton had written his own version of her reply, a spin on Shylock's "If you prick us, do we not bleed?" speech from *The Merchant of Venice*:

JOANNA:

Because he's my child . . . Because I love him. I know I left my son, I know that's a terrible thing to do. Believe me, I have to live with that every day of my life. But just because I'm a woman, don't I have a right to the same hopes and dreams as a man? Don't I have a right to a life of my own? Is that so awful? Is my pain any less just because I'm a woman? Are my feelings any cheaper? I left my child—I know there is no excuse for that. But since then, I have gotten help. I have worked hard to become a whole human being. I don't think I should be punished for that. Billy's only six. He needs me. I'm not saying he doesn't need his father, but he needs me more. I'm his mother.

Benton wasn't happy with it. At the end of the second day of shooting—right after Dustin slapped her and goaded her in the elevator—the director had taken Meryl aside. "There's a speech you give in the courtroom," he told her, "but I don't think it's a woman's speech. I think it's a man trying to write a woman's speech." Would she take a crack at it? Meryl said yes. Then Benton walked home and promptly forgot he'd asked her.

Now, several weeks and many frayed nerves later, Meryl was handing the director a legal pad scrawled with her handwriting and telling him brightly, "I have the speech you told me to write." She had written it on the way back from Indiana, where she was visiting Don Gummer's parents.

Oh, why did I do that? Benton thought. He had no time for this. Now he'd have to overrule her. *I'm going to lose a friend. I'm going to lose a day of shooting. I'm going to maybe destroy a performance.*

Then he read the speech, and exhaled. It was wonderful—though about a quarter too long. Working fast, he and Meryl crossed out a few redundant lines, then had it typed up.

She took the stand in a tan blazer and a matching skirt, her hair in a ponytail flung over her left shoulder. As the cameras rolled, Meryl delivered her lines with the precarious certitude of a woman who'd rehearsed them carefully. Unlike Kate or Jill, or certainly Meryl, Joanna is always one inch from collapse, even as she reveals that her new salary as a sportswear designer is more than what Ted makes.

When it came time for the big speech, Meryl spoke the words she had written herself:

JOANNA:

Because he's my child . . . And because I love him. I know I left my son, I know that that's a terrible thing to do. Believe me, I have to live with that every day of my life. But in order to leave him, I had to believe that it was the only thing I could do. And that it was the best thing for him. I was incapable of functioning in that home, and I didn't know what the alternative was going to be. So I thought it was not best that I take him with me. However, I've since gotten some help, and I have worked very, very hard to become a whole human being. And I don't think I should be punished for that. And I don't think my little boy should be punished. Billy's only seven years old. He needs me. I'm not saying he doesn't need his father. But I really believe he needs me more. I was his mommy for five and a half years. And Ted took over that role for eighteen months. But I don't know how anybody can possibly believe that I have less of a stake in mothering that little boy than Mr. Kramer does. I'm his mother.

Tearily, she repeated, "I'm his *mother*." But the word that slayed Benton was "mommy." "I could have never imagined writing that," he said. No longer the aloof tennis addict of Avery Corman's novel, Joanna now had a vivid inner life, full of yearning and tenderness and regret.

Benton filmed the speech in wide shot first, reminding Meryl to save her energy for the close-up. But she delivered it with "the same sense of richness" each time, even when the cameras turned on Dustin for his reaction. "Part of the pleasure she must have taken is showing to Dustin she didn't need to be slapped," the director said. "She could have delivered anything to anybody at any time."

They wrapped for the day. When they returned to Tweed Courthouse, it was to shoot one of the most wrenching scenes in the film: Joanna's cross-examination by Ted's lawyer, Shaunessy, played with cowboy-like bluster by Howard Duff. Benton had taken this sequence nearly word for word from the book, and its purpose was clear: to dismantle Joanna's tenuous self-esteem in a way that even Ted finds heartless.

Right away, Shaunessy badgers Joanna with questions: Did Mr. Kramer ever strike you? Was he unfaithful? Did he drink? How many lovers have you had? Do you have one now? As Joanna begins to falter, he goes in for the kill. Hunching over her on his cane, he asks her to name the "longest personal relationship" of her life. Wasn't it with her ex-husband?

"Yes," she murmurs.

So, hadn't she failed at the most important relationship in her life?

"It did not succeed," she answers weakly.

"Not *it*, Mrs. Kramer," he bellows, sticking an accusatory finger in her face. "*You*. Were you a failure at the one most important relationship in your life? *Were you?*" It's at that moment we see the "whole human being" Joanna believes herself to be crumble before our eyes, trapped like a sea creature in a fisherman's net.

Before the take, Dustin had gone over to the witness stand to talk to Meryl. He needed her to implode on camera, and he knew the magic words to make it happen: "John Cazale." Out of Benton's earshot, he started whispering the name in her ear, planting the seeds of anguish as he had in the elevator scene. He knew she wasn't over the loss. That's why she'd gotten the part. Wasn't it?

Now, with a fat finger waving three inches from her face, Meryl heard the words "Were you a failure at the one most important relationship in your life?" Her eyes watered. Her lips tensed. Dustin had instructed her to look at him when she heard that line. When she did, he gave a little shake of his head, as if to say, "No, Meryl, you weren't a failure."

Who exactly was up on the stand? Was it the actress who had stormed into the hotel room, guns blazing, telling three powerful men to rewrite their screenplay? Wasn't that who she had always been: self-assured, proficient at everything, the girl who could swim three lengths without taking a breath? Or was Dustin right? Was she "barely there," just like Joanna Kramer?

Since *Miss Julie*, acting was the one thing that had never failed her. She had willed herself through the wasp's nest of Yale Drama School. She'd done Constance Garnett in a wheelchair, Shakespeare in the rain, Tennessee Williams in a fat suit. She'd learned Hallelujah Lil on three days' notice. She'd danced the troika and done pratfalls. There was only one problem her talent hadn't been able to solve: it hadn't kept John alive.

Had she been a failure at the most important relationship of her life? The question wasn't a fair one, but it had been asked, and answered, by Dustin Hoffman. "No," he said, with a shake of his head.

As she sat on the witness stand, defending her life, was she thinking about John? Or was she acting *despite* Dustin's meddling? By her own admission, the grief was still with her. "I didn't get over it," she said soon after. "I don't want to get over it. No matter what you do, the pain is always there in some recess of your mind, and it affects everything that happens afterwards. John's death is still very much with me. But, just as a child does, I think you can assimilate the pain and go on without making an obsession of it."

She had never believed that actors had to suffer. With almost alien precision, she could simulate any emotion she needed to. But if Meryl was now an emotional wreck playing an emotional wreck, could anyone (including her) really say whether she was faking it? Could she be "real" and a simulacrum at the exact same time?

When Benton saw Meryl glance to the side, he noticed Dustin shaking his head. "What was that? What was that?" the director said, bounding over to Dustin. Unwittingly, Dustin had created a new moment, one that Benton wanted in the scene. He turned the cameras around and had Meryl act the cross-examination again, this time recording Dustin's reactions. Now, the head shake meant something else. It was Ted Kramer telling Joanna Kramer, "No, you didn't fail as a wife. You didn't fail as a mother." Amid the rancor of the court proceeding, it was a final gesture of the love they once had.

They filmed the remaining testimonies, and the court sequence was in the can. At one point between takes, Dustin went up to the actual court stenographer they'd hired to sit behind the typewriter.

"Is this what you do?" he asked. "Divorces?"

"Oh, I did them for years," the woman said, "but I burned out. I couldn't do it anymore. It was just too painful." She added cheerfully, "I really love what I'm doing now."

"What?" Dustin asked.

"Homicides."

ON SEPTEMBER 30, 1978, an Indian-summer day, Meryl Streep married Don Gummer. The Episcopal ceremony took place in the garden of her parents' home on Mason's Island, in front of about fifty guests. Don, who was still recuperating from the motorcycle accident, limped down the aisle on crutches. Some of the guests may have been forgiven for thinking, *Wait a second. Who is this guy?*

"I was worried at the time that it was a rebound thing," said Robyn Goodman, even though she'd encouraged it. Meryl and Don had been dating for just a few months. How could she possibly be sure? Was she really over John? Did it matter?

Even the mother of the bride was a little confused. "What is she thinking about?" she asked Joe Papp at the wedding. Papp sensed some "strain" between mother and daughter, despite the appearance of good fellowship. *The Taming of the Shrew* had closed earlier in the month, and he could see that Meryl had "not recovered by any means" from John's death.

But he knew that she had a clear head, because he had seen how she worked. In a way, it all made sense: after everything that had happened, she was making her life stable again. "She does the right thing for herself at the moment," he said later. "She is a shrewd analyst of herself." The old leftist that he was, he observed that she was marrying "within her class."

Ten days later, at her mother's insistence, Meryl wrote to Joe and Gail Papp to thank them for the clock they'd given as a wedding gift. "What immense support you have provided throughout some insupportable times," she wrote to the couple who had once guided her and John through the medical maze. "You have been there at the bottom and top of things. We are all now in each other's lives indelibly, forever."

Some thirteen years later, as he was dying of prostate cancer, Papp began looking for a successor to run the Public. His first choice was Meryl Streep. By then, she had three young children and lived in Connecticut, and hadn't been in a play for a decade. She said no right away, stunned that Joe would ever think her capable of all the schmoozing and the fund-raising. She kissed him goodbye and went back to Connecticut, feeling "unspeakably touched that he would choose me to be his successor, stupefied that he could misconceive me so thoroughly, and sad to realize that there was no one, *no one*, who could fill his shoes."

ROBERT BENTON KNEW there was something wrong with the ending of *Kramer vs. Kramer* virtually the moment he shot it. He had toyed with the idea of closing the movie on a reunited Ted and Billy walking through Central Park. The camera pans out to reveal that they're just two out of thousands of parents and children enjoying a sunny afternoon in New York City.

But he realized early on that there were two stories embedded in the movie. One is Ted's relationship with Billy, which is resolved somewhere around the playground-accident scene, when Ted realizes that nothing in the world comes before his love for his son. The second story is about Ted and Joanna: After the brutality of the custody hearing, how can they ever be functioning coparents?

That's the conflict Benton needed to resolve in the final scene, which he set in the lobby of Ted's building. It's the day Joanna comes to take Billy, some time after she wins the custody battle. She buzzes up and asks Ted to come downstairs, where he finds her leaning against the wall in her trench coat. She tells him she isn't taking Billy after all.

JOANNA:

After I left . . . when I was in California, I began to think, what kind of mother was I that I could walk out on my own child. It got to where I couldn't tell anybody about Billy—I couldn't stand that look in their faces when I said he wasn't living with me. Finally it seemed like the most important thing in the world to come back here and prove to Billy and to me and to the world how much I loved him . . . And I did . . . And I won. Only . . . it was just another "should."

(she begins to break down)

Then Joanna asks if she can go upstairs and talk to Billy, and both parents get in the elevator. The picture ends with the doors closing on the Kramers, united as parents, if not as spouses.

They shot the scene in late 1978, in the lobby of a Manhattan apartment building. But as Benton pieced the film together, the ending didn't sit right. One problem was Joanna's reasoning. If she had really come back because of how people looked at her in California, that meant she was the same deluded narcissist of Avery's novel, not the ambivalent, vulnerable woman Meryl was playing. It was too much about *her*: her pride, her guilt, her endless search for self-actualization.

The second problem was the final shot in the elevator. It looked too much like Ted and Joanna were getting back together. This couldn't be a Hollywood ending, with the audience imagining the final kiss behind the elevator door. Benton wanted to leave no doubt: even if the Kramers were moving forward as parents, their marriage was definitively over.

Early in 1979, the director called back Dustin and Meryl for reshoots. Meryl had been rehearsing a new play at the Public called *Taken in Marriage*, an all-female ensemble piece by Thomas Babe. She had ended 1978 with a disappointment, playing the title character in Elizabeth Swados's musical adaptation of *Alice's Adventures in Wonderland*. The twenty-seven-year-old Swados was overwhelmed with her directing duties, and shortly before previews Papp scuttled the production. Instead, he offered a three-night concert version over Christmas. Meryl played not only Alice but Humpty Dumpty and other denizens of Wonderland. "This is a mature actress who has reinvented herself as a magical, ageless child," the *Times* review said. "By the end of the concert we are convinced that Alice is tall, blond and lovely—just like Meryl Streep."

The lobby where Benton had filmed the first ending of *Kramer vs. Kramer* was unavailable, so the crew built a replica. It had been the cinematographer Néstor Almendros's idea to paint Billy's room with clouds around his bed. They would symbolize the cocoon of home and act as a reminder, like Justin Henry's flaxen hair, of the missing mother. In the rewritten ending, the clouds were the catalyst for Joanna's change of heart, which was no longer about her but about her son.

JOANNA:

I woke up this morning . . . kept thinking about Billy. And I was thinking about him waking up in his room with his little clouds all around that I painted. And I thought I should have painted clouds downtown, because . . . then he would think that he was waking up at home. I came here to take my son home. And I realized he already is home.

Meryl delivered the speech with trembling certainty, inserting a fortifying gasp between "painted" and "clouds." It was Joanna, as Benton saw it, who now performed the film's ultimate heroic act: sacrificing custody not *despite* her love for Billy but *because* of it.

This time, Joanna got in the elevator alone. In the final moments, she wipes the tear-drenched mascara from her eyes and asks Ted how she looks. "Terrific," he says, as the door closes between them. Her wordless, split-second reaction was as richly textured as Dustin's stare at the end of *The Graduate*—both flattered and disbelieving, the face of someone who's been given just the right gift at just the right moment, by the most unlikely person. What does the future hold for this woman, dangling between fragility and conviction?

"This picture started out belonging to Ted Kramer, and by the end it belonged to both of them," Benton said. "And there was no way Dustin could shake her. No way he could do anything to shake her. She was just there, and she was an incredible force." When she told Dustin she planned on going back to the theater, he said, "You're never going back."

Something else had changed between the first ending and the second: this time, Meryl was pregnant. Not enough to show, but enough that Joanna's choice—a harbinger of Sophie's—suddenly seemed unconscionable. She told Benton, "I could never have done this role now."

"THIS IS THE SEASON of Meryl Streep," Mel Gussow wrote to his editor at the *New York Times Magazine* in the fall of 1978:

> *On Dec. 14, "The Deer Hunter," her first starring movie, opens. Advance reports (I have not seen it yet) indicate that it is a powerhouse and an Academy Award contender—both the movie and her performance in it. She co-stars in this Vietnam period movie with Robert De Niro and the late John Cazale (her former love; she was recently married to someone else). Meryl also plays*

*the title role in Liz Swados's "Alice in Wonderland," now in
rehearsal at the Public Theater, and beginning previews Dec.
27. This fall she also filmed "Kramer Vs. Kramer," playing the
female lead opposite Dustin Hoffman, as well as Woody Allen's
"Manhattan."*

*Before her "season," she was clearly the most interesting and
original actress on the American stage. I say this having followed
her career from its genesis at the Yale Repertory Theater, where
she did everything from Strindberg to Christopher Durang
and Albert Innaurato. What makes her special is that before
she became a lovely leading lady, she was already a versatile
character actress. Her most notable Yale appearance was as
an octogenarian, wheelchair-confined Constance Garnett in
a Durang-Innaurato mad musical travesty of all arts and
literature called "The Idiots Karamazov." Shall we be the first to
do the complete Streep?*

On November 13, 1979, a year after Mel Gussow's pitch, Meryl gave
birth to a six-pound, fourteen-ounce baby boy, whom she and Don
named Henry Wolfe Gummer. He was due on Halloween but arrived
two weeks late, delivered by Caesarean section to avoid a breech birth.
The father, *Variety* noted, was a "non-pro."

She had spent the final months of her pregnancy like a student
cramming for a test, reading *The First Twelve Months of Life* and *Our
Bodies, Ourselves*. But she still felt unprepared for motherhood. When
she saw Don holding the newborn, it felt, she said, like "the most natural thing in the world." They brought the baby home, where Don had
made him a nursery. To avoid confusion with the other Henrys in her
family, she nicknamed him "Gippy."

Any journalist looking for the "complete Streep"—there were now
many—would have to be prepared to pause the interview for breast-
feeding. "My work has been very important," she told one of them,
"because if you want a career, I feel that you have to build a foundation

in your twenties. But we wanted to have a child because we felt that not enough people in our circle of friends were having children. Friends of mine from college, who are very accomplished, are delaying children until they are older because of their careers."

She had turned thirty that summer, during her second trimester. While they still had their freedom, she and Don took a cruise ship to France and spent two and a half months driving a rental car through Europe, stopping at the tiny towns between Paris and Florence. They got back for the premiere of *The Senator*, in August. At the insistence of Lew Wasserman, the chairman of Universal, Alan Alda had retitled it *The Seduction of Joe Tynan*, lest anyone assume that the adulterous "senator" was based on Wasserman's friend Ted Kennedy. The movie was a modest success, with cordial reviews. But the "season of Streep," which began with her Oscar nomination for *The Deer Hunter* and continued with the April release of *Manhattan*, was now in full swing.

Robert Benton spent the intervening months finishing *Kramer vs. Kramer* with his editor, Jerry Greenberg. It was beginning to feel less like a total disaster. (Too bad his wife had already canceled that ski trip.) In test screenings, he would stand in the back of the theater and watch the audience, taking note of every fidget and cough. Wondering how a divorce movie would play in middle America, he screened the film in Kansas City, Missouri. He was dismayed when he saw a man get up during a critical scene. How could anyone go to the bathroom *now*? He followed the man outside. Instead of going to the men's room, the guy stopped at a pay phone and called his babysitter to check on his child.

We're home free, Benton thought.

The film opened on December 19, 1979. As the producers had hoped, it was received less as a movie than as a cultural benchmark, a snapshot of the fractured American family, circa now. "Though the movie has no answers to the questions it raises, it recharges the debate by restating issues in new and disturbing terms, or perhaps in the oldest terms of all: through agonizingly ambiguous human truths," Frank

Rich wrote in *Time*. From Vincent Canby, in the *Times*: "'Kramer vs. Kramer' is a Manhattan movie, yet it seems to speak for an entire generation of middle-class Americans who came to maturity in the late 60's and early 70's, sophisticated in superficial ways but still expecting the fulfillment of promises made in the more pious Eisenhower era."

Avery Corman had not been involved in the film adaptation of his novel. He was shown a rough cut, which he found "tremendously powerful." (A colleague of his remembered him being "pissed" that so many secondary characters had been cut.) Shortly after it opened, Avery took his wife and two sons to a public screening, at Loews Tower East on Seventy-second Street. He recalled, "When the movie ended and the lights came on and I looked around, gathered throughout the theater were a bunch of teenagers sitting sort of silently, quietly in their seats. They didn't get up to leave. They were just sitting there. And I said to my wife, 'Oh, my God. That's the secret audience for all of this: children of divorce.'"

Indeed, the public greeted the film with open wallets. On its opening weekend, it played in 524 theaters, grossing more than $5.5 million. In the filmmaking world that *Star Wars* had wrought, a chamber drama about a failed marriage was no longer Hollywood's idea of big money. But the U.S. gross of *Kramer vs. Kramer* would total more than $106 million, making it the biggest domestic moneymaker of 1979—beating out even *Star Wars* progeny like *Star Trek* and *Alien*, starring Meryl's former classmate Sigourney Weaver.

It was a movie people wept over and argued over, a well-made tear-jerker about a father and son. Anyone who was or ever had a loving parent could relate to that story. But there was a trickier story lurking within—the shadow narrative of Joanna Kramer. In celebrating the bond between Ted and Billy, had the movie sold out not only her but the feminist movement? Some people seemed to think so. The *Washington Post*'s Gary Arnold found it "difficult to escape the conclusion that Dear Mrs. Kramer is a dim-witted victim of some of the sorriest cultural cant lately in vogue."

Leaving the theater with her fifteen-year-old daughter, the writer Barbara Grizzuti Harrison felt a trifle manipulated. Why do we applaud the noble self-sacrifice of Ted Kramer, she wondered, when the same thing is merely expected of women? How does Joanna land a re-entry job for $31,000 a year? Why can't Ted seem to hire a babysitter? And what to make of Joanna's hazy quest for fulfillment? "I keep thinking of Joanna," Harrison wrote in *Ms.* magazine, the standard-bearer of mainstream feminism. "Is she outside howling at the gates of happiness, or is she satisfied with her job, her lover, and occasional visits to Billy. Who *is* Joanna, and did she spend those 18 months in California in vain?"

More and more journalists, not to mention the vast ticket-buying public, were asking themselves a related question: Who is Meryl Streep?

HERE ARE A few things you might have been interested to know, if you were *Time* or *People* or *Vogue* or even *Ms.* magazine: Meryl Streep bought her dungarees on MacDougal Street. One of her favorite articles of clothing was a Hawaiian jacket she'd had since college. She was partial to pearl earrings and ate apple slices and took out the garbage herself. If you called her answering machine, you got a recorded message saying, "Hello . . . um . . . if you want to leave a message, please wait for the beep, because . . . um . . . I don't know . . . otherwise the thing cuts off. Thank you."

She loved visiting art galleries. She loved riding the subway. She thought that all politicians should ride the subway and be forced to confront the "reality of life." She was outspoken about male contraception, because too many of her female friends had fertility problems after using IUDs or the pill. She was looking, for the first time, for a lawyer and an accountant. Also, a part-time nanny. She preferred doing theater to movies, and she hoped one day to play Hamlet. Her dream was to put together an all-star Shakespeare troupe that would perform in repertory across the country, with actors like Al Pacino and Robert De

Niro and Mary Beth Hurt. Joe Papp would produce, and they would go to places "less glamorous than Gary." If not now, maybe when they were all fifty-five.

She did not always get what she wanted. She had put out her "feelers" for *Evita* on Broadway, because "charismatic leaders are very interesting," but she was pregnant and the part went to Patti LuPone. She was approached about a remake of *The Postman Always Rings Twice*, but it required nudity, and when she asked if Jack Nicholson would be willing to show the same amount of skin, the role went to Jessica Lange. She thought people who described French actresses as "mysterious" and "sexy" because they talked in a babyish whisper were "full of shit." She loved Bette Davis and Rosalind Russell and Lina Wertmüller and *Amarcord*. She admired Zero Mostel because he "put his life on the line for comedy." She hated parties—the most boring thing in the world was a night at Studio 54. She disapproved of the new "slink" in fashion, preferring the green cowboy boots her husband bought her for Christmas.

She was, various journalists suggested, one of the "anti-ingénues" who were now on the rise in Hollywood. She was like Faye Dunaway, but less vampy. Jane Fonda, but less self-satisfied. Jill Clayburgh, but less ingratiating. Diane Keaton, but less neurotic. She was a throwback to Katharine Hepburn or Carole Lombard. Her name sounded like the "cry of a bird." She looked like a "tapered candle" or a "Flemish master's angel." She was a dead ringer for Alesso Baldovinetti's *Portrait of a Lady in Yellow*. Her cheekbones were "exquisite." Her nose was "patrician." There wasn't even a word for her pale blue eyes—maybe "merulean"? She was "more than just a gorgeous face." She could make you "identify with Medea." She was living, by her own admission, a "Cinderella story." She evinced a "go with the flow" philosophy. She hated hot weather, which made her feel like cheese left in the sun. She had never been south of Alexandria, Virginia.

In truth, she had no idea why anyone should care where she bought her dungarees, or why her face should appear on the covers of *Parade*,

Playgirl, and *Ladies' Home Journal.* The "excessive hype" mystified her at best and irritated her at worst. "For a while there it was either me or the Ayatollah on the covers of national magazines," she complained two years later, in a cover story for a national magazine (*Time*). Perhaps Brustein's admonitions about Hollywood "personalities" still lingered, but she saw celebrity as an unwelcome side effect to her craft. Also, it was becoming harder and harder for her and Don to visit art galleries.

When the magazines came to call, she could be charming and self-effacing, but sometimes she was just impatient. For *Vogue,* she gamely did cheerleader splits for the photographer. But the writer who showed up at the loft couldn't help but feel intrusive as Meryl nursed the two-month-old Gippy while complaining into the tape recorder, "I think that the notion that you owe it to your public is kind of odd. Nobody else does that except elected officials, and I'm not elected, I never ran for anything . . . And it seems bizarre to think that I have to share the few private moments I have with other people."

She and Dustin did their best to qualify their on-set sparring, at least in front of journalists. But the results could sound passive-aggressive. "Dustin has a technician's thoroughness and he is very demanding, but it isn't the star temperament I'd been led to expect," she told the *Times.* "It isn't vanity. He is a perfectionist about the craft and the structuring of the film, and his own ego is subjugated to that." Dustin gave similarly tortured compliments. "I hated her guts," he said when the movie came out. "But I respected her. She's ultimately not fighting for herself, but for the scene. She sticks with her guns and doesn't let anyone mess with her when she thinks she's right."

The press infatuation hit a crescendo the first week of 1980, when Meryl appeared on the cover of *Newsweek.* She wore her (by then) signature pearl earrings and a Mona Lisa smile, accompanied by big white letters: "A Star for the '80s." The article posited that Meryl Streep may well become "the first American woman since Jane Fonda to rival the power, versatility and impact of such male stars as Dustin

252

Hoffman, Jack Nicholson, Robert De Niro and Al Pacino." She had not yet had a leading role in a movie, and already evoked the language of superlatives. When the *Time* cover followed, in 1981, she "didn't feel anything."

It seemed to her she had already passed the sweet spot, when she could focus solely on the pleasure of acting. When she started out, she would spend 80 percent of her time on headshots or auditions or résumés, and the other 20 percent on her work. Now it was again 80 percent on peripheral things, like talking to *Newsweek* and *Vogue*. Part of her wished she had remained a "middling successful actor," the kind nobody wants to know anything about. She was high on the homecoming float once again, flabbergasted by how thin the air was up there. Somehow it always came as a disappointment, as if someone had put her there other than herself.

THE STAR FOR the '80s spent the first moments of the eighties at a New Year's Eve party thrown by Woody Allen. The director, still at work on *Stardust Memories*, had taken over a ballet school on Seventy-fifth Street, and its rehearsal studios and winding marble staircase were now peopled with boldface names. On the second floor, Bianca Jagger leaned against a barre talking with Andy Warhol. One flight up, Kurt Vonnegut danced on a red disco floor with his wife, Jill Krementz, as George Plimpton and Jane Alexander watched from the sidelines. Gloria Vanderbilt came early; Mick Jagger came late. There were movie stars (Lauren Bacall, Bette Midler, Jill Clayburgh), literary grandees (Norman Mailer, Lillian Hellman, Arthur Miller). Ruth Gordon, of *Harold and Maude*, could be overheard saying, "I'm astonished that anybody *knows* this many people."

Earlier in the day, some teenagers had sneaked in, pretending to be with the caterers, and now wandered among the beau monde, eating appetizers. Much of the talk was about how the host, known for his shyness, was either courageous or masochistic to be throwing such a lavish affair. When the sentiment got back to Woody, he deadpanned,

"There is a lot of valiancy going around." Up in the dining room, Tom Brokaw fought through the crowd to talk to Meryl Streep, who had attended despite her apparent misgivings about the host. In a party where everybody was a somebody, she now made as big a ripple as the rest. Famousland may have been where she belonged, but she was already plotting her retreat.

She and Don had found a ninety-two-acre property in Dutchess County, which they bought for around $140,000. It was a furnished three-floor house, surrounded by five thousand Christmas trees. There was a free-standing garage that Don could turn into a studio, and they were talking about installing a windmill and a solar-power system and freeing themselves of utility companies completely. Mostly, they wanted a place where they could avoid the grime and noise of downtown Manhattan, not to mention the autograph-seekers. Before having Henry, Meryl would wander SoHo contemplating the interesting characters lurking behind each window. Now, for the first time, it seemed ugly. She had nowhere to bring the baby, and buying Tampax at the drug store made her self-conscious. They'd keep the apartment, of course, but in their wooded oasis they'd feel like homesteaders on a vast frontier. In the rush of fame, some self-protective instinct had kicked in. She would need to draw the curtain to keep a part of herself small and quiet and private.

When the clocks struck midnight at the ballet school, Meryl Streep and practically every celebrity in New York said farewell to the seventies. People were already talking about a "new conservatism," which would penetrate not just politics but the movies. Some people saw it in Meryl's refined face and pearl earrings—"the Lady," as *Vogue* called her—but that was mostly a projection. In any case, the new conservatism couldn't have been much in evidence at Woody Allen's New Year's party: this was the man, after all, who in *Annie Hall* had affectionately described his city as the epicenter of "left-wing Communist Jewish homosexual pornographers."

In February, *Kramer vs. Kramer* was nominated for nine Academy

Awards, including Best Picture (Stanley Jaffe, producer), Best Actor (Hoffman), Best Director (Benton), and Best Adapted Screenplay (Benton again). Eight-year-old Justin Henry, nominated for Best Supporting Actor, became the youngest Oscar nominee in history. And Meryl, along with Barbara Barrie (*Breaking Away*) and Candice Bergen (*Starting Over*), would compete for Best Supporting Actress against two of her costars: Jane Alexander from *Kramer vs. Kramer* and Mariel Hemingway from *Manhattan*.

There was no doubt now that Meryl could carry a leading role in a movie, and Sam Cohn set to work finding the right project—or projects. After *Manhattan* and *Kramer vs. Kramer*, she wanted to play anyone but another contemporary New Yorker. "Put me on the moon," she told Cohn; he got her as far as the end of a stone pier on the English Channel. By mid-February, she was contracted to star in *The French Lieutenant's Woman*, a costume drama based on the John Fowles novel, with a screenplay by Harold Pinter. It would begin shooting in Dorset in May. She would play two characters: a mysterious Victorian siren and the modern-day actress portraying her in a big-budget film.

At the same time, she was in contention for a screen adaptation of William Styron's novel *Sophie's Choice*, about a Polish Holocaust survivor living in Brooklyn. Landing the role would be a fight: the director, Alan J. Pakula, had a Czech actress in mind, and Meryl would beg him to reconsider. And as early as March, her name was being tossed around in connection with a project about the Oklahoma nuclear-plant worker Karen Silkwood. Nineteen-eighty had hardly begun, and her next three years of work were already mapped out—as was her niche as an accent-wielding tragedian. It would be a long time before anyone thought of Meryl Streep as funny.

Meanwhile, *Kramer vs. Kramer* was cleaning up the awards season. At the Golden Globes, Meryl wore her white-silk wedding dress and began lactating during the ceremony. She accepted the award with one arm across her chest. The movie was now opening on screens around the world, from Sweden to Japan. On March 17th, it was shown at a special screening in London at the Odeon Leicester Square, for an audience that included Queen Elizabeth II and Prince Philip. Meryl flew over, along with Dustin Hoffman, Robert Benton, Stanley Jaffe, and Justin Henry. She wore a long white dress and a matching blazer with the collar turned up. As Liv Ullmann and Peter Sellers looked on, she held out a hand to Her Majesty, touching white glove to white glove. The queen leaned in to talk to Justin. Was this his first acting job?

"Yes," he told her.

The queen asked if the movie would make her cry.

"Yes," he replied. "My mom cried four times."

APRIL 14, 1980. Outside the Dorothy Chandler Pavilion, the stars of the new decade arrived in style: Goldie Hawn, Richard Gere, Liza Minnelli, George Hamilton. Among the movie gods was Meryl Streep, one of the only women not in sequins. She wore the same white dress she'd worn to meet the queen, minus the gloves.

Inside, she took her seat between her husband and Sally Field, nominated for Best Actress for *Norma Rae*. Henry Mancini, in a huge bow tie, opened the show by conducting the theme from *Star Trek*. Meryl applauded when the Academy president, Fay Kanin, spoke of the institution's "glorious heritage." She sat nervously through Johnny Carson's monologue, with zingers covering *The Muppet Movie*, Bo Derek's cornrows in *10*, the Iranian hostage crisis, Dolly Parton's chest ("Mammary vs. Mammary"), and the fact that three of the big films that year were about divorce. "It says something about our times when the only lasting relationship was the one in *La Cage aux Folles*," Carson joked. "Who says they're not writing good feminine roles anymore?"

Two gentlemen from Price Waterhouse, charged with guarding the envelopes, came onstage and took a bow. Then Jack Lemmon and Cloris Leachman came out to deliver the first award of the night: Best Supporting Actress.

When she heard her name, last among the nominees, Meryl rubbed her hands together and mumbled something to herself. "And the winner is . . . ," Leachman said, before handing the envelope to Lemmon.

"Thank you, my dear."

"You're welcome, my dear."

"Meryl Streep in *Kramer vs. Kramer.*"

The hall reverberated with Vivaldi's Mandolin Concerto in C Major, the movie's theme. As she hurried to the stage, she leaned over and kissed Dustin on the cheek. Then she glided up the stairs to the microphone and took hold of her first Academy Award.

"Holy mackerel," she began, glancing down at the statuette. Her tone was placid. "I'd like to thank Dustin Hoffman and Robert Benton, to whom I owe . . . this. Stanley Jaffe, for giving me the chance to play Joanna. And Jane Alexander, and Justin"—she blew a kiss—"for the love and support during this very, very delightful experience."

To the people in the audience, and to the millions watching at home, she seemed like a star fully hatched, a poised Venus on the half shell. Only she knew how unlikely the whole thing was: that "movie star" was her job description. It was another metamorphosis, like the one that had set her course a decade ago, as she stood amid the ersatz scent of lilacs as Miss Julie. That she had scaled the mountain of show business in ten short years was merely a reflection of what Clint Atkinson knew then, and what Joe knew, and what John knew, and what perhaps even she knew: that Meryl Streep had it in her all along.

After one last "thank you very much," she held up the Oscar and headed left, before Jack Lemmon was kind enough to point her right.

Vivaldi played again for Best Adapted Screenplay, Best Director, and Best Actor. Dustin Hoffman, accepting his Oscar from Jane Fonda, reiterated his well-known contempt for award shows ("I've been critical of the Academy, and for reason"). Justin Henry lost to Melvyn Douglas (*Being There*), seventy-one years his senior, becoming so distraught that Christopher Reeve, a.k.a. Superman, had to be called over to console him. At the end of the night, Charlton

Heston announced the winner for Best Picture: it was a *Kramer vs. Kramer* sweep.

In the moments after the ceremony, the *Kramer* winners were shown into a room of about a hundred reporters. "Well, the soap opera won," Dustin boomed as he walked in, anticipating their disdain. It was clear that this wouldn't be a typical glad-handing press conference, and the reporters were eager to match Dustin's feistiness. The columnist Rona Barrett remarked that many women, particularly feminists, "feel this picture was a slap to them."

"That wasn't said at all," Dustin snapped back. "I can't stop people from feeling what they are feeling, but I don't think everyone feels that way."

As they argued, Meryl bounded onto the platform. "Here comes a feminist," she said. "I don't feel that's true at all." Having commandeered the stage, she continued, "I feel that the basis of feminism is something that has to do with liberating men *and* women from prescribed roles."

She could have said the same about acting—or at least her version of it, the kind she had fought so hard to achieve. She was no longer the college freshman who thought that feminism had to do with nice nails and clean hair. In fact, it was inseparable from her art, because both required radical acts of imagination. Like an actress stretching her versatility, Joanna Kramer had to imagine herself as someone other than a wife and a mother in order to become a "whole human being," however flawed. That may not have been apparent to Avery Corman, but it was to Meryl, and tonight's triumph seemed to underscore that she was right.

No longer would she have to sneak her character through the back door, the forgotten woman in the screenplay. In the decade to come, she would bend the movies toward her, stretching her ability to reveal the wrinkles of consciousness as wide as the screen could allow. With the help of Sam Cohn, who remained her agent until 1991, she would command the kind of complicated female roles she had thought impossible in Hollywood: a Danish adventurer, a Washington grandee, a Depression-era wino, an Australian murder suspect. After 1981, she would all but give up theater, returning only for stints at the Delacorte. Part of the reason would be her children: three more after Henry, named Mamie, Grace, and Louisa, raised with nary a gap on her résumé. Her marriage to Don Gummer, which seemed almost impetuous at the time, would prove one of the most enduring in Hollywood.

In later years, she would voice her politics more firmly, urging Congress to revive the Equal Rights Amendment and describing Walt Disney as a "gender bigot" at the 2014 National Board of Review gala. She would note with dismay that of all her characters, men her age—Bill Clinton among them—always told her that their favorite was Linda, the pliant checkout girl from *The Deer Hunter*. No wonder she had taken the role with such trepidation; she knew how easily the world could turn a woman into an ingénue. It was a measure of how much times had changed, she said in 2010, that men had finally started mentioning another favorite character: Miranda Priestly, the power-fluent fashion editor from *The Devil Wears Prada*. "They relate to Miranda," she reasoned. "They wanted to date Linda."

For now, she stood in front of a room of reporters, Oscar in hand, with a simple declaration: "Here comes a feminist."

Someone asked her, "How does it feel?"

"Incomparable," she said. "I'm trying to hear your questions above my heartbeat." If she seemed composed, it was all an act. Earlier, as she wandered backstage after her acceptance speech, she had stopped in the ladies' room to catch her breath. Her head was spinning. Her heart was pounding. After a moment of solitude, she headed back out the door, ready to face the big Hollywood hoopla. "Hey," she heard a woman yell, "someone left an Oscar in here!" Somehow, in her tizzy, she had left the statuette on the bathroom floor.

SUPPORTING CHARACTERS

ALAN ALDA—Actor best known for the long-running TV show *M*A*S*H*. Writer and star of *The Seduction of Joe Tynan*.

JANE ALEXANDER—Stage and screen actress and four-time Oscar nominee, for her roles in *The Great White Hope*, *All the President's Men*, *Kramer vs. Kramer*, and *Testament*.

CLINT ATKINSON—Streep's drama teacher at Vassar who directed her in *Miss Julie* and other plays. He died in 2002.

LINDA ATKINSON—Yale acting student, class of 1975.

BLANCHE BAKER—Streep's costar in *The Seduction of Joe Tynan* and *Holocaust*, for which she won an Emmy Award. Later played the title role in *Lolita* on Broadway.

ROBERT BENTON—Oscar-winning writer and director of *Kramer vs. Kramer*. Also known as the cowriter of *Bonnie and Clyde* and as the director of *The Late Show*, *Places in the Heart*, and *Nobody's Fool*.

MIKE BOOTH—Streep's high school boyfriend, with whom she corresponded from Vassar while he served in the Vietnam War.

ARVIN BROWN—Director of *27 Wagons Full of Cotton* and *A Memory of Two Mondays*. He was the longtime artistic director of the Long Wharf Theatre, in New Haven, Connecticut.

ROBERT BRUSTEIN—Dean of the Yale School of Drama from 1966 to 1979 and the founding director of the Yale Repertory Theatre. He later founded the American Repertory Theater, in Cambridge, Massachusetts.

STEPHEN CASALE—Brother of John Cazale. As a young man, he changed his last name from "Cazale" to its original Italian spelling.

PHILIP CASNOFF—Stage and television actor who dated Streep while she was at Yale.

JOHN CAZALE—Stage and screen actor best known as Fredo Corleone in *The Godfather* and *The Godfather: Part II*. His other films include *The Conversation*, *Dog Day Afternoon*, and *The Deer Hunter*. Co-starred with Streep in *Measure for Measure* in 1976 and dated her until his death, in 1978.

MICHAEL CIMINO—Oscar-winning director of *The Deer Hunter*. His other films include *Thunderbolt and Lightfoot*, *Year of the Dragon*, and *Heaven's Gate*, considered one of the most disastrous financial flops in movie history.

SAM COHN—Talent agent at ICM who represented Streep until 1991. His clients also included Bob Fosse, Woody Allen, Mike Nichols, Nora Ephron, Robert Benton, Paul Newman, and Whoopi Goldberg. He died in 2009.

AVERY CORMAN—Author of the novels *Kramer vs. Kramer*, *The Old Neighborhood*, and *Oh, God!*

MICHAEL DEELEY—Former president of EMI Films and producer of *The Deer Hunter*, *Blade Runner*, and *The Man Who Fell to Earth*.

CHRISTOPHER DURANG—Playwriting student, class of 1974, at Yale, where he cowrote *The Idiots Karamazov* with Albert Innaurato. His later plays include *Beyond Therapy*, *Sister Mary Ignatius Explains It All for You*, and the Tony-winning *Vanya and Sonia and Masha and Spike*.

MICHAEL FEINGOLD—First literary manager of the Yale Repertory Theatre, for which he adapted *Happy End*. He began writing for the *Village Voice* in 1971 and was its chief theater critic from 1983 to 2013.

RICHARD FISCHOFF—Associate producer of *Kramer vs. Kramer*.

CONSTANCE GARNETT—British translator who lived from 1861 to 1946. She was one of the first English translators of Russian classics by Tolstoy, Dostoyevsky, and Chekhov.

ROBYN GOODMAN—Theater producer, former actress, and friend of John Cazale, through her late husband, Walter McGinn. She cofounded the theater company Second Stage in 1979.

JOE "GRIFO" GRIFASI—Yale acting student, class of 1975. He appeared with Streep onstage in *A Midsummer Night's Dream*, *A Memory of Two Mondays*, *Secret Service*, and *Happy End* and onscreen in *The Deer Hunter*, *Still of the Night*, and *Ironweed*.

DON GUMMER—Sculptor and husband of Meryl Streep.

HENRY WOLFE GUMMER—Son of Meryl Streep and Don Gummer, nicknamed "Gippy" as a baby. He is now an actor and musician.

MEL GUSSOW—Longtime theater critic and cultural reporter for the *New York Times*. He died in 2005.

TOM HAAS—Acting teacher at the Yale School of Drama. He later became the artistic director of the Indiana Repertory Theatre, and died in 1991.

J. ROY HELLAND—Streep's longtime hair stylist and makeup artist. In 2012, he won an Academy Award for *The Iron Lady*.

LILLIAN HELLMAN—Playwright whose works include *The Children's Hour*, *The Little Foxes*, and *Toys in the Attic*. Her memoir *Pentimento* was the source for *Julia*. She died in 1984.

JUSTIN HENRY—Former child actor who played Billy Kramer in *Kramer vs. Kramer*.

ISRAEL HOROVITZ—Playwright and director. John Cazale starred in his plays *The Indian Wants the Bronx* and *Line*.

MARY BETH HURT—Streep's costar in *Trelawny of the "Wells,"* *Secret Service*, and *The Cherry Orchard*. Also known for the films *Interiors* and *The World According to Garp*.

ALBERT INNAURATO— Playwriting student, class of 1974, at Yale, where he cowrote *The Idiots Karamazov* with Christopher Durang. His later plays include *Gemini* and *Passione*.

STANLEY R. JAFFE—Producer of *Kramer vs. Kramer*. His later credits include *Fatal Attraction*, *The Accused*, and *School Ties*.

WALT JONES—Yale directing student, class of 1975. He later wrote and directed the Broadway production *The 1940's Radio Hour*.

RAÚL JULIÁ—Stage and screen actor who costarred with Streep in *The Cherry Orchard* and *The Taming of the Shrew*. Known to film audiences as Gomez in *The Addams Family*. He died in 1994.

PAULINE KAEL—Film critic for *The New Yorker*, who wrote for the magazine from 1968 to 1991. She died in 2001.

SHIRLEY KNIGHT—Actress best known for her Oscar-nominated roles in *The Dark at the Top of the Stairs* and *Sweet Bird of Youth*. Replaced by Streep in *Happy End*.

BOB LEVIN—Streep's college boyfriend when she was a Vassar student and he was the fullback for the Yale football team.

CHARLES "CHUCK" LEVIN—Yale acting student, class of 1974. Brother of Bob Levin.

ROBERT "BOBBY" LEWIS—Cofounder of the Actors Studio and original member of the Group Theatre. Later served as head of the acting and directing departments at the Yale School of Drama. He died in 1997.

ESTELLE LIEBLING—Influential singing coach who taught the adolescent Streep. She died in 1970.

JOHN LITHGOW—Streep's costar in *Trelawny of the "Wells," A Memory of Two Mondays*, and *Secret Service*. He was later Oscar-nominated for his roles in *The World According to Garp* and *Terms of Endearment*.

CHRISTOPHER LLOYD—Costarred with Streep in *The Possessed* and *A Midsummer Night's Dream* at Yale and in *Happy End* on Broadway. Best known for his roles in *Taxi, Back to the Future*, and *The Addams Family*.

WILLIAM IVEY LONG—Yale design student, class of 1975. As a Broadway costume designer, he won Tony Awards for *Nine, The Producers, Hairspray*, and others. In 2012, he was elected chair of the American Theatre Wing.

WALTER MCGINN—Actor and college friend of John Cazale. He was married to Robyn Goodman, and died in 1977.

KATE MCGREGOR-STEWART—Yale acting student, class of 1974.

ALLAN MILLER—Acting coach who directed Streep in *Major Barbara* at Yale.

MICHAEL MORIARTY—Stage and screen actor who costarred with Streep in *The Playboy of Seville*, *Henry V*, and *Holocaust*. Later known for his role as Benjamin Stone in *Law & Order*.

GAIL MERRIFIELD PAPP—Widow of Joseph Papp and former head of the play-development department at the Public Theater.

JOSEPH PAPP—Founder of the New York Shakespeare Festival, Shakespeare in the Park, and the Public Theater, which was renamed the Joseph Papp Public Theater after his death, in 1991.

RALPH REDPATH—Yale acting student, class of 1975.

ALAN ROSENBERG—Yale acting student (dropped out). Later known for his roles on *Civil Wars*, *L.A. Law*, and *Cybill*. President of the Screen Actors Guild from 2005 to 2009.

JOHN SAVAGE—Screen actor who played Steven in *The Deer Hunter*. Also known for *Hair*, *The Onion Field*, and *Salvador*.

JERRY SCHATZBERG—Director of *The Seduction of Joe Tynan*. His other films include *The Panic in Needle Park*, *Scarecrow*, and *Honeysuckle Rose*.

ANDREI SERBAN—Romanian stage director who directed *The Cherry Orchard* and *Agamemnon* at Lincoln Center.

BARRY SPIKINGS—Film producer, formerly of British Lion and EMI Films, whose credits include *The Deer Hunter* and *Convoy*.

EVERT SPRINCHORN—Former head of Vassar College's Drama Department, now Professor Emeritus of Drama.

MARVIN STARKMAN—Filmmaker and friend of John Cazale, whom he directed in the short film *The American Way*.

HARRY STREEP, JR.—Father of Meryl Streep. He died in 2003.

HARRY STREEP III—Younger brother of Meryl Streep, known as "Third."

MARY WOLF WILKINSON STREEP—Mother of Meryl Streep. She died in 2001.

ELIZABETH SWADOS—Experimental theater composer whose musical *Alice in Concert* starred Streep in its various incarnations. Best known for *Runaways*, which ran on Broadway in 1978.

BRUCE THOMSON—Streep's boyfriend her senior year of high school.

ROSEMARIE TICHLER—Head of casting at the Public Theater from 1975 to 1991 and then its artistic producer until 2001.

RIP TORN—Costarred with Streep in *The Father* and *The Seduction of Joe Tynan*. Best known for his roles in *Payday*, *Cross Creek*, and *The Larry Sanders Show*.

DERIC WASHBURN—Screenwriter of *The Deer Hunter*.

WENDY WASSERSTEIN—Yale playwriting student, class of 1976. Her plays include *Uncommon Women and Others*, *The Sisters Rosensweig*, and the Pulitzer Prize- and Tony Award–winning *The Heidi Chronicles*. She died in 2006.

SAM WATERSTON—Streep and Cazale's costar in *Measure for Measure*. Later known for his roles in *The Killing Fields* and on *Law & Order* and *The Newsroom*.

SIGOURNEY WEAVER—Yale acting student, class of 1974, best known for her roles in *Alien*, *Working Girl*, *Gorillas in the Mist*, and *Avatar*. In 2013, she starred in Christopher Durang's Tony Award–winning *Vanya and Sonia and Masha and Spike*.

IRENE WORTH—Streep's costar in *The Cherry Orchard* and the winner of three Tony Awards, for *Tiny Alice*, *Sweet Bird of Youth*, and *Lost in Yonkers*. She died in 2002.

FRED ZINNEMANN—Director of *Julia*; best known for *High Noon*, *From Here to Eternity*, and *A Man for All Seasons*. He died in 1997.

ACKNOWLEDGMENTS

My GRATITUDE, FIRST and foremost, belongs to my agent, David Kuhn, who all but commanded me to write this book, in that remarkable way he has of knowing what people have in them before they know it themselves. Thanks, as well, to Becky Sweren, for making sure I got it all done.

Thank you to my wonderful editor, Gail Winston, for her insight, her vision, and her endless class, and to everyone at HarperCollins, including Sofia Groopman, Beth Silfin, Martin Wilson, and Jonathan Burnham.

I would not have gotten anywhere without the generosity, of time and of spirit, of the many people I interviewed. Researching this book was a scavenger hunt that took me to all kinds of unexpected places, nudged along by a motley crew of spirit guides. I am indebted to everyone who rooted through a box in the garage, dusted off an old photograph, or called forth an old memory (or many), just to help me piece it all together.

Thank you to the librarians and archivists at the Paley Center for Media (especially the indefatigable Jane Klain), the Robert B. Haas Family Arts Library at Yale University, the Harry Ransom Center at the University of Texas at Austin, the Howard Gotlieb Archival Research Center at Boston University, Kent State University Libraries, the Bernardsville Public Library Local History Collection, the Cleveland Public Library, the New Haven Free Public Library, the Adriance

Memorial Library in Poughkeepsie, the Public Library of Steubenville and Jefferson County, the Margaret Herrick Library in Beverly Hills, and, especially, the New York Public Library for the Performing Arts. I would move in there if I could.

For permission to use material, thank you to Christopher Durang, Albert Innaurato, Christopher Lippincott, William Baker, Michael Booth, William Ivey Long, Paul Davis, Israel Horovitz, Robert Marx, Ann Gussow, Robert Brustein, the European American Music Corporation, and the Liveright Publishing Corporation.

For their encouragement, their wisdom, and their friendship, my deepest thanks to Natalia Payne, Laura Millendorf, Ben Rimalower and everyone from Theaterists, Jesse Oxfeld, Rachel Shukert, Shira Milikowsky, Deb Margolin, and the ingenious Dan Fishback. For advice, pep talks, and commiseration: Daniel Kurtz-Phelan, Christopher Heaney, Jason Zinoman, James Sanders, Michael Barbaro, and Sam Wasson, whose book *Fifth Avenue, 5 A.M.* I took around with me like a talisman. Thank you to my colleagues at *The New Yorker*, particularly Rhonda Sherman, Richard Brody, John Lahr, Rebecca Mead, Shauna Lyon, Paul Rudnick, and Susan Morrison. Thanks to Molly Mirhashem, for fact-checking, and Ed Cohen, for copy-editing. For various indispensible things, thanks to Frederik Ernst, Michael Feingold, Barbara De Dubovay, Richard Shepard, Candi Adams, Aimee Bell, and Leslee Dart.

Thank you, also, to Meryl Streep, for living a fascinating life, and for not throwing up any significant roadblocks.

Thank you to my endlessly supportive family: my father, Richard, my sister, Alissa, and my mother, Nancy, who also grew up in suburbia in the fifties, had long hair and loved folk music in the sixties, moved to dirty old New York City in the seventies, juggled motherhood and a career in the eighties (and to this day), and painted clouds in my bedroom.

And, above all, my love and gratitude to Jaime Donate, who endured countless evenings of Streepiana. Everything I value most in our lives, you've given me.

NOTES

In researching the early life and career of Meryl Streep, I was helped tremendously not only by the eighty-odd people who were kind enough to give me interviews but by the work of the journalists who had the privilege of interviewing her as an up-and-comer. Especially useful were Mel Gussow's notes and transcripts for his February 4, 1979, *New York Times Magazine* profile "The Rising Star of Meryl Streep," which are available in the Mel Gussow Collection at the Harry Ransom Center, the University of Texas at Austin, Series II, Container 144, abbreviated in the notes below as "MG."

I spent many happy afternoons at the New York Public Library for the Performing Arts, which is not only an exalting place to work but a trove of theater and film ephemera. Anyone wishing to see Meryl Streep in *27 Wagons Full of Cotton*, *A Memory of Two Mondays*, or *The Taming of the Shrew* need only call up the Theatre on Film and Tape Archive and make an appointment. (Do it!) Particularly helpful were the New York Shakespeare Festival records in the Billy Rose Theatre Division, indicated below by "NYSF," followed by a box number. Materials found at the Robert B. Haas Family Arts Library at Yale University are abbreviated "HAAS."

PROLOGUE

2 "Do you agree": Catherine Kallon, "Meryl Streep in Lanvin—2012 Oscars," www .redcarpet-fashionawards.com, Feb. 27, 2012.

3 "Stiff legged and slow moving": A. O. Scott, "Polarizing Leader Fades into the Twilight," *New York Times*, Dec. 30, 2011.

3 "Do you ever get nervous": Full dialogue from Hollyscoop at https://www.you-tube.com/watch?v=p72eu8tKlbM.

4 "Oh, I didn't have anything prepared": 60th Golden Globe Awards, Jan. 19, 2003.

4 "There are some days": 56th Primetime Emmy Awards, Sept. 19, 2004.

4 "I think I've worked with everybody": 64th Golden Globe Awards, Jan. 15, 2007.

5 "I didn't even buy a dress!": 15th Screen Actors Guild Awards, Jan. 25, 2009.

5 "Oh, my God. Oh, *come on*": Onstage remarks from the 84th Academy Awards, Feb. 26, 2012.

6 "Spare him, spare him!": William Shakespeare, *Measure for Measure*, Act II, Scene ii.

8 "It's like church for me": "Meryl Streep: Inside the Actors Studio," Bravo TV, Nov. 22, 1998.

8 "She has, as usual, put thought and effort": Pauline Kael, "The Current Cinema: Tootsie, Gandhi, and Sophie," *The New Yorker*, Dec. 27, 1982.

9 "Women . . . are better at acting": Commencement address delivered by Meryl Streep at Barnard College, May 17, 2010.

9 "I have come to the brink": From the private collection of Michael Booth.

MARY

11 On the first Saturday of November: "Miss Streep Is Crowned," *Bernardsville News*, Nov. 10, 1966.

12 "Streep has the clear-eyed blond handsomeness": Pauline Kael, "The Current Cinema: The God-Bless-America Symphony," *The New Yorker*, Dec. 18, 1978.

13 "I was six": Commencement address delivered by Meryl Streep at Barnard College, May 17, 2010.

13 "I remember taking my mother's eyebrow pencil": Ibid.

14 Her mother's side was Quaker stock: Streep's lineage and her recollections of her father and grandparents are detailed in Henry Louis Gates, Jr., *Faces of America: How 12 Extraordinary People Discovered Their Pasts* (New York: New York University Press, 2010), 34–50.

14 "joie de vivre": *Good Morning America*, ABC, Aug. 3, 2009.

16 "special days": "Meryl Streep: Inside the Actors Studio," Bravo TV, Nov. 22, 1998.

16 "shooting out sparks": MG.

16 "pretty ghastly": Paul Gray, "A Mother Finds Herself," *Time*, Dec. 3, 1979.

16 "I didn't have what you'd call a happy childhood": Ibid.

17 Her father had studied with Franz Liszt: Biographical information about Estelle Liebling from Charlotte Greenspan's entry on Liebling in the Jewish Women's Archive Encyclopedia, www.jwa.org.

17 "There's room in the back!": "Meryl Streep: The *Fresh Air* Interview," National Public Radio, Feb. 6, 2012.

18 "Miss Liebling was very strict": Beverly Sills, *Beverly: An Autobiography* (Toronto: Bantam Books, 1987), 41.

18 "Cover! Cover! Cover!": Gerald Moore, "Beverly Sills," *Opera Magazine*, Dec., 2006.

18 *The Wings of the Dove*: Gray, "A Mother Finds Herself."

19 "Empathy . . . is at the heart": Commencement address delivered by Meryl Streep at Barnard College, May 17, 2010.

19 "tricky negotiation": Ibid.

19 "I worked harder on this characterization": Ibid.

19 "*Seventeen* magazine knockout": Gray, "A Mother Finds Herself."

20 "We felt like we were in a little shell": Debbie Bozack's quotations are from an author interview, Apr. 30, 2014.

21 "Just remember Biology": Streep gave her signed 1965 *Bernardian* yearbook to Michael Booth, and it remains in his possession.

21 Opinions, for now, took a backseat: "Meryl Streep: The *Fresh Air* Interview," Feb. 6, 2012.

21 she met Mike Booth: Booth's high school recollections are from an author interview, July 10, 2014, and from his piece "Meryl & Me," *US*, Aug. 25, 1986.

24 "Songbird": "An Interview with Meryl Streep," *The Charlie Rose Show*, WNET, Nov. 5, 1999.

24 "Almost every day for the past two months": " . . . And the Music Lingers On," *The Crimson*, Apr., 1966.

24 "I thought about the singing part": Rosemarie Tichler and Barry Jay Kaplan, *Actors at Work* (New York: Faber and Faber, 2007), 290.

24 "I thought that if I looked pretty": Diane de Dubovay, "Meryl Streep," *Ladies' Home Journal*, March, 1980.

25 Barbra Streisand albums: "Meryl Streep: The *Fresh Air* Interview," Feb. 6, 2012.

25 "Often success in one area": Commencement address delivered by Meryl Streep at Barnard College, May 17, 2010.

27 "I reached a point senior year": Ibid.

27 first plane ride: "Spotlight: Meryl Streep," *Seventeen*, Feb., 1977.

28 "Handsome quarterback of our football team": Senior testimonials from *The Bernardian*, 1967.

28 Bennington College admissions office: Susan Dworkin, "Meryl Streep to the Rescue!," *Ms.*, Feb., 1979.

29 "a nice girl, pretty, athletic": Commencement address delivered by Meryl Streep at Vassar College, May 22, 1983.

JULIE

31 "successful in preparing young women": Elizabeth A. Daniels and Clyde Griffen, *Full Steam Ahead in Poughkeepsie: The Story of Coeducation at Vassar, 1966–1974* (Poughkeepsie: Vassar College, 2000), 18.

32 *Though we have had our chances*: Wendy Wasserstein, *Uncommon Women and Others* (New York: Dramatists Play Service, 1978), 36.

32 "I suppose this isn't a very impressive sentiment": Ibid., 21.

32 "On entering Vassar": Commencement address delivered by Meryl Streep at Vassar College, May 22, 1983.

33 The repertoire: This drawing, and Streep's letters from her freshman year, are from the private collection of Michael Booth.

34 "I made some very quick": Commencement address delivered by Meryl Streep at Barnard College, May 17, 2010.

34 Bob Levin, the fullback: Author interview with Bob Levin, Dec. 16, 2014. Kevin Rafferty's 2008 documentary *Harvard Beats Yale 29–29* tells the full story of the legendary 1968 football game.

35 "I remember when I was, like, a sophomore": "Meryl Streep: The *Fresh Air* Interview," National Public Radio, Feb. 6, 2012.

35 "Welcome, O life!": James Joyce, *A Portrait of the Artist as a Young Man* (New York: B. W. Huebsch, 1916), 299.

36 At two o'clock in the morning: Booth's recollections throughout are from an author interview, July 10, 2014.

38 By 1967, nearly two-thirds: This account of Vassar's transition to coeducation comes largely from Daniels and Griffen, *Full Steam Ahead in Poughkeepsie*.

39 "How unthinkable": Ibid., 29.

39 A survey in the spring: Ibid., 34–35.

40 "Vassar to Pursue Complete Coeducation": *Vassar Miscellany News*, Oct. 4, 1968.

40 "Vassar Men—Facing a Comic Doom": Susan Casteras, *Vassar Miscellany News*, Oct. 11, 1968.

40 "genuine sense of identity": Diane de Dubovay, "Meryl Streep," *Ladies' Home Journal*, March, 1980.

43 "Read *Miss Julie*": Susan Dworkin, "Meryl Streep to the Rescue!," *Ms.*, Feb., 1979.

43 "You can't do that!": Evert Sprinchorn's quotations are from an author interview, Apr. 7, 2014.

44 "Tonight she's wild again": From Evert Sprinchorn's translation, which was used in the Vassar College production. Collected in Robert Brustein, ed., *Strindberg: Selected Plays and Prose* (New York: Holt, Rinehart and Winston, 1964), 73.

44 lilac scent: Author interview with set designer C. Otis Sweezey, Sept. 26, 2014.

44 "She just seemed much more mature": Author interview with Judy Ringer, Apr. 12, 2014.

44 "I don't remember her having any particular investment in it": Author interview with Lee Devin, Apr. 7, 2014.

45 "It was a very serious play": "Meryl Streep: Inside the Actors Studio," Bravo TV, Nov. 22, 1998.

45 "She is the first neurotic": Michel Bouche, "Don't Miss 'Miss Julie' in Vassar Performance," *Poughkeepsie Journal*, Dec. 13, 1969.

45 "I loved my father": In Brustein, ed., *Strindberg: Selected Plays and Prose*, 99.

45 "modern characters, living in a transitional era": Ibid., 61.

46 "Being the only man": Daniels and Griffen, *Full Steam Ahead in Poughkeepsie*, 124–25.

46 "The men came my junior and senior years": Commencement address delivered by Meryl Streep at Vassar College, May 22, 1983.

47 "That was the Garden of Eden": In Brustein, ed., *Strindberg: Selected Plays and Prose*, 85.

49 "They really didn't want us here": Except where noted, Streep's recollections of Dartmouth come from Mark Bubriski, "From Vassar (to Hanover) to Hollywood: Meryl Streep's College Years," *The Dartmouth*, May 19, 2000.

49 Meryl's classmate Carol Dudley: Dudley's recollections are from an author interview, May 5, 2014.

49 "I got straight A's": Commencement address delivered by Meryl Streep at Vassar College, May 22, 1983.

50 "highly symbolic": MG.

50 "Living the Revolution": Commencement address delivered by Gloria Steinem at Vassar College, May 31, 1970.

51 "I don't even think that question is *valid*": *The Dartmouth*, May 19, 2000.

52 "Men of all degrees": George Lillo, *The London Merchant*, Act IV, Scene ii.

52 "Meryl Streep coos, connives, weeps": Debi Erb, "Meryl Streep Excels in 'London Merchant,'" *Miscellany News*, March 12, 1971.

53 "Even in production": Author interview with Philip LeStrange, May 21, 2014.

54 "I had never given it to anybody before": Author interview with Sondra Green, May 21, 2014.

54 "I'd never made myself cry": "Meryl Streep: Inside the Actors Studio," Nov. 22, 1998.

55 "You lackey! You shoeshine boy!": In Brustein, ed., *Strindberg: Selected Plays and Prose*, 95.

56 Meryl sang jazz standards: E-mail to author from Marj O'Neill-Butler, July 10, 2014.

57 Left to their own devices: Author interview with Peter Parnell, May 28, 2014.

57 "It was really quite idyllic": Author interview with Peter Maeck, May 22, 2014.

57 "dilettante group": MG.

58 "This just shows what kind of cross-section": Jack Kroll, "A Star for the '80s," *Newsweek*, Jan. 7, 1980.

58 "The quality of mercy": William Shakespeare, *The Merchant of Venice*, Act IV, Scene i.

58 "You want to provide for her?": Recalled by Levin, Dec. 16, 2014.

CONSTANCE

61 "I feel instinctively": Christopher Durang, "New Again: Sigourney Weaver," *Interview*, July, 1988.

61 "The first year sent me into therapy": Kate McGregor-Stewart's quotations are from an author interview, Feb. 10, 2014.

61 "They didn't take your strong points": Linda Atkinson's quotations are from an author interview, Jan. 22, 2014.

62 "When I was in drama school": Hilary de Vries, "Meryl Acts Up," *Los Angeles Times*, Sept. 9, 1990.

63 green pajama pants: Durang, "New Again: Sigourney Weaver."

63 "I'm sullen in the hallways": Author interview with Sigourney Weaver, June 9, 2015.

63 "I didn't know what was happening": William Ivey Long's quotations are from an author interview, Jan. 19, 2014.

64 "Every class at the drama school": Walt Jones's quotations, except where noted, are from an author interview, Jan. 30, 2014.

65 "It was all fans and flutterings": Author interview with Robert Brustein, Jan. 14, 2014.

65 "stagnant ponds": Robert Brustein, *Making Scenes: A Personal History of the Turbulent Years at Yale 1966–1979* (New York: Random House, 1981), 8.

65 "My plan was to transform the place": Ibid., 10.

65 "the liberal on a white horse": Author interview with Gordon Rogoff, Jan. 16, 2014.

65 "I wanted to develop an actor": Brustein, *Making Scenes*, 15.

65 "blasphemous ritual sacrifice": Ibid., 104.

66 "I had tried to be a mellow": Ibid., 90.

66 "You know the Sara Lee slogan": Thomas Meehan, "The Yale Faculty Makes the Scene," *New York Times Magazine*, Feb. 7, 1971.

66 official Drama School bulletin: Class schedules and descriptions can be found in the Yale Repertory Theatre and Yale School of Drama Ephemera Collection, HAAS, Box 16.

67 "The things that I honestly really think about": Rosemarie Tichler and Barry Jay Kaplan, *Actors at Work* (New York: Faber and Faber, 2007), 291.

68 "Tom Haas was Meryl's bane": Author interview with Robert Brustein, Jan. 14, 2014.

68 "one of the luminaries": Steve Rowe's quotations are from an author interview, Feb. 16, 2014.

69 "I was knocked out": Alan Rosenberg's quotations are from an author interview, March 10, 2014.

70 "She was more flexible": Ralph Redpath's quotations are from an author interview, Jan. 13, 2014.

71 "What do you mean, you dreadful man?": Jean-Claude van Itallie, trans., *Anton Chekhov's Three Sisters* (New York: Dramatists Play Service, 1979), 9.

72 "Center stage was a sofa": Michael Posnick's quotations are from an author interview, Jan. 16, 2014.

73 "He said that I was holding back my talent": Mel Gussow, "The Rising Star of Meryl Streep," *New York Times Magazine*, Feb. 4, 1979.

73 "Everyone was saying, 'They're awful' ": Albert Innaurato's quotations are from an author interview, Jan. 10, 2014.

74 "I knew this girl was obviously destined": Michael Feingold's quotations are from an author interview, Feb. 11, 2014.

74 "I took special note": Brustein, *Making Scenes*, 152.

74 "languorous sexual quality": MG.

75 "hardly ever visceral": Allan Miller's quotations are from an author interview, July 28, 2014.

75 "They expressed their vociferous": E-mail to author from Walt Jones, March 30, 2014.

75 "How come I'm sleeping with the director": Recalled by Miller, July 28, 2014.

76 "He delved into personal lives": MG.

76 "It was a bloodbath": Several other students remembered a "bloodbath" as well. Miller, for his part, had no memory of the evaluation and said that Streep was "a pleasure to work with."

77 "It's a curious sensation": Robert Brustein Collection, Howard Gotlieb Archival Research Center at Boston University, Box 34.

78 "rife with factionalism": Brustein, *Making Scenes*, 168.

79 "Every year, there'd be a coup d'état": Diana Maychick, *Meryl Streep: The Reluctant Superstar* (New York: St. Martin's Press, 1984), 37.

79 Cast as an old woman: Recalled by Jones, Jan. 30, 2014.

80 "We rehearsed it for a couple of weeks": David Rosenthal, "Meryl Streep Stepping In and Out of Roles," *Rolling Stone*, Oct. 15, 1981.

81 "deadly piranha": Brustein, *Making Scenes*, 240.

82 "Constance: *The Brothers Karamazov*": Christopher Durang and Albert Innaurato, *The Idiots Karamazov* (New York: Dramatists Play Service, 1981), 22.

82 "Have you ever *seen* Meryl be good?": Recalled by Christopher Durang, whose quotations, except where noted, are from an author interview, Sept. 26, 2014.

83 "had it in for Meryl": Rosenthal, "Meryl Streep Stepping In and Out of Roles."

84 "That was the most unpleasant thing": Recalled by Durang, Sept. 26, 2014.

84 *You may ask*: Durang and Innaurato, *The Idiots Karamazov*, 51.

85 "Meryl was totally disguised": Brustein, *Making Scenes*, 188.

85 Things came to a head: The events in this section were recalled by Rosenberg, March 10, 2014.

86 *The Limits to Growth*: Recalled by Streep in the interview tapes for Diane de Dubovay's March, 1980, profile in *Ladies' Home Journal*, provided to the author by the de Dubovay family.

86 "I later found out": Terry Curtis Fox, "Meryl Streep: Her 'I Can't Wait' Jumps Right Out at You," *Village Voice*, May 31, 1976.

88 mortifyingly unprofessional: Stephen Sondheim gives his perspective in his book *Finishing the Hat: Collected Lyrics (1954–1981) with Attendant Comments, Principles, Heresies, Grudges, Whines and Anecdotes* (New York: Knopf, 2010), 285–87. Brustein recalls his own frustrations and campus responses to *The Frogs* in *Making Scenes*, 178–82.

88 "The echo sometimes lasts": Aristophanes, Burt Shevelove, Stephen Sondheim, *The Frogs* (Chicago: Dramatic Publishing Co., 1975), 8.

89 "a splashy M-G-M epic": Mel Gussow, "Stage: 'Frogs' in a Pool," *New York Times*, May 23, 1974.

89 "How many plays about women": Brustein, *Making Scenes*, 218.

90 "I just can't get into all this chick stuff": Julie Salamon's excellent *Wendy and the Lost Boys: The Uncommon Life of Wendy Wasserstein* (New York: Penguin Press, 2011), 135.

90 "There was something about Wendy": Ibid., 126.

90 "She'll never pass you a poison apple": Wendy Wasserstein, *Bachelor Girls* (New York: Knopf, 1990), 78.

90 "To me she always seemed lonely": Salamon, *Wendy and the Lost Boys*, 177.

91 Summer Cabaret: Recollections of the Summer Cabaret from Walt Jones, Jan. 30, 2014.

92 "straight-out, unabashed performing": Gussow, "The Rising Star of Meryl Streep."

92 "If I were not protected": Ibid.

93 "I cut scene in Kraków": Recalled by Feingold, Feb. 11, 2014.

93 Elzbieta Czyzewska: Bruce Weber, "Elzbieta Czyzewska, 72, Polish Actress Unwelcome in Her Own Country, Dies," *New York Times*, June 18, 2010.

93 without the direction of Tom Haas: Haas became the artistic director of the Indiana Repertory Theatre. He died in 1991, after getting hit by a van while jogging.

94 "You can get out of my school!": Recalled by Atkinson, Jan. 22, 2014.

94 "She's supposed to be a whore": Recalled by Long, Jan. 19, 2014.

94 "You're limited, and it frees you": MG.

94 "The star role is the translator": Mel Gussow, "Play: 'Idiots Karamazov,' Zany Musical," *New York Times*, Nov. 11, 1974.

95 "distressing job": Brustein, *Making Scenes*, 190.

96 the red tie: Ibid., 198.

96 "More resistant": Recalled by Rowe, Feb. 16, 2014.

96 "the same cruel contempt": Brustein, *Making Scenes*, 199.

96 "You just want the *New York Times* to kiss your ass": Recalled by Redpath, Jan. 13, 2014.

96 "Torn scares everyone": Ira Hauptman's dramaturgical log for this production of *The Father* can be found in the Yale School of Drama Production Casebook Collection, HAAS, Box 1.

97 "The competition in the acting program": Andrea Stevens, "Getting Personal about Yale's Drama School," *New York Times*, Nov. 12, 2000.

97 "I'm under too much pressure": Ibid.

97 "Rip would never stand for it": Brustein, *Making Scenes*, 199.

98 "You're going to graduate in eleven weeks": Stevens, "Getting Personal about Yale's Drama School."

98 "surprise" and "disappointment": Brustein, *Making Scenes*, 192.

98 "Jealousy and meanness of spirit": Ibid., 191.

98 "Genghis Khan presiding": Ibid., 194.

99 "lovers want more rehearsal time": Robert Marx's dramaturgical log for *A Midsummer Night's Dream* can be found in the Yale School of Drama Production Casebook Collection, HAAS, Box 1.

100 "the culmination of everything": Brustein, *Making Scenes*, 201.

100 "The production falters a bit": Mel Gussow, "Stage: Haunting Shakespeare 'Dream,'" *New York Times*, May 15, 1975.

100 "That kind of grab-bag": Jack Kroll, "A Star for the '80s," *Newsweek*, Jan. 7, 1980.

101 "The Rep is home": Robert Brustein Collection, Howard Gotlieb Archival Research Center at Boston University, Box 8.

ISABELLA

103 "Unfortunately, the jobs selling gloves": Michael Lassell, "Waiting for That 'First Break,'" *New Haven Register*, July 13, 1975.

104 *I'm twenty-six*: Mel Gussow, "The Rising Star of Meryl Streep," *New York Times Magazine*, Feb. 4, 1979.

104 "Gawd, where's Meryl?": Susan Dworkin, "Meryl Streep to the Rescue!," *Ms.*, Feb., 1979.

104 "I want you to meet someone": Tichler's recollections are from Kenneth Turan and Joseph Papp, *Free For All: Joe Papp, The Public, and the Greatest Theater Story Ever Told* (New York: Doubleday, 2009), 363–64; and from an author interview, June 25, 2014.

105 "Off with the crown": William Shakespeare, *Henry VI, Part 3*, Act I, Scene iv.

105 "I grew up right here in Houston": Terrence McNally, *Whiskey: A One-Act Play* (New York: Dramatists Play Service, 1973), 48.

107 "Well, you can't make a *Hamlet*": Biographical information about Joseph Papp is drawn from Helen Epstein's indispensable *Joe Papp: An American Life* (Boston: Little, Brown, 1994). This quotation appears on p. 11.

107 "an irresponsible Commie": Ibid., 158.

108 "We seek blood-and-guts actors": Ibid., 167.

108 "He always felt under duress": Gail Papp's quotations are from an author interview, June 19, 2014.

109 "expansionist period": Epstein, *Joe Papp: An American Life*, 345.

109 "one of the lily white subscribers": Ibid., 296.

110 "should follow, to the closest detail": Arthur Wing Pinero, *Trelawny of the "Wells"* (Chicago: Dramatic Publishing Co., 1898), "A Direction to the Stage Manager."

110 "Tryout town, USA": The history of the Eugene O'Neill Theater Center is available at its website: www.theoneill.org.

111 "glossy enameled cinderblock": Grifasi's recollections of the summer of 1975 were delivered in a speech honoring Streep at the O'Neill's Monte Cristo Awards, held in New York City on Apr. 21, 2014.

111 "motley, idiosyncratic bunch": Jeffrey Sweet, *The O'Neill: The Transformation of Modern American Theater* (New Haven: Yale University Press, 2014); Foreword by Meryl Streep.

112 A "dull" achievement: Ibid.

112 She and Grifo borrowed a car: Grifasi's and Tichler's accounts differ slightly; Tichler remembers Streep getting stuck on a train.

112 *They're not going to hire me*: Rosemarie Tichler and Barry Jay Kaplan, *Actors at Work* (New York: Faber and Faber, 2007), 305.

113 "Ninety-five percent of actresses": Turan and Papp, *Free for All*, 363.

114 "I got three bills a month": Commencement address delivered by Meryl Streep at Vassar College, May 22, 1983.

115 "I thought that I had really failed": Mary Beth Hurt's quotations are from an author interview, July 16, 2014.

115 "The curvaceous, desperately subtle flirtation": Turan and Papp, *Free for All*, 364.

115 "a pale, wispy girl": John Lithgow, *Drama: An Actor's Education* (New York: Harper, 2011), 275–76.

116 "And from that moment": Tichler and Kaplan, *Actors at Work*, 305–6.

116 "Mr. Antoon has transposed": Clive Barnes, "The Stage: Papp Transplants Pinero's 'Trelawny,'" *New York Times*, Oct. 16, 1976.

117 "The lights are no sooner up": Walter Kerr, "'A Chorus Line' Soars, 'Trelawny' Falls Flat," *New York Times*, Oct. 26, 1975.

118 hunky *Playgirl* centerfolds: Dave Karger, "Oscars 2012: Love Story," *Entertainment Weekly*, March 2, 2012.

118 "Well, when *we* get to do movies": Recalled by J. Roy Helland at "Extreme Makeover," a panel discussion at the New Yorker Festival, held in New York on Oct. 11, 2014.

118 "He wasn't just a guy": Author interview with Jeffrey Jones, June 26, 2014.

118 "Forget about being a character actress": Terry Curtis Fox, "Meryl Streep: Her 'I Can't Wait' Jumps Right Out at You," *Village Voice*, May 31, 1976.

120 "As she made small talk": Lithgow, *Drama*, 277.

120 "She was so slim and blond": Arvin Brown's quotations are from an author interview, Apr. 8, 2014.

121 "I've lost m' white kid purse!": Tennessee Williams, *27 Wagons Full of Cotton: And Other Plays* (New York: New Directions, 1966), 3.

121 "a tall, well-upholstered": Julius Novick, "The Phoenix Rises—Again," *Village Voice*, Feb. 9, 1976.

123 *"Che brutta!"*: "Meryl Streep: The *Fresh Air* Interview," National Public Radio, Feb. 6, 2012.

124 "What is it—love and Good-bye?": William Gillette, *Secret Service* (New York: Samuel French, 1898), 182.

125 "Those two plays at the Phoenix Theatre": Joan Juliet Buck, "More of a Woman," *Vogue*, June, 1980.

125 "profoundly uncomfortable": MG.

126 "What I thought was great about him": Epstein, *Joe Papp: An American Life*, 334.

127 "When I was at Yale": Fox, "Meryl Streep: Her 'I Can't Wait' Jumps Right Out at You."

128 "What infinite heart's-ease": William Shakespeare, *Henry V*, Act IV, Scene i.

128 "They had a whole group": Author interview with Tony Simotes, May 2, 2014.

129 "O, for a muse of fire": William Shakespeare, *Henry V*, Act I, Prologue.

129 "the first time I realized": Eric Grode, "The City's Stage, in Rain, Heat and Ribald Lines," *New York Times*, May 27, 2012.

129 "Michael Moriarty couldn't give two shits": Author interview with Gabriel Gribetz, Apr. 23, 2014.

129 "I envy the wealth": Thomas Lask, "Rudd, Meryl Streep, Actors to Hilt," *New York Times*, June 19, 1976.

130 Snaking counterclockwise: This description of the line comes from George Vecsey, "Waiting for Shakespeare," *New York Times*, July 16, 1976.

131 "Then, Isabel, live chaste": Shakespeare, *Measure for Measure*, Act II, Scene iv.

131 "The role is so beautiful": Judy Klemesrud, "From Yale Drama to 'Fanatic Nun,'" *New York Times*, Aug. 13, 1976.

131 "Men have *always* rejected Isabella . . . quite a scholar": Fox, "Meryl Streep: Her 'I Can't Wait' Jumps Right Out at You."

132 "I'll tell him yet": Shakespeare, *Measure for Measure,* Act II, Scene iv.

132 "It's ludicrous": Klemesrud, "From Yale Drama to 'Fanatic Nun.'"

133 "Plainly conceive, I love you": Shakespeare, *Measure for Measure*, Act II, Scene iv.

133 "It was their dynamic": Author interview with Judith Light, June 18, 2014.

133 "The physical attraction between them": Author interview with Michael Feingold, Feb. 11, 2014.

133 "We sense the sexual give-and-take": Mel Gussow, "Stage: A 'Measure' to Test the Mettle of Actors," *New York Times*, Aug. 13, 1976.

134 "I've been shot through with luck": Klemesrud, "From Yale Drama to 'Fanatic Nun.'"

FREDO

135 "We had a house up in the country": Marvin Starkman's quotations are from an author interview, Apr. 24, 2014.

135 "We got a color television": Robyn Goodman's quotations are from an author interview, June 5, 2014.

135 "We had to give him a key": Israel Horovitz's quotations are from an author interview, Apr. 17, 2014.

136 "You eat a meal with him": Richard Shepard, dir., *I Knew It Was You: Rediscovering John Cazale*, Oscilloscope Laboratories, 2010.

137 "There was an undercurrent of sadness": Stephen Casale's quotations are from an author interview, Apr. 2, 2014.

137 "I've always taken care of you, Fredo": Francis Ford Coppola, dir., *The Godfather: Part II*, Paramount Pictures, 1974.

138 "He was mad as hell": The details of Cazale's ancestry and childhood come from an author interview with Stephen Casale, Apr. 2, 2014, and from Clemente Manenti, "The Making of Americans," *Una Città*, Sept., 2011.

138 "Giovanni Cazale": John's brother, Stephen, changed his own name back to "Casale" in 1967.

140 "I'm going to Marvin's house": Recalled by Starkman, Apr. 24, 2014.

141 "You again": Recalled by Pacino in *I Knew It Was You* (Shepard, dir.).

142 "Everybody wants to be first, right?": Israel Horovitz, *Plays: 1* (London: Methuen Drama, 2006), 64.

142 "That's Fredo": *I Knew It Was You* (Shepard, dir.).

142 "The second son, Frederico": Mario Puzo, *The Godfather* (New York: Putnam, 1969), 17.

142 "In an Italian family": Francis Ford Coppola, director's commentary, *The Godfather: DVD Collection*, Paramount Pictures, 2001.

143 "the best bugger on the West Coast": Francis Ford Coppola, dir., *The Conversation*, Paramount Pictures, 1974.

143 "I know it was you, Fredo": *The Godfather: Part II* (Coppola, dir.).

144 "There is a kind of moral decay": Tim Lewis, "Icon: John Cazale," *British GQ*, Jan., 2010.

145 "You know what a No. 10 can is?": Recalled by Starkman, Apr. 24, 2014.

146 "It's yours": Sidney Lumet, director's commentary, *Dog Day Afternoon*, Warner Home Video, 2006.

146 "Wyoming": *Dog Day Afternoon*, Sidney Lumet (dir.), Warner Bros., 1975.

147 Papp had given Sam Waterston the choice: Author interview with Sam Waterston, June 26, 2015.

147 "These are Cubans": Author interview with Tony Simotes, May 2, 2014.

148 "He brought menacing": Author interview with Rosemarie Tichler, June 25, 2014.

148 "Never could the strumpet": William Shakespeare, *Measure for Measure*, Act II, Scene ii.

149 "Oh, man, I have met the greatest actress": *I Knew It Was You* (Shepard, dir.).

149 "He wasn't like anybody I'd ever met": Ibid.

149 "We would talk about the process": Ibid.

150 "He knows Italian": Recalled by Casale, Apr. 2, 2014.

150 "The jerk made everything mean something": Brock Brower, "Shakespeare's 'Shrew' with No Apologies," *New York Times*, Aug. 6, 1978.

151 "He took his time with stuff": *I Knew It Was You* (Shepard, dir.).

152 "She had an almost feral alertness": From Streep's tribute speech at "The 42nd AFI Life Achievement Award: A Tribute to Jane Fonda," held in Los Angeles on June 5, 2014.

152 "I admire Jane Fonda": Susan Dworkin, "Meryl Streep to the Rescue!," *Ms.*, Feb., 1979.

152 politics and Leon Trotsky: From Streep's tribute speech at "An Academy Salute to Vanessa Redgrave," held in London on Nov. 13, 2011.

152 On days off, she would hang out with John Glover: Author interview with John Glover, Apr. 7, 2015.

153 "Beautifully!": Joan Juliet Buck, "More of a Woman," *Vogue*, June, 1980.

153 "What do you mean, you couldn't find me?": Recalled by Starkman, Apr. 24, 2014.

153 *I've made a terrible mistake*: "Streep's Debut Turned Her Against Hollywood," *WENN*, Nov. 1, 2004.

153 "You can't do the classics": Helen Epstein, *Joe Papp: An American Life* (Boston: Little, Brown, 1994), 343.

154 "That's when you can really work": Terry Curtis Fox, "Meryl Streep: Her 'I Can't Wait' Jumps Right Out at You," *Village Voice*, May 31, 1976.

154 "something much lighter and closer": Andrei Serban's quotations, except where noted, are from an e-mail from Serban to the author on June 2, 2014.

155 "you could have taken away": Fox, "Meryl Streep: Her 'I Can't Wait' Jumps Right Out at You."

155 "Think about *The Cherry Orchard*": Diana Maychick, *Meryl Streep: The Reluctant Superstar* (New York: St. Martin's Press, 1984), 53.

156 "You're not fat!": Recalled by Michael Feingold, whose quotations are from an author interview, Feb. 11, 2014.

156 "I've never seen an angrier improvisation": Author interview with Mary Beth Hurt, July 16, 2014.

156 "Falling down *verrry verrry* funny": Mel Gussow, "The Rising Star of Meryl Streep," *New York Times Magazine*, Feb. 4, 1979.

157 "We are not interested in the truth": John Simon, "Deadly Revivals," *The New Leader*, March 14, 1977.

157 "It is a celebration of genius": Clive Barnes, "Stage: A 'Cherry Orchard' That Celebrates Genius," *New York Times*, Feb. 18, 1977.

157 "I think that if this horrifying production": The outraged letters are lovingly collected in NYSF, Box 2-56.

158 "She was like a centrifugal force": Robert Markowitz's quotations are from an author interview, Oct. 6, 2014.

158 "When I watched you in a game": *The Deadliest Season* (Robert Markowitz, dir.), CBS, March 16, 1977.

159 "I felt this production was a disaster": Author interview with Christopher Lloyd, June 28, 2014. More on this disaster-prone production can be found in Davi Napoleon, *Chelsea on the Edge* (Ames: Iowa State University Press, 1991), 212–16.

LINDA

164 "John Cazale was out most of the day": NYSF, Box 5-114.

164 "disturbing symptoms": Helen Epstein, *Joe Papp: An American Life* (Boston: Little, Brown, 1994), 4.

164 An Austrian-born septuagenarian: Ronald Sullivan, "Dr. William M. Hitzig, 78, Aided War Victims," *New York Times*, Aug. 30, 1983.

164 "some outrageous color like citron": Gail Papp's quotations are from an author interview, June 19, 2014.

165 "He checked us in": Epstein, *Joe Papp: An American Life*, 4.

166 "After tonight, Jamil Zakkai": NYSF, Box 5-114.

166 Manganaro's: Author interview with cast member Prudence Wright Holmes, June 17, 2014.

166 "She had a kind of a tough love": Author interview with Christopher Lloyd, June 28, 2014.

166 "Did you ever think of quitting smoking?": Author interview with Stephen Casale, Apr. 2, 2014.

166 "We're gonna get this thing!": Richard Shepard, dir., *I Knew It Was You: Rediscovering John Cazale*, Oscilloscope Laboratories, 2010.

167 *Surabaya Johnny, why'm I feeling so blue?*: Bertolt Brecht, lyrics; Kurt Weill, music; original German play by Dorothy Lane; book and lyrics adapted by Michael Feingold, *Happy End: A Melodrama with Songs* (New York: Samuel French, 1982), 59.

167 "No, I don't have enough confidence": Recalled by Holmes, June 17, 2014.

167 "When I'm kidding, I'm serious": Steve Garbarino, "Michael Cimino's Final Cut," *Vanity Fair*, March, 2002.

168 "like Michelangelo": Ibid.

168 Redeker had based it on a photo spread: This account of the origins of *The Deer Hunter* derives from an author interview with Quinn Redeker on Nov. 11, 2014, an author interview with Michael Deeley on Sept. 27, 2014, and Deeley's book *Blade Runners, Deer Hunters, and Blowing the Bloody Doors Off* (New York: Pegasus Books, 2009), 130–31.

169 "All I can possibly say": Author interview with Michael Deeley, Sept. 27, 2014.

169 "very guarded": Deric Washburn's quotations are from an author interview, Sept. 29, 2014.

169 "Well, Deric, it's fuck-off time": Peter Biskind, "The Vietnam Oscars," *Vanity Fair*, March, 2008.

170 "You know what that Russian roulette thing is?": Barry Spikings's recollections, except where noted, are from an author interview, Sept. 26, 2014.

170 "a fragile slip of a thing": Michael Cimino, *The Deer Hunter*, second draft written with Deric Washburn (Feb. 20, 1977), 12. Robert De Niro Papers, Harry Ransom Center, the University of Texas at Austin, Series I, Box 44.

171 EMI paid the asking price: Deeley, *Blade Runners, Deer Hunters, and Blowing the Bloody Doors Off*, 168–69.

171 "the forgotten person in the screenplay": Mel Gussow, "The Rising Star of Meryl Streep," *New York Times Magazine*, Feb. 4, 1979.

171 "hitting it big as some starlet": MG.

171 "They needed a girl": Susan Dworkin, "Meryl Streep to the Rescue!," *Ms.*, Feb., 1979.

172 "failed alpha male": Michael Cimino, director's commentary, *The Deer Hunter*, StudioCanal, 2006.

172 Finally, he came to Cimino: Jean Vallely, "Michael Cimino's Battle to Make a Great Movie," *Esquire*, Jan. 2–16, 1979.

172 "the morons at EMI": David Gregory, dir., *Realising "The Deer Hunter": An Interview with Michael Cimino*, Blue Underground, 2003.

172 "I told him he was crazy": Vallely, "Michael Cimino's Battle to Make a Great Movie."

172 The medical advice they received: Deeley, *Blade Runners, Deer Hunters, and Blowing the Bloody Doors Off*, 170.

173 *I'm getting out*: Vallely, "Michael Cimino's Battle to Make a Great Movie."

173 "absolute dreadful piece of shit": *Realising "The Deer Hunter"* (Gregory, dir.).

173 "He was sicker than we thought": *I Knew It Was You* (Shepard, dir.).

173 repeated the story decades later: As she does in *I Knew It Was You* (Shepard, dir.).

173 asked to sign an agreement: Recalled by John Savage, whose quotations, except where noted, are from an author interview, Sept. 19, 2014.

174 "Mingo Citizens Elated by Film": *Herald-Star* (Steubenville), July 6, 1977.

174 "Movie Makers Leave Cash": *Sunday Plain Dealer* (Cleveland), July 31, 1977.

174 "They say the nature of the scenes": Steve Weiss, "Mingo Gets Robbed—No Name in Lights," *Herald-Star*, July 1, 1977.

175 Weisberger's clothing store: Dolly Zimber, "Mingo Citizens Elated by Film," *Herald-Star*, July 6, 1977.

175 "Linda is essentially a man's view": Roger Copeland, "A Vietnam Movie That Does Not Knock America," *New York Times*, Aug. 7, 1977.

177 Olga Gaydos: Interview with Olga Gaydos, The Cleveland Memory Project, Cleveland State University Libraries, www.clevelandmemory.org.

177 "That's enough": Recalled by Mary Ann Haenel, whose quotations are from an author interview, Sept. 21, 2014.

177 "Being in a movie was like the smallest part": *I Knew It Was You* (Shepard, dir.).

177 Outside Lemko Hall: Chris Colombi, "Where's the Glamour?," *Plain Dealer* (Cleveland), Dec. 9, 1977.

178 They were paid twenty-five dollars: Donna Chernin, "Clevelander Finds Extras for Film-Shooting Here," *Plain Dealer*, July 22, 1977.

178 "Michael, everybody brought a gift!": Cimino, director's commentary, *The Deer Hunter*.

178 Cimino said that his uncle: Ibid.

179 "I thought of all the girls": Dworkin, "Meryl Streep to the Rescue!"

179 "stockpiled": Commencement address delivered by Meryl Streep at Barnard College, May 17, 2010.

179 how to kill a fly: Recalled by Haenel, Sept. 21, 2014.

180 "It was such a beautiful wedding": Cimino, director's commentary, *The Deer Hunter*.

180 "This is this": Michael Cimino (dir.), *The Deer Hunter*, Columbia-EMI-Warner/Universal Pictures, 1978.

180 "some strange prefiguration": Cimino's account of shooting in the mountains is from his director's commentary for *The Deer Hunter*.

182 "unrelentingly Austrian": Dworkin, "Meryl Streep to the Rescue!"

182 "I've had to do things": Marvin J. Chomsky, dir., *Holocaust*, NBC, 1978.

182 "extraordinarily beautiful and oppressive": NYSF, Box 1-160. The front of the postcard is a photo of the Johann Strauss Monument.

183 "too much for me": Dworkin, "Meryl Streep to the Rescue!"

183 she was in prison: Paul Gray, "A Mother Finds Herself," *Time*, Dec. 3, 1979.

183 "She may have made associations": Marvin Chomsky's quotations are from an author interview, Nov. 6, 2014.

183 "The reason was that we felt so awful": Jane Hall, "From Homecoming Queen to 'Holocaust,'" *TV Guide*, June 24, 1978.

183 Blanche Baker, the twenty-year-old: Author interview with Blanche Baker, Oct. 9, 2014.

184 "that damn eiderdown": Brock Brower, "Shakespeare's 'Shrew' with No Apologies," *New York Times*, Aug. 6, 1978.

184 "It was not a side of her": Author interview with Albert Innaurato, Jan. 10, 2014.

185 "One that I hope to keep seeing": William G. Cahan, M.D., *No Stranger to Tears: A Surgeon's Story* (New York: Random House, 1992), 264.

185 "My beau is terribly ill": Undated letter, Robert Lewis Papers, Kent State University Libraries, Special Collections and Archives, Sub-Series 3B, Box 33.

185 "I was so close": Diane de Dubovay, "Meryl Streep," *Ladies' Home Journal*, March, 1980.

185 "snow emergency": Andy Newman, "A Couple of Weeks Without Parking Rules? Try a Couple Months," www.nytimes.com, Jan. 7, 2011.

186 "smelled to high heaven": Cimino, director's commentary, *The Deer Hunter*.

186 Mid-shoot, he summoned Spikings: Unpublished recollections by Barry Spikings, provided to author.

187 "We'll do it": Ibid.

187 "We're not in the fucking movie!": Biskind, "The Vietnam Oscars."

188 "pretty fucking amazing": Wendy Wasserstein, *Uncommon Women and Others* (New York: Dramatists Play Service, 1978), 33.

189 Her air of confidence: Recalled by Steven Robman, whose quotations are from an author interview, Dec. 21, 2014.

189 "Steve, do we have a camera": Author interview with Ellen Parker, Dec. 3, 2014.

189 "He's not doing so good": Gussow, "The Rising Star of Meryl Streep."

190 Warner "Let's go to the videotape!" Wolf: Brower, "Shakespeare's 'Shrew' with No Apologies."

190 "She took care of him": MG.

190 "When I saw that girl": *I Knew It Was You* (Shepard, dir.).

190 "It's all right, Meryl": This story was told by Israel Horovitz in Tim Lewis, "Icon: John Cazale," *British GQ*, Jan., 2010, as well as to the author by another of Cazale's friends.

190–91 "negotiate the stairs": Epstein, *Joe Papp: An American Life*, 4.

191 "John Cazale happens once in a lifetime": Israel Horovitz, "A Eulogy: John Cazale (1936–1978)," *Village Voice*, March 27, 1978. Used by permission of Israel Horovitz.

191 "emotionally blitzed": Gray, "A Mother Finds Herself."

191 she drew sketches: Epstein, *Joe Papp: An American Life*, 4.

192 "deceitful" and "selfish": Deeley, *Blade Runners, Deer Hunters, and Blowing the Bloody Doors Off*, 178.

192 "That's it! We lost the audience!": *Realising "The Deer Hunter"* (Gregory, dir.).

192 "The Deer Hunter and the Hunter and the Hunter": Biskind, "The Vietnam Oscars."

192 "I told them I would do everything I could": Vallely, "Michael Cimino's Battle to Make a Great Movie."

193 he bribed the projectionist: *Realising "The Deer Hunter"* (Gregory, dir.). Barry Spikings said of this story, "I would describe that as artistic liberty."

193 She always shielded her eyes: MG.

193 One Sunday morning: Recalled by Casale, Apr. 2, 2014.

193 "I don't want to stop replaying the past": Hall, "From Homecoming Queen to 'Holocaust.'"

194 "When I want something, I go git it": Jerry Schatzberg, dir., *The Seduction of Joe Tynan*, Universal Pictures, 1979.

194 "modern woman": MG.

194 Campaigning for the ERA: Howard Kissel, "The Equal Opportunity Politics of Alan Alda," *Chicago Tribune*, Aug. 12, 1979.

194 He could sense the sadness: Jerry Schatzberg's quotations are from an author interview, Oct. 6, 2014.

194 "I did that film on automatic pilot": Dworkin, "Meryl Streep to the Rescue!"

194 "Oh," she responded: Recalled by Schatzberg, Oct. 6, 2014.

195 "It's there": Recalled by Baker, Oct. 9, 2014.

195 "I'm actually his lawyer": Karen Hosler, "Tinseltown Entourage Reveals Star-Struck City," *Baltimore Sun*, May 7, 1978.

195 "Anytime he wants to change *his* dialogue": Recalled by Schatzberg, Oct. 6, 2014.

195 "a more lovely, more understanding person": Dworkin, "Meryl Streep to the Rescue!"

195 "It's a scene that demands": Jack Kroll, "A Star for the '80s," *Newsweek*, Jan. 7, 1980.

196 "It's true, things *do* contract in the cold!": *The Seduction of Joe Tynan* (Schatzberg, dir.).

196 "She looked at the movie": Kroll, "A Star for the '80s."

196 "untrue, offensive, cheap": Elie Wiesel, "Trivializing the Holocaust: Semi-Fact and Semi-Fiction," *New York Times*, Apr. 16, 1978.

196 "Errol Flynn heroics": Joseph Papp, "The 'Holocaust' Controversy Continues," *New York Times*, Apr. 30, 1978.

196 In Germany: Nicholas Kulish and Souad Mekhennet, "How Meryl Streep Helped the Nazi Hunters," www.salon.com, May 9, 2014, from their book *The Eternal Nazi: From Mauthausen to Cairo, the Relentless Pursuit of SS Doctor Aribert Heim* (New York: Doubleday, 2014).

197 Wandering Annapolis: Hosler, "Tinseltown Entourage Reveals Star-Struck City."

197 *"Hey, Holocaust!"*: Scot Haller, "Star Treks," *Horizon*, Aug., 1978.

197 "I wish I could assign": MG.

197 The day after the Emmys: Tony Scherman, "'Holocaust' Survivor Shoots 'Deer Hunter,' Shuns Fame," *Feature*, Feb., 1979.

198 "a big, awkward, crazily ambitious": Vincent Canby, "Blue-Collar Epic," *New York Times*, Dec. 15, 1978.

198 "Like the Viet Nam War itself": Frank Rich, "Cinema: In Hell Without a Map," *Time*, Dec. 18, 1978.

198 "the mystic bond of male comradeship": Pauline Kael, "The Current Cinema: The God-Bless-America Symphony," *The New Yorker*, Dec. 18, 1978.

199 "fighting a phantom": Leticia Kent, "Ready for Vietnam? A Talk with Michael Cimino," *New York Times*, Dec. 10, 1978. Cimino's later dealings with the press seem to have wounded him; he declined an interview for this book via his associate Joann Carelli, who said, "You can thank your peers for this response."

200 "He was no more a medic": Biskind, "The Vietnam Oscars."

200 "The political and moral issues": Tom Buckley, "Hollywood's War," *Harper's*, Apr. 1979.

200 Jan Scruggs, a former infantry corporal: Mary Vespa and Pat Gallagher, "His Dream Was to Heal a Nation with the Vietnam Memorial, but Jan Scruggs's Healing Isn't Over Yet," *People*, May 30, 1988.

200 One veteran who agreed: Michael Booth's recollections are from an author interview, July 10, 2014.

202 "I wanted something my mother": Bettijane Levine and Timothy Hawkins, "Oscar: Puttin' on the Glitz," *Los Angeles Times*, Apr. 6, 1979.

202 She even took a dip: Janet Maslin, "At the Movies: Meryl Streep Pauses for Family Matters," *New York Times*, Aug. 24, 1979.

202 thirteen people had been arrested: Aljean Harmetz, "Oscar-Winning 'Deer Hunter' Is Under Attack as 'Racist' Film," *New York Times*, Apr. 26, 1979.

202 "not endorsing anything": Lance Morrow, "Viet Nam Comes Home," *Time*, Apr. 23, 1979.

202 "It shows the value of people": Gussow, "The Rising Star of Meryl Streep."

203 "I see a lot of new faces": Onstage remarks from the 51st Academy Awards, Apr. 9, 1979.

203 "respectful but well short of thunderous": Charles Champlin, "'Deer Hunter'—A Life of Its Own," *Los Angeles Times*, Apr. 11, 1979.

203 "racist, Pentagon version of the war": Morrow, "Viet Nam Comes Home." Cimino relates his elevator encounter with Fonda in his director's commentary for *The Deer Hunter*.

JOANNA

206 "We just assumed": Robyn Goodman's quotations are from an author interview, June 5, 2014.

207 "international art center": Grace Glueck, "Art People: The Name's Only SoSo, But Loft-Rich TriBeCa Is Getting the Action," *New York Times*, Apr. 30, 1976.

208 Left alone, she started to wonder: The story of the apartment is recounted in Diane de Dubovay, "Meryl Streep," *Ladies' Home Journal*, March, 1980.

208 "If you're going to be an artist": Donor Highlight, "Don Gummer," Herron School of Art + Design, www.herron.iupui.edu.

208 He was born in Louisville: Biographical information about Don Gummer comes from Irving Sandler, "Deconstructive Constructivist," *Art in America*, Jan., 2005.

210 Tatami floor mats: Gallery label, *Nara and Lana*, Indianapolis Museum of Art, www.imamuseum.org.

210 "I think he's trying to say something": Recalled by Goodman, June 5, 2014.

211 "greedy for work": Michael Arick, dir., *Finding the Truth: The Making of "Kramer vs. Kramer,"* Columbia TriStar Home Video, 2001.

211 "Sam gets away with more": Mark Singer, "Dealmaker," *The New Yorker*, Jan. 11, 1982. Many more wonderful details about Sam Cohn lie therein.

212 "a confident staccato": Ibid.

212 "We had a rolling list": Susan Anderson's quotations are from an author interview, Oct. 6, 2014.

213 "It was never one on one": Arlene Donovan's quotations are from an author interview, Sept. 22, 2014.

214 Avery got suspicious: The details of Avery Corman's childhood are recounted in his book *My Old Neighborhood Remembered: A Memoir* (Fort Lee: Barricade Books, 2014), 5–6, 80–86. Otherwise, Corman's recollections are from an author interview, Sept. 30, 2014.

216 "a striking, slender woman": Avery Corman, *Kramer vs. Kramer* (New York: Random House, 1977), 6.

216 "Feminists will applaud me": Ibid., 44.

216 "linked to his nervous system": Ibid., 161.

217 "That was my main concern": Judy Klemesrud, "Avery Corman on His Latest Book: A Father's Love Note to His Family," *New York Times*, Oct. 21, 1977. Judy

Corman later became the head publicist for Scholastic, Inc., where she oversaw the publicity launch for several *Harry Potter* books. She died in 2004.

217 In 1975, divorces in the United States: Keith Love, "For First Time in U.S., Divorces Pass 1 Million," *New York Times*, Feb. 18, 1976.

217 "range, depth, and complexity of feeling": Richard Fischoff's quotations are from an author interview, Nov. 9, 2014.

218 *How am I going to do this?*: Robert Benton's quotations, except where noted, are from an author interview, Oct. 15, 2014.

219 She wanted to pursue her acting and dancing career: Tony Schwartz, "Dustin Hoffman Vs. Nearly Everybody," *New York Times*, Dec. 16, 1979.

219 "I was getting divorced": Stuart Kemp, "Dustin Hoffman Breaks Down While Recounting His Past Movie Choices," *Hollywood Reporter*, Oct. 16, 2012.

219 "It was almost like group therapy": *Finding the Truth* (Arick, dir.).

220 "what makes divorce so painful": Ibid.

220 "irksome, brawling scold": William Shakespeare, *The Taming of the Shrew*, Act I, Scene ii.

221 "I am ashamed": Ibid., Act V, Scene ii.

221 "She swings as sweetly": Brock Brower, "Shakespeare's 'Shrew' with No Apologies," *New York Times*, Aug. 6, 1978.

221 When she first met Raúl: Eric Pace, "Raul Julia Is Remembered, with All His Panache," *New York Times*, Nov. 7, 1994.

221 "The girl is an *acting factory*!": Author interview with cast member George Guidall, Dec. 12, 2014.

221 "He wants her spirit": Germaine Greer, *The Female Eunuch* (New York: McGraw-Hill, 1971), 206.

222 "Feminists tend to see this play": Brower, "Shakespeare's 'Shrew' with No Apologies." She was paraphrasing Greer, who writes, in *The Female Eunuch* (206), "Kate's speech at the close of the play is the greatest defense of Christian monogamy ever written. It rests upon the role of a husband as protector and friend, and it is valid because Kate has a man who is capable of being both, for Petruchio is both gentle and strong (it is a vile distortion of the play to have him strike her ever)."

222 "She's learned how to look": Jack Kroll, "A Star for the '80s," *Newsweek*, Jan. 7, 1980.

223 *What an obnoxious pig*: Ronald Bergan, *Dustin Hoffman* (London: Virgin, 1991), 137.

223 "an ogre, a princess": Stephen M. Silverman, "Life Without Mother," *American Film*, July–Aug., 1979.

224 "She never opened her mouth": *Dustin Hoffman: Private Sessions*, A&E, Dec. 21, 2008.

225 "funny-looking kid": *Finding the Truth* (Arick, dir.).

226 "All my friends at one point": Susan Dworkin, "Meryl Streep to the Rescue!," *Ms.*, Feb., 1979.

226 "dilemma of how to be a woman": MG.

226 Part of her wished: Ibid.

226 "The more I thought about it": Kroll, "A Star for the '80s."

226 While brushing her teeth one morning: MG.

226 "I did *Kramer vs. Kramer* before I had children": Ken Burns, "Meryl Streep," *USA Weekend*, Dec. 1, 2002.

227 "My character wouldn't live": Recalled by Fischoff, Nov. 9, 2014.

227 Dustin slapped her hard: As told by Streep on *Friday Night with Jonathan Ross*, BBC One, July 4, 2008, and recalled by Fischoff and Benton.

227 "Don't make me go in there!": Robert Benton, dir., *Kramer vs. Kramer*, Columbia Pictures, 1979.

229 "very, very lucky": Juliet Taylor's quotations are from an author interview, Nov. 17, 2014.

229 "more of an authors' idea": E-mail to author from Marshall Brickman, Nov. 6, 2014.

229 "I think he just hated my character": Rachel Abramowitz, "Streep Fighter," *Premiere*, June, 1997.

229 "Woody would say": *Finding the Truth* (Arick, dir.).

230 "Let's pretend that we've just made passionate love": Recalled by Karen Ludwig in an author interview, Oct. 16, 2014.

230 "I don't think Woody Allen even remembers me": de Dubovay, "Meryl Streep."

230 "On a certain level": Ibid.

231 "You're an actor, then": Recalled by Hoffman in *Finding the Truth* (Arick, dir.).

232 "artistic differences": Clarke Taylor, " 'Kramer': Love on the Set," *Los Angeles Times*, Nov. 12, 1978.

232 She was taken aback: Author interview with Jane Alexander, May 8, 2015.

232 "somebody's wife or somebody's mother": *Kramer vs. Kramer* (Benton, dir.).

232 "Meryl, why don't you stop": Christian Williams, "Scenes from the Battle of the Sexes," *Washington Post*, Dec. 17, 1982.

233 "See that glass there on the table?": Recalled by Hoffman in *Finding the Truth* (Arick, dir.).

233 "*Don't talk to me that way*": *Kramer vs. Kramer* (Benton, dir.).

233 "Next time you do that": Nick Smurthwaite, *The Meryl Streep Story* (New York: Beaufort Books, 1984), 53.

233 "Dear Mr. Papp": NYSF, Box 2-122.

234 "my horse, my ox, my ass": William Shakespeare, *The Taming of the Shrew*, Act III, Scene ii.

235 "but she was not injured": NYSF, Box 5-121.

235 "I can't believe how many people": Christopher Dixon, dir., *Kiss Me, Petruchio*, 1981.

235 "I feel very ambiguous": Ibid.

236 "When you give": Ibid.

236 "Joe had no problem": Helen Epstein, *Joe Papp: An American Life* (Boston: Little, Brown, 1994), 335.

237 Tweed Courthouse: The history of the courthouse appears on its webpage at www .nyc.gov.

237 "Because he's my child": The first version of the speech appears in the shooting script, dated Sept. 5, 1978, provided to the author by Richard Fischoff. The second is transcribed from the final film.

240 "longest personal relationship": *Kramer vs. Kramer* (Benton, dir.).

240 Before the take, Dustin had gone over: Hoffman himself tells this story, with some pride, in *Finding the Truth* (Arick, dir.).

241 "I didn't get over it": de Dubovay, "Meryl Streep."

242 "Homicides": Recalled by Hoffman in *Finding the Truth* (Arick, dir.).

243 "She does the right thing": MG.

243 "What immense support": NYSF, Box 1-173.

243 "unspeakably touched": Epstein, *Joe Papp: An American Life*, 427. Papp's eventual successor was JoAnne Akalaitis. He died on Oct. 31, 1991.

244 "After I left": Benton, *Kramer vs. Kramer*, shooting script, Sept. 5, 1978.

245 "This is a mature actress": Mel Gussow, "Stage: 'Alice' Downtown, with Meryl Streep," *New York Times*, Dec. 29, 1978.

245 "I woke up this morning": As transcribed from the final film.

246 "This is the season of Meryl Streep": MG.

247 "non-pro": "Births," *Variety*, Nov. 28, 1979.

247 *The First Twelve Months of Life*: Streep talks about her preparations for motherhood and the trip to Europe in her interview tapes for Diane de Dubovay's March, 1980, profile in *Ladies' Home Journal*, provided to the author by the de Dubovay family.

247 "the most natural thing in the world": de Dubovay, "Meryl Streep."

247 "My work has been very important": Ibid.

248 At the insistence of Lew Wasserman: Alan Alda, *Things I Overheard While Talking to Myself* (New York: Random House, 2007), 116.

248 "Though the movie has no answers": Frank Rich, "Grownups, A Child, Divorce, And Tears," *Time*, Dec. 3, 1979.

249 "'Kramer vs. Kramer' is a Manhattan movie": Vincent Canby, "Screen: 'Kramer vs. Kramer,'" *New York Times*, Dec. 19, 1979.

249 the U.S. gross: Box Office Mojo.

249 "difficult to escape": Gary Arnold, "'Kramer vs. Kramer': The Family Divided," *Washington Post*, Dec. 19, 1979.

250 "I keep thinking of Joanna": Barbara Grizzuti Harrison, "'Kramer vs. Kramer': Madonna, Child, and Mensch," *Ms.*, Jan., 1980.

250 dungarees on MacDougal Street: MG.

250 Hawaiian jacket: Mel Gussow, "The Rising Star of Meryl Streep," *New York Times Magazine*, Feb. 4, 1979.

250 She was partial to pearl earrings: Joan Juliet Buck, "More of a Woman," *Vogue*, June, 1980.

250 "Hello . . . um . . .": Paul Gray, "A Mother Finds Herself," *Time*, Dec. 3, 1979.

250 "reality of life": de Dubovay, "Meryl Streep."

250 male contraception: "Meryl Streep," *People*, Dec. 24, 1979.

251 "less glamorous than Gary": Tony Scherman, "'Holocaust' Survivor Shoots 'Deer Hunter,' Shuns Fame," *Feature*, Feb., 1979.

251 "charismatic leaders are very interesting": MG.

251 *The Postman Always Rings Twice*: Kroll, "A Star for the '80s."

251 "full of shit": MG.

251 "put his life on the line": Kroll, "A Star for the '80s."

251 the new "slink": MG.

251 "cry of a bird": Buck, "More of a Woman."

251 "tapered candle": Dworkin, "Meryl Streep to the Rescue!"

251 "Flemish master's angel": "People Are Talking About . . . ," *Vogue*, July, 1979.

251 *Portrait of a Lady in Yellow*: Buck, "More of a Woman."

251 "merulean . . . more than just a gorgeous face": Gray, "A Mother Finds Herself."

251 "identify with Medea": Buck, "More of a Woman."

251 "Cinderella story": Gray, "A Mother Finds Herself."

251 "go with the flow": de Dubovay, "Meryl Streep."

251 Alexandria, Virginia: MG.

252 "excessive hype": John Skow, "What Makes Meryl Magic," *Time*, Sept. 7, 1981.

252 "I think that the notion": Buck, "More of a Woman."

252 "Dustin has a technician's thoroughness": Schwartz, "Dustin Hoffman Vs. Nearly Everybody."

252 "I hated her guts": Kroll, "A Star for the '80s."

252 "the first American woman": Ibid.

253 "didn't feel anything": Bob Greene, "Streep," *Esquire*, Dec., 1984.

253 "middling successful actor": Buck, "More of a Woman."

253 New Year's Eve party: The details of the party come from Charles Champlin, "An 'A' Party for Woody," *Los Angeles Times*, Jan. 4, 1980.

254 homesteaders on a vast frontier: de Dubovay, "Meryl Streep."

254 "the Lady": Buck, "More of a Woman."

254 "left-wing Communist Jewish": Woody Allen, dir., *Annie Hall*, United Artists, 1977.

255 "Put me on the moon": David Rosenthal, "Meryl Streep Stepping In and Out of Roles," *Rolling Stone*, Oct. 15, 1981.

255 At the Golden Globes: As told by Streep on *The Graham Norton Show*, BBC, Jan. 9, 2015.

256 "My mom cried four times": Beverly Beyette, "Justin Henry: A Little Speech, Just in Case . . . ," *Los Angeles Times*, Apr. 14, 1980.

256 "glorious heritage": Onstage remarks from the 52nd Academy Awards, Apr. 14, 1980.

258 "Well, the soap opera won": The details of the press conference come from Lee Grant, "Oscars Backstage: A Predictable Year," *Los Angeles Times*, Apr. 15, 1980, and from " 'Kramer' Family Faces the Hollywood Press," UPI, Apr. 15, 1980.

259 "They relate to Miranda": Commencement address delivered by Meryl Streep at Barnard College, May 17, 2010.

259 "someone left an Oscar in here!": "The Crossed Fingers Worked, but Then Meryl Left Her Oscar in the John," *People*, Apr. 28, 1980.